MW00879309

From the Bayou To The Big League

Also By Linda Hebert Todd

Wild Justice A Novel

Sidonie and the Loup-Garou: Stories From The Bayou

Stardust In My Hand: Selected Poems

From the Bayou

To

The Big League

The Odyssey Of Wally "Preacher" Hebert

Linda Hebert Todd

Bald Cypress Press
Westlake, Louisiana

BALD CYPRESS PRESS
From The Bayou To The Big League—The Odyssey of Wally "Preacher" Hebert
Linda Hebert Todd

Copyright © 2019 by Linda Hebert Todd
All Rights Reserved

Cover Design: Heather Duff
Cover Photograph: Courtesy of Bill Swank

All rights reserved. This book was self-published by the author Linda Hebert Todd under Bald
Cypress Press. No part of this book may be reproduced in any form by any means without the
express permission of the author.

Published in the United States by Bald Cypress Press

Printed by Kindle Direct Publishing

ISBN:9781542343558

I just played for fun.

Wally Preacher Hebert

This is for the guys who played for fun.

In Memory of John David Hebert

March 3, 1951 - June 18, 2010

TABLE OF CONTENTS

PREFACE

Yankee Stadium
May 1931
Browns versus Yankees

"You can put that slow curve right up your ass."

The Sultan of Swat—aka Babe Ruth—had this piece of advice for the young, curly-haired rookie standing on the pitcher's mound. Ruth handed the admonition out as he trotted back to the dugout after being thrown out on first base in the double play he had hit into.

Before that, the tall southpaw for the St. Louis Browns had taken the pitcher's mound in relief. He was greeted by 40,000 screaming Yankee fans in the *House That Ruth Built*. This was the dark-haired Cajun's initiation into the major leagues. His first pitch in the big leagues resulted in a base hit that advanced two base runners. The next man up strolled to the plate and took his stance. Who was the batter standing some sixty feet away? The Bambino himself—swinging his bat and smiling.

With the bases loaded and one away, the rookie faced the most dangerous hitter in baseball. What a way to start a major league career. He served Ruth a curve ball, and the Caliph of Clout hit into a double play that ended the inning and stranded two runners.

The Browns went on to win that game, and the young man from Louisiana beat the Yankees three more times that season. In one game he pitched an eight-inning shutout against the World Champion Philadelphia Athletics. In another game against the Yankees he struck Babe Ruth out three times, and in one inning fanned Ruth and Gehrig back to back. What follows is the story of my father, Wallace "Preacher" Hebert, and his journey from the bayous of Louisiana to the merry-go-round of professional baseball in St. Louis, Hollywood, San Diego, and Pittsburgh, and back to the swamps of home—a ninety-two year romp through the Twentieth Century.

INTRODUCTION

It survived several moves, and followed the Heberts from Lake Charles, Louisiana, to St. Louis to Hollywood to San Diego to Pittsburgh, back to Lake Charles, and finally to its final resting place in Westlake, Louisiana. One might wonder what in the world I'm talking about. A battered cardboard box filled with a hodge-podge of newspaper clippings about one Wallace "Preacher" Hebert sat for years in an attic in a gabled house on the outskirts of a village in southwest Louisiana.

These clippings were cut from a variety of newspapers located in the cities mentioned above. They were clipped lovingly by my mother — Nannie Locke Bostick Hebert, aka Bobbie — and deposited in the box. Every time she ran across my dad's name in a paper, out came the scissors and into the box it would go.

Why, one might ask, would my father's name be in so many different periodicals? Starting with his high school years his name was found quite often in the sports section of the Lake Charles American Press, depending on the time of year and whichever sport was in season. In the fall it was football and the Lake Charles Wildcats. In the winter basketball was front and center. Springtime brought track and baseball.

In football he was a hard-charging fullback who was known around the state as the Ramming Preacher. He starred in basketball, usually being the high scorer. He hurled the javelin and discus in track, and he was one of the two pitchers on the baseball team. After qualifying for the state finals in baseball the team had to cancel because Hebert came down with the mumps. You can't go to a tournament with one pitcher.

One afternoon my younger siblings were looking around in the attic, and they ran across the box. That's when we started to learn more about our father's previous life. To us he was the one who put a lot of good food from his garden on our table. The one who worked strange hours — sometimes at night, sometimes during the day, sometimes in the evening.

What we didn't know was that he had spent thirteen years tossing a baseball around and terrorizing batters in St. Louis, Hollywood, Los Angeles, and Pittsburgh. I remember San Diego and Pittsburgh vaguely, but I didn't know what he did while there. I do remember him being gone for days at a time.

Bill Swank, a San Diego baseball historian, took the mess in the box and put it in chronological order for a scrapbook. I want to put that scrapbook into book form for descendants and other family members to learn about my father's life. This book is not only about his baseball years but those years make up the largest section. His early years and later years are interesting as well. He hunted and skinned alligators as a thirteen-year-old and came full circle, doing the same thing when he was in his eighties. I've used these newspaper accounts along with my memories of family stories told over the years.

Several books served to refresh my memories and are listed in the source section. One in particular — *Baseball's Forgotten Heroes* by Tony Salin — was a treasure trove for me. When my father was eighty-seven, Mr. Salin called our house one night asking for an interview for a book he was writing. Daddy was there alone as Mom was in Tennessee visiting my brother Wally. Mr. Salin recorded the interview and sent us a copy of the tape after he published the book. My daughter Mollie transcribed the tape for me, so I have a hard copy of stories in my dad's own words.

While this book was written mainly for family, anyone who enjoys baseball may find it interesting. I have described many of the games he was in, so those who don't have access to the scrapbook can see how baseball was conducted in the thirties and early forties. Somewhat different from today's norm. No million-dollar contracts. No giving one's self a leg up with artificial enhancements. They played with the talent God gave them.

RIVERBANK ON THE CALCASIEU

Cypress knees jut from shaded water.

Pine needles eclipse the sodden bank.

Spanish moss, velvety and curled,

Drips from laden branches.

Brush-tailed squirrels scurry

Up and down prickled pine tree trunks.

Serene water, cloudy, sun-dappled,

Surround the wharf, boards parched and warped,

And await the rowdy arrival

Of the ones who will roil the tranquility.

PART I
Born on the Bayou

THE EARLY YEARS
1907 To 1930

Austin, Wallace, Charlie, Bessie Hebert

ONE

CAMERON PARISH

Le Grand Derangement

They had lived in peace for more than 150 years, those people known as Acadians. They called their homeland Acadie, known today as Nova Scotia in Canada. Their distinct culture established a prosperous way of life and instilled a strong sense of independence. Their original homeland was France, so they were a devoutly Catholic society.

Trouble was on the horizon when Acadie became a possession of the British Empire. The king of England wanted them to sign a loyalty oath to him, which they refused to do. The British officials, in their infinite wisdom and mercy, decided the Acadians were no longer welcome in Canada so they had soldiers seize their farms in 1755. The farms were turned over to Anglo-American Protestants, and the Acadians were forced into exile. This expulsion from their homeland of more than a century and a half is known as *le Grand Derangement*.

The British separated husbands and wives, parents and children, and scattered some of the Acadians throughout the thirteen colonies. Others were sent to Europe where they were not welcomed by the native inhabitants. Half of the entire Acadian population died during this time. Among the survivors many roamed the world seeking lost family members and a new homeland.

Those Acadians who entered British colonies and territories had left French law for life under English law, where a plethora of written records chronicled virtually any decision or transaction. In the process, many Acadian families such as Breau, Boudreau, and Gautreau acquired their "X" as they signed documents as best they could. Hence the old Acadian records read Breau, and the Louisiana families today are spelled Breaux.

Between 1765 and 1785, after the French and Indian War, some three thousand exiled souls made their way to Louisiana where they were welcomed. Among the Broussards, the Boudreaux, and the Thibodeaux were some Hebert forebears who established a family tree in what became known as *la Nouvelle Acadie*—the New Acadia. Many of these hardy souls found their way to Cameron Parish in the extreme southwest corner of Louisiana.

To paraphrase Julius Caesar, our Hebert ancestors and their fellow exiles said, "We came, we saw, we conquered." Known today as Cajuns, we're famous for the distinct culture that has evolved. Our food: what's better than seafood gumbo on a winter night or crawfish etouffee anytime? Our music: what's more fun than the two-step or waltz twirled to the accordion and fiddle?

Plunk Wally "Preacher" Hebert down in the 18th Century and he would have done just fine. He would have survived the exile and conquered his new homeland with all its challenges. Meat on the table? No problem—go out to the field and kill a rabbit. Vegetables? Plow up the ground and drop a few corn seeds. Need cash? Skin a few gators. Scared of Babe Ruth? I don't think so.

Unnamed Hurricane of 1918

"The house is breaking apart. We got to leave. Now." The young father was trying to shepherd his little family out before the wind took their house away with them in it.

His seven-year-old daughter, crying because she couldn't find her new doll, tried to pull away and go back.

"We can't take anything. We got to leave now." He picked her up and carried her down the steps, her waist-length dark hair whipping around both of them as he leaned into the wind, trying to get to the strongest section of fence.

His wife followed, pulling their young son toward the fence. The boy was crying for his puppy who had disappeared, but his pleas were blown away by the roaring of the wind.

They got to the fence and each grabbed a post, knowing if they let go they would be blown wherever the wind took them. The blasts got so strong the little girl lost her grip on the post. Her long hair got tangled in the barbed wire and kept her from blowing away, even though at times her little body was parallel to the ground.

This was the unnamed storm that roared ashore on the Cameron Parish coast in 1918 when Wallace was a youngster. The memory of what happened to the little neighbor girl and her family stayed with him for the remainder of his life. That family ultimately survived, but everyone had broken bones and other injuries. The Hebert family also survived the storm, but it changed their lives forever.

He was born Wallace Andrew Hebert in a Cameron Parish sharecropper's house on August, 1907, but there was some confusion about when he came into the world. His mother said August 21. A baptismal certificate indicated otherwise—August 22. The family always celebrated on the 21st like his mother said. After all, she was there. Born to Mathilde Smith Hebert and John Aurelian Hebert, he was the second of eight children—five girls and three boys.

Residents of the swamp country of southwest Louisiana learned early on to catch, trap, and shoot whatever they could find to put food on the table. For the first ten years of his life, Wallace roamed the bayous and marshes of Cameron Parish. A skilled fisherman by the age of nine, the fish were not safe from his mother's frying pan. He dismantled wooden barrels and used the staves as weapons to bring down rabbits who had the bad luck of crossing his path. Even at that age he had the uncanny ability to throw with a deadly left-handed accuracy. His mother Mathilde (pronounced Mah-teel) said by age 3 he was planting his own garden, and he did so every year of his life.

The Hebert siblings, who eventually numbered 8, were all lifelong avid and successful fishermen (and women.) On one occasion when Wallace was about five years of age, he and his father whom everyone called Gros Ian ("Big John") went fishing. Not having a barbed fishhook, Wallace was using a stick, line, and a bent pin. When he got a bite, he flipped the fish up the bank. After several successful catches, he launched a catfish into the air and it landed by its fin fully impaled into his side. The pain was immediate and excruciating, but his father quickly laid him on the ground, put his foot on his son, grabbed the fish, and yanked the barbed fin out. Gros Ian rubbed the slime from the catfish into the wound, and Wallace said the pain stopped and it healed without a scar.

Those idyllic days came to an end during his eleventh year when the 1918 storm made its unexpected appearance on Louisiana's Gulf Coast. In addition to the horror of their neighbors' ordeal, he saw his own family's best horse with a two-by-four blown through it, and a vacant lot where their house had stood. From the dubious safety of a ditch, his family spent the duration of the storm watching nature's fury obliterate everything they had worked for.

After the wind abated and the waters receded, the Hebert clan packed what was left and headed north to the city of Lake Charles in Calcasieu Parish. John Hebert drove a delivery truck, repaired sewing machines, and worked as a duck hunting guide to put food on the table. So began the next phase of Wallace's journey.

TWO

LAKE CHARLES

School Days at Central

On their first day at Central School in Lake Charles, after their move from Cameron Parish, my grandmother dressed the school-age Hebert siblings in their Sunday best. All three brothers wore hats. The more casually dressed schoolmates laughed at them. "Here come the preacher brothers," they would taunt. As time went on it got shortened to "Preacher," and soon only applied to my father. That nickname followed him the rest of his life and caused much confusion concerning his vocation.

For the most part the school days went smoothly for him at Central—except for one thing. According to his teachers he had the misfortune to be born left-handed. They insisted he use his right hand to write. When he kept reverting back to his left hand, they tied it behind his back. For the remainder of his life he wrote right-handed, and for everything else he used his left—shooting a basketball, pitching a baseball or football, batting, golfing, fishing, shooting a shotgun. Thanks to the well-meaning teachers at Central School his handwriting always resembled a third-grader's.

Long Before Little League

According to Hebert he started playing baseball long before high school. He was still in elementary school at Central when he fell in love with the national pastime. He and his friends had their diamond in a field full of cypress stumps. Every now and then one of the fly-chasers would disappear into a sinkhole. After a few mishaps they memorized the locations of these hazards. Soon they could run all over the field without even looking. However, they still had to sidestep snakes, especially in high water.

Connie Mack brought his Philadelphia Athletics for several years to Lake Charles for spring training. The youngsters in the area, including young Preacher, spent their afternoons chasing batting practice balls for the boys from Philly.

Summer in the Swamp

In the summer of 1921 Preacher was thirteen years of age. After school ended that year, his father took him into the swamp with a cast iron skillet, a shotgun, some clothes, and a pirogue. A pirogue was the Cajun's answer to a Native American canoe and just as difficult to keep right side up. A frail shell of a boat, it was hewn out of a single log, averaged thirteen feet in length, and a mere twenty-two inches in width. It took lot of coordination to operate one.

His father returned to town, and Preacher set up camp in an old houseboat with a wood-burning stove. He was alone all summer, living off the land. If he wanted to eat he had to catch it himself—fish, ducks, squirrels or whatever else was available. What thirteen-year-old in this day and age would spend an entire summer alone in a swamp catching, gutting, and cooking his food?

In the southwest Louisiana of 1921, money was tight for the Heberts. His reason for being in the swamp was to hunt alligators; night time was when he hunted. With no gator season to keep the population down the big reptiles roamed everywhere. They had no natural enemies. Undisputed lords of the bayous, all that was required of them was to find food and make baby alligators.

The swamps and bayous of the area teemed with small fur-bearing animals—mink, muskrat, and nutria. Their pelts were worth a lot of money. Alligators, on the other hand, weren't worth much and ate those little animals faster than a Cajun could suck the heads off twenty pounds of crawfish.

A wealthy landowner from Lake Charles put a price on alligator hides— $1.50 for hides from four to seven feet; $5.50 for anything from seven and a half to twenty feet long. That was a lot of money in 1921.

When darkness descended he would paddle the pirogue through inky waters carrying the lantern and shotgun. The full moon kept the obscurity of night at bay, but when the moon was on the wane the darkness was smothering. He shone the lantern out into the water, and the only thing shining back at him were red gator eyes. He paddled to within two or three feet of the eyes, keeping the light trained on them, and shot at the space between the eyes.

He had to be careful. Once the gators had been shot their tails became lethal weapons. He could find himself in the black waters of the bayou. After he was certain the alligator was dead, he paddled to the bank holding on to its mouth with one hand. After dragging it out of the water, he left it there until morning; then he paddled back and skinned it. He hunted all night, skinned all day, and slept when he found time. Did I mention he was thirteen?

He stored the hides in brine-filled barrels, and his father came on weekends to pick up the hides and bring more shells for the shotgun. Sometimes his mother sent a cake—a welcome respite from his regular diet of fish and other swamp creatures.

One steamy night several of those bayou monarchs came close to wiping out the entire Wallace branch of the Hebert clan. The mist hung low everywhere, a hot, foggy Louisiana summer night with no stars or moon in the cloying darkness. He had the lantern, but it wasn't much help; it only shone out about five feet. The gators seemed thicker and closer together that night. Red eyes were everywhere, and the noises coming through the fog were terrifying. He saw one set of eyes on an extra wide head; it had to be at least ten feet long.

He shot the wide-headed beast between the eyes. The next thing he knew he was in the water with an overturned pirogue. His gun and lantern lay on the bottom of the bayou, and he found himself surrounded by a bunch of gators, one of them mortally wounded. He thought about diving for his gun, but he couldn't see anything, and all he could hear was the wounded gator thrashing beside him. He swam in the direction of the bank, pulled himself up, and sat there until daylight.

At first light he spotted the pirogue upside down bumping against the opposite bank. He swam across, righted the small boat, dove down and found the gun buried in the mud. He then dragged the dead twelve-foot gator onto the bank for skinning.

He passed his fourteenth birthday in August, shooting up six inches in height, and bulking up from dragging 400 pound alligators around seven days a week. His own mother didn't recognize him at first when he got home that fall. When school started in the autumn of 1921, Preacher Hebert went out for football and found it quite a bit easier than his summer vacation.

He got almost 300 hides that summer. I did some math, and it looks like he brought in about $1,650.00. That was a lot of money in 1921. There were seven children in the family by then, and the fruits of his labor were much appreciated.

$1650 today would be $23,146.72 according the inflation rate table.

1928 Football 3 Games

WILDCATS ADD ANOTHER VICTORY TO THEIR STRING
Took Game From Lafayette By 41-0 Score
HEBERT AGAIN WAS OUTSTANDING FACTOR
Literally Passed, Plunged His Team To Its Fourth Win

This game was played on October 29 in Lake Charles. The headlines are a thumbnail sketch of the whole game. The week before in the Alexandria game the feature of the contest was Hebert's receiving prowess in catching passes. In the Lafayette game it was his ability to deliver accurate, bullet-like passes to his receivers — three backs and two ends.

After an evenly-played first quarter that ended in a 7-0 lead for the Wildcats, it was a punting contest between the two quarterbacks until the Lafayette punter's kick ended up on his own twenty-five yard line. Hebert took it over the goal line, banging it across in three attempts. He added the extra point with a pass to right halfback Ferber.

That set the scene for the remainder of the game. Get close to the goal line with passes from Hebert to his able receivers and broken-field running by halfback Don Zimmerman, then give the ball to Hebert to blast through the opposing line — with the help of his offensive line.

When the timekeeper's gun ended the game the final score was 41-0.

WILDCATS SCORED AND SCORED BIG OVER DERIDDER

Added Another Boost To Chance for State Crown

IT WAS LAKE CHARLES DAY IN BEAUREGARD

Parades In Honor of the Victors Both Before and After Game

On a crisp sunny day in mid-November, 1928, the Wildcats of Lake Charles invaded Deridder, the parish seat of neighboring Beauregard Parish, to take on the blue-and-white clad Dragons of Deridder High School. Thanks to the slamming broadsides of fullback Preacher Hebert and the open-field running of halfback Don Zimmerman, Deridder was eliminated from their chance for sectional honors. The Wildcats, however, stayed alive in their quest for the state crown.

The first half was a nail-biter for both teams. It was a punting duel for two quarters, as neither team could get anything going. After one such punt the Wildcats recovered the ball on Deridder's four-yard line, causing much elation of fans and players alike. What could be better? Four downs to get the ball four yards. Should be a piece of cake, especially with the Ramming Preacher carrying the pigskin.

A Deridder fan was heard shouting from the sidelines that if the Dragons kept the Wildcats out of the end zone they would be the best team in the state. At the end of the second quarter it looked like he might be right. The Dragons held them then and for the remainder of the half. Both teams left the field with big fat zeroes on the board.

Coach Killen must have been quite persuasive during the halftime chat with his charges. The Wildcats that took the field at the beginning of the third quarter were a totally different eleven from the ones who straggled off the field at the end of the second frame. The Deridder boys didn't know what hit them. The plan seemed to be: let Zimmerman carry for long gains; let battering ram Hebert take it across the line. Turn the gazelle and the elephant loose. Before the final gun was fired the Wildcats had crossed the goal line four times.

Hebert scored all but one of the touchdowns for the Wildcats. Allen Dees made it into the scoring column when he grabbed a pass deep in Deridder territory and fell across the line. 26-0, Lake Charles.

Deridder finally emerged from the doldrums just before the game ended and scored their lone touchdown. Final: 26-6.

Approximately 8,000 people witnessed the contest. The Deridder officials said the game was the biggest football classic ever staged in Beauregard Parish. Fans had converged from all over the parish to see the game.

Over 1,000 of the ones yelling from the sidelines were fans from the Lake Charles contingent. Three-hundred of them had made the trip on the eight-coach special train of the Southern-Pacific. Also, the parking lot was jammed with automobiles from the Lake Charles area some forty minutes to the south.

When the train arrived in Deridder at 2:00 p.m., almost 1,000 people followed the Red and Blue Band through the business section of town and on to the ball park. After the game ended the same group paraded back through Deridder in triumph while the band led the way playing "Here's to Lake Charles High School to Whom All Others Yield."

I think this was the game that figured in a family story our mother told us. She and her best friend, Fay Malloy, were still attending Central School. They were fourteen—probably in eighth grade. Our dad was in high school—the big football hero. Mom and Fay were on that train, and guess who was in the seat ahead of them. My dad and his current girlfriend.

He had been banged around by the Deridder line and wasn't feeling too good. She was trying to make him forget his aches and pains. Mom and Fay were carrying on as only fourteen-year-old girls can. It would be another four years before she caught his eye.

Monday morning after the Deridder victory Lake Charles High students filed in and took their seats at the Monday assembly. After the round of routine announcements the principle, G.W. Ford, placed an oblong box on the lectern and called for Preacher Hebert to come forward.

A belt bearing the Wildcat insignia on the buckle was presented to him in appreciation for the fine work he did against the Deridder Dragons football team the preceding Saturday. The existence of the belt, donated by Kushner Brothers, local jewelers, was unknown to any of the players. I suppose this was a precursor of the MVP awards of today.

The Deridder game was just one in an undefeated season for Coach Killen's Wildcats. When the final whistle blew on the last game of the season LCHS had scored 215 points to their opponents' thirty. Known around the state as the Ramming Preacher, he scored more points for the Wildcats than any other player on the squad; his total for the year was seventy-eight.

During a special banquet at the close of the season Preacher was elected captain of the team for the next season along with fellow all-state recipient Homer Robinson as co-captain. Preacher enjoyed his football years, but baseball remained his passion.

WILDCATS AND WARREN EASTON GAME WAS TIED

Lake Charles Lost Title By Virtue of Agreement

ZIMMERMAN CLOSED HIGH SCHOOL CAREER

Played Flashy, Sensational Game, As Did Preacher Hebert Also

December 10, 1928. Southwestern Louisiana University's football field in Lafayette. Lake Charles High School Wildcats versus the Warren Easton Eagles of New Orleans. At stake: the championship of South Louisiana. The headlines give a good thumbnail sketch of how the game unfolded. Don Zimmerman racked up the yardage; Preacher Hebert brought the bacon home.

Since there was no such thing as overtime in 1928, the game was over when the final gun sounded at the end of the fourth quarter. Before a game was started, team reps agreed on how to declare a winner in a playoff game in case of a knotted score. The most popular way to decide this was to award the victory to whichever team had racked up the most first downs.

Late in the first quarter Zimmerman went on one of his rampages. After a punt he made an end run around the left end for eighteen yards and got the ball to the Eagle forty-yard marker. Hebert plowed through right tackle for six yards. Zimmerman, the Galloping Wildcat, made it to the seven-yard line on the next play.

The Ramming Preacher busted through the Eagle line and came to rest on the three-yard mark just as the first quarter ended. On the first play of the second quarter Hebert brought it a yard closer to the prize. He made it to the Promised Land on the next try. 6-0, Wildcats. A swarm of disgruntled Eagles smothered Zimmerman as he attempted a drop kick for the point after. Still 6-0.

The second half started, and the fans on both sides of the gridiron were treated to both teams marching up and down the field with nothing to show for it the entire third quarter. Warren Easton's football angel woke up in the fourth quarter, and they managed to make it across that hallowed line. The point-after try failed, and it was tied at 6-6.

The remainder of the fourth quarter saw both teams exchange punts and turnovers. With two minutes to play, Lake Charles got the ball at mid-field. Zimmerman ate up thirty yards before being stopped twenty yards from pay dirt and victory. The final gun sounded before they could mount another play.

All eyes were on the scoreboard. 6-6. Nothing left to do but count first downs. Both teams and their coaches crowded around the counters — the head linesman, the field judge, and the newspapermen. Final tally — Warren Easton, 10, Lake Charles, 9. The Eagles were named champions of South Louisiana and would go to the final game for the state championship. The Wildcats would return home to Lake Charles, lick their wounds for awhile, and gear up for the next year.

How Nannie Locke Bostick Became Bobbie Hebert

The phone rang in the Bostick house, and my granddaddy answered. "Bobbie? There's no one here by that name."

My mother ran into the room. "It's for me. It's for me," she said, and took the phone out of his hand. "Oh, that was my father," she continued speaking into the phone. "He was just kidding around."

I don't know if that's how it really went down, because I wasn't around when it happened. My mother was in junior high at Central School in Lake Charles, but we heard that story many times as we were growing up. Her real name was Nannie Locke Bostick, and everyone in her family called her Nannie Locke. When she started school at Central she decided she didn't want to be called Nannie Goat any longer , and she told them her name was Bobbie Bostick. She went through school and her life in Louisiana as Bobbie. My father called her Bob until the day he died. To her Texas relatives she was Nannie Locke – always with the middle name.

All her friends in Louisiana and her in-laws called her Bobbie. To all the nieces and nephews in Louisiana she was Aunt Bobbie. To the nieces and nephews on her side of the family she was Aunt Nannie Locke. To all the baseball players over the years she was known as Bobbie Hebert. She was always the one to take control of any situation.

Nannie "Bobbie" Bostick

1929 Football Games

WILDCATS SHOWED LOTS OF FIGHT IN CROWLEY GAME
Won Second Contest of Year by 19-0
PREACHER HEBERT DID MOST OF SCORING
Baldwin and Khoury Played Good Game for Home Team

The last day of September, 1929, dawned hot and muggy in Lake Charles, Louisiana. Definitely not a day for football, but that's what the Wildcats were offering up to their fans that day in a game against the Crowley Gents. The semi-tropical heat slowed everyone down—fans as well as players, but the intrepid boys in red and blue showed enough flashes of brilliance throughout the afternoon at American Legion Park to keep the rooting section on their feet most of the time.

The offensive punch that had taken the day off the week before against Beaumont was supplied mostly by team captain, fullback Preacher Hebert, and his deadly line smashes. He earned his reputation as one of the hardest hitting backs in the state by accounting for most of the yardage gained that day.

The first score of the game came in the second quarter that started out on the forty-yard line. A series of short gains brought the ball down to easy striking distance for him. He rammed through two more times, and finally hit pay dirt on the third try. He finished up by plunging through to add the extra point. 7-0.

The Wildcat defense scored the second touchdown in the third quarter. The Gents had been backed up to their own ten-yard line. Their quarterback attempted to punt out of the hole. Kamiel Khoury, the big Wildcat, tore through the line and blocked the punt. It went skittering into the end zone, and Marvin Baldwin, Wildcat left tackle, jumped on it for the score. 13-0. Hebert tried another run for the extra point, but that time the Crowley line held.

The fourth quarter rolled around, and the local boys got their final tally. The Crowley quarterback was trying to kick out of his own end zone. He got rattled and decided to pass. Hebert intercepted and took it in for another six points. 19-0. This time they tried to kick the point-after. No dice.

The defense won that game. They scored two of the three touchdowns. They held the highly-touted Gents to two first downs. Of course, back then the offense and the defense were the same players. In that game Coach Killen substituted one time only. Ten of those players were on that field the whole game. Unheard of nowadays.

BULLDOGS DOWNED WILDCATS BEFORE RECORD CROWD
Game Was Hard-Fought From Start To Finish
Hebert, Tritico, and Robinson Played Well for Red and Blue

October 19, 1929.

Lest the reader think Preacher Hebert just had to show up, and the game was in the "W" column, take a look at the game between the Wildcats and the Bulldogs of Jennings. The 'Cats had made the trip eastward on Highway 90 to the small town of Jennings, Louisiana, in mid-October to take on the maroon and white Bulldogs. They returned to Lake Charles bloodied but unbowed, having been handed a 12-7 defeat by the host team.

Both of the Jennings touchdowns were scored in the first half—one in the first quarter and the other in the second. Both of them came about as a result of Wildcat fumbles in their own territory. The Bulldogs recovered a miscue on the Wildcat thirty-five yard line and took it over in two plays. Extra point try failed.

The second give-away saw the Wildcats sitting on the Jennings nineteen yard line, poised to take it in to tie the game. This time it was not to be. This time the 'Cats handed the ball back to their hosts, who marched back down field and scored their second touchdown. Point-after try failed again. 12-0.

Coach Killen obviously had a serious discussion with his team since they returned to the field in the third quarter seemingly ready to play football. A series of line blasts by Hebert, and a long pass from Hebert to Shaheen resulted in a Lake Charles gain near enough to the goal line for Stevenson to carry the ball in for the score. Giovanni kicked the extra point, bringing the score to 12-7.

The Wildcats knew all they had to do was score one more touchdown, and the game was theirs. Of course, they also had to hold Jennings scoreless. Which they did. The 'Dogs threatened to score several times in the final period, but it was as though an invisible barrier was in place across the goal lines. Neither team seemed able to break through, and 12-7 remained the final score.

Hebert was easily the outstanding Wildcat, according to the American Press sportswriter. Time and again he shredded the Jennings line for long gains. His passes to his halfbacks gained more ground for Lake Charles than any other method of attack. Tritico and Robinson added yardage to the ground gains.

Hebert also shone on defense, as did ends Allen and Shaheen, as well as tackles Khoury and Baldwin. Jennings halfbacks Langley and Biggs teamed up with the other two Jennings backs to cause mayhem on the gridiron for the Wildcats. Those two fumbles were costly to Lake Charles.

WILDCATS DOWNED ALEXANDRIA ON AN ICY GRIDIRON
Lake Charles Gridsters Outplayed Bolton Bears Throughout Game

November 22, 1929. Alexandria, Louisiana. Lake Charles Wildcats versus Bolton Bears. This game was far different from the one Lake Charles played against Crowley in late September. That game was played in near-tropical temperatures, warm enough to send players and fans alike into mid-summer doldrums even though the summer of 1929 was officially a thing of the past.

Late November was the opposite. This time around the sidelines were ablaze with bonfires warming the intrepid fans who braved the blizzard as they cheered their teams on, hoping for the elusive "W."

The game was filled with fumbles, and while one may try to blame a defeat on the weather, the fact remains that both teams played amidst the same conditions. Usually in that situation the superior team would prevail—and that's what happened in Alexandria that icy November day.

The season was coming to a close along with Wally Hebert's football career at Lake Charles High. It was one of his better games in spite of the weather. He scored both Wildcat touchdowns—one in the first quarter and one in the fourth.

He was ably assisted by Joe Tritico, fleet-footed Wildcat halfback, who was the leading ground-gainer for the 'Cats. Lest their heads got too big for their helmets, let's not forget the guys on the forward line—Shaheen, Hall, Guidry, Watson, Khoury, and Allen—who kept the backfield—Hebert, Tritico, Robinson, and Stevenson—from getting plowed under by the young men from Alexandria.

Hebert closed out his high school career with a selection to the all-state team. He enjoyed his football years, but it was time to shed the shoulder pads for a pitcher's mitt.

Will Lead Wildcats This Year

PREACHER HEBERT   **HOMER ROBINSON**

"Preacher" Hebert, plunging Wildcat full back, and Homer Robinson, all-state lineman, who will lead the Lake Charles high school football team through the season which opens against Beaumont here next Saturday. Hebert and Robinson are captain and alternate captain, respectively. They were elected to lead the Wildcats this year at a special banquet given at the close of last season for the expressed purpose of choosing leaders for the '29 squad.

Wallace "Preacher" Hebert

Basketball

Football season came to an end, but that didn't mean it was time for rest and relaxation for the Ramming Preacher. He traded in a bullet-shaped ball for a round one. He still wore the red and blue of Coach Curtis Cooke's Lake Charles Wildcat basketball team as the right forward. In his spare time he filled the same position for the Gulf States Utilities' cagers.

One night in mid-January the Gulf States five handed a defeat to the boys of the Krause and Managan Lumbermen by the strange score of 34-12. More like a football score than basketball. Gulf States took an early lead and held it throughout the game thanks in part to the "brilliant goal tossing of Preacher Hebert" and his game-high sixteen points.

Poor K&M—they just couldn't catch a break. A week after the Gulf States five whacked them 34-12, the high school quintet did even more damage by a score of 36-9. Preacher Hebert was once again high scorer with eleven points. One might wonder about the low scores and individual output. Back then there was no such thing as a three-point shot.

Anything depending on hand-eye coordination was no problem for Hebert. Hitting rabbits with barrel staves. Shooting alligators between the eyes. Knocking a smokestack off a tractor—but that's another story. He could hit a moving receiver in football. Round ball in the net? No problem. He also excelled in track and field with the javelin and discus, but he found his greatest joy when he was on the pitcher's mound whipping that little ball across home plate.

End of an Era

Preacher Hebert stepped on the pitcher's mound while his teammates on the Gulf States Utilities ball club took the field against a strong Houston Electric Company team. When it was all over the rangy lefthander from Louisiana had handed the opposing team its first defeat in five years, tossing a no-hit, no-run game against the boys from Texas.

After high school Preacher had started working at Gulf States Utilities. Good job, plenty of money, he said. During the summer they played baseball against other semi-pro teams. He pitched three seasons for Gulf States, and during one season pitched twelve games — winning ten and losing two. Of these twelve games three were two-hitters, one was a one-hitter, and four were shut-outs. During the no-hit game Ray Cahill, a pro scout for the St. Louis Browns, was sitting in the stands watching a relative of his play for the Houston team.

He liked what he saw when the young southpaw for Gulf States took the mound and shut the Texas team down. He passed his information on to the home office. The Browns signed Hebert to play on the Class C Springfield Midgets for the 1930 season. The other teams in that league were Joplin, Missouri; Fort Smith, Arkansas; Shawnee, Oklahoma; and Independence, Missouri. Hebert never forgot that hot, dry summer and those uncomfortable bus rides to different cities.

On a Sunday morning in March, 1930, he was to report to Springfield, Missouri, and begin spring training with the Western League club of that city. Before he left Lake Charles, members of the Gulf States baseball team presented him with a pitcher's glove and a leather Gladstone bag. The team spokesman had some farewell words for him.

"We all hate to see Preacher go, but we know that it is a step forward for him, and some day we hope to be reading of Preacher pitching one-and-two-hit games in the big leagues." Turns out the speaker got his wish. Read on.

PART II
Leaving the Bayou

THE BASEBALL YEARS

1930 To 1943

Wally Hebert and Ted Lyons

Never let the fear of striking out get in your way.

George Herman "Babe" Ruth

THREE

1930

4-24-30 Midgets/Miners

Lefty Hebert Plays Hero In Thrilling First Game
Youthful Southpaw Silences Big Bats of Joplin Club
Preacher Hebert Won First Tilt For Springfield
Hebert Hero Of 15-Inning Mound Duel

On opening day for the Class C Western Association, the Springfield Midgets were scheduled to meet the Joplin Miners on Joplin home turf. Wally Hebert and the rest of the Springfield team blew into town on April 24 raring to get the 1930 season under way. This was unknown territory for new recruit Hebert, who hadn't done much traveling out of Louisiana until then.

Since they were the visitors they got first bat, so they filed into the dugout and took their seats. Manager Kid Eberfield had designated Dick Gray to start on the mound, so Hebert knew he needed to get comfortable since he wouldn't be seeing any action that day. Little did he know.

The Miners scattered to their positions on the diamond, the first pitch was tossed, and the umpire yelled "Play ball." The 1930 season officially got under way. The Midgets got down to business right away, putting men on base and sending them across the plate. When inning number one ended the Midgets led by a score of 2-0.

Then came a five-inning drought of action at home plate for both teams. It was like the Midgets decided they had done all that was necessary. Now all they had to do was hold their opponent scoreless. It was fun while it lasted. Then along came the sixth inning.

The Midgets, batting first, ended up with another zero on the scoreboard. Joplin decided enough was enough. Their fans were getting antsy. Gray, Springfield's starting pitcher, had been humming along nicely, keeping runs off the scoreboard, but the Miners bore down on him, and by the time the third out was called the score was tied. 2-2. That was all for Gray, and Eberfield sent Hebert to the mound. This was it. What he had dreamed of ever since he hefted his first baseball. Pitching in the pros.

He took his warm-up pitches and faced his first professional batter. The game groaned on for the next eight innings with nothing happening offensively on either side. Along the way Hebert struck out five Miners, allowed six hits, and walked two. His team mates helped keep Miner runs off the scoreboard.

The top of the *fifteenth* inning rolled around. Dusk threatened to stop the game. The Midget players decided to end it all and got to Joplin's pitcher for three runs, including one scored by Hebert. The Miners had one more chance to eke out a win.

Hebert was having none of that. He had been pitching nine and two-thirds innings—a whole game and then some. He was ready to hang it up. He stymied the Joplin bats in the bottom of the fifteenth, and the game was mercifully over. 5-2.

The 1200 or so Joplin fans who showed up to cheer for their team left the ballpark worn out and heart-broken. They had been glued to their seats agonizing over a three hour contest that in the end didn't go their way. The victorious Midgets, who I'm sure were too exhausted to do much celebrating, boarded a bus for a night ride to the next battle.

During the 1930 season with Springfield Hebert pitched thirty-six games, winning fifteen and losing sixteen. One newspaper reported some of the losses were not all his fault. For example, in one of those losses he allowed but one base hit, but five fielding errors proved costly and led to defeat, for which the pitcher always gets blamed in the stats.

He spent one season playing for Springfield, and in 1931 he was on his way to St. Louis and the big league.

Pitching Statistics for 1930:

Games Played: 36

Innings Pitched: 251

Won: 15

Lost: 16

Percentage: .484

Hits: 265

Strike-outs: 154

Bases on Balls: 83

FOUR

1931

6-12-31 Browns/Athletics

Wallace Hebert Had Athletics at His Mercy During League Debut
Preacher Hebert Humbles World's Champions by 8 to 2
LAKE CHARLES BOY'S DEBUT IS IMPRESSIVE
19-Year-Old Southpaw Gives Up Only Seven Hits As Browns Cut Mack's First Place Lead

The headlines above are somewhat misleading about Wally Hebert's first start in the major leagues against the reigning world champion Philadelphia Athletics. He really was a southpaw, and he really did hand Philly an 8-2 shellacking in his first major league start. The misinformation was about his age at the time. He was not nineteen. He was born in 1907. In June 1931 he would have been twenty-three, turning twenty-four in August.

The courthouse in Lake Charles caught fire and burned all the birth certificates. With no way to prove anyone's age, some of the guys stayed in high school and played sports for a couple of extra years. Back then they weren't as strict as they are now about eligibility. It made good copy to write about a nineteen-year-old rookie popping it to the world champions. It was still quite a feat no matter the age.

Even though this was his first starting assignment, the Browns had benefitted earlier from his relief work on the mound. His debut start was touted as the greatest of the year among the rookies who came up that spring.

His mound opponent that day was Rube Walberg, considered one of the best pitchers in the game and riding a seven-game winning streak. Hebert and his teammates put the quietus on that, sending Walberg packing in the seventh inning.

He had the Philly bats at his mercy throughout the nine innings, scattering seven hits around, and had such hitters as Al Simmons and Jimmy Foxx swinging at thin air. Simmons, generally conceded to be one of the best hitters in baseball, went to the plate four times with nothing to show for it. Foxx didn't do much better—one single out of four times up.

Browns' Goose Goslin did his part in the win, going four for four at the plate, including a homer, a triple, and two runs batted in. Irving Burns hit a home run, and all but one of the Browns got at least one hit. Heady stuff for a young man who had been playing for his high school team two short years earlier.

St. Louis started off like gangbusters, scoring three runs in the first inning. With a three run lead they decided to take a batting hiatus. They hopped along for four innings, taking that lead for granted. In the bottom of the fifth frame the Athletics scored. 3-1. That still didn't wake up the Browns. Another zero in the top of the sixth. Philadelphia came back in their half and scored another. 3-2. Uh-oh.

Top of the seventh rolled around, and the Browns decided to get busy. They scored three more times, increasing their lead to 6-2. That's when Walberg made his exit. Hebert shut the host team down the next three innings while his mates added two more in the top of the eighth. Final score, 8-2.

Two weeks later, on June 24, Hebert did it again—just to prove the first time around was no fluke. This time the Athletics made their trip to St. Louis and were again put down by a much closer score. This was Hebert's third major league victory, and once again he shut down the bats of Simmons and Foxx, as well as another dangerous hitter, Mickey Cochrane. This time around Simmons got one hit out of four at-bats. Foxx went zero for four, and Cochrane went zilch for five.

Goose Goslin again came through with two home runs, and the second baseman also hit a homer. Walberg was credited with the loss to the rookie from Louisiana for the second time in two weeks.

Meanwhile, back in Lake Charles no one was surprised at Hebert's great start. Everyone there knew all along Preacher would make good when given a chance. Safe to say it was gratifying to hear of him trouncing the world champions. After all, they had been watching him for years at Lake Charles High where he was an all-state fullback in football, as well as excelling in basketball and track.

Baseball was always his first love. The good citizens of Lake Charles remember the kid who once chased down balls for Connie Mack's Athletics during spring training, and who always dreamed of growing up to be like them.

The following poem appeared the next day, June 13, in the St. Louis Post-Dispatch. The column was titled "Sport Salad," written by L.C. Davis.

Fans, Meet Mr. Hebert

Young Wallace Hebert Brown recruit,
Put on his junior baseball suit,
And neatly trimmed the A's.
When Wallace gave the Browns a leg,
And moved his playmates up a peg
The fans were in a daze.

The world-renowned White Elephants
Could do but little with his slants,
And proved an easy mark.
Though Wally still is in his teens
He spilled the scrapple and the beans,
All over Connie's park.

The A's were eating from his mitt,
And as the pill they couldn't hit
He had them on the run.
Not only that, the youthful ace
Struck Simmons out with three on base,
A thing that's seldom done.

White Elephants was a nickname used by the Athletics. The "Connie" mentioned here is Connie Mack, longtime head of the A's.

6-21-31 Browns/Yankees

PREACHER HAS ONLY A BREEZE IN NIGHTCAP
BROWNS TWICE DEFEAT YANKS
Wally Stewart Wins Opener; Hebert, Rookie, Caps Nightcap

Sandwiched between those two games against the Athletics Hebert pitched in the second game of a double-header against the New York Yankees where he finally got to start a game in front of the hometown crowd at Sportsman Park in St. Louis.

The Browns hosted the Yankees on Sunday afternoon, June 21, and decided to treat their fans to two games of baseball for a change. Wally Stewart was on the mound for the Brownies in the first game and eked out a 9-7 victory while serving up seven hits. Three of those hits happened to be home runs—one each for Ruth, Gehrig, and Lazzeri.

Rookie Wally Hebert had an easier time with his stint on the mound. He pitched five innings of shutout ball before letting the visitors on the scoreboard. They scored once in the sixth and once in the eighth, but it was too little too late. Hebert went the distance for St. Louis while New York threw three pitchers at the Browns to no avail.

Hebert didn't seem intimidated by the big guns in the Yankee batting order. He wasn't afraid to pitch to Babe Ruth or Lou Gehrig, and disdained walking them on purpose. Gehrig managed one single, and Ruth got two hits out of four trips to the plate. Indeed, Ruth with his two scratch hits, was the only man in the Yankee lineup who had any luck at all against Hebert's offerings.

St. Louis started the scoring glut in the second inning with two runs, and added four more in the next frame. This brought the score to 6-0, basically putting the game in the "W" column right then. After the Yanks put their run up the Browns came right back at them with a run of their own. 7-1 Browns. Eighth inning: same song, second verse. One for the Yankees, one for the Browns. 8-2. Another goose egg for New York in the top of the ninth, and the game was over.

Hebert allowed one home run by Yankee shortstop Lary. At the plate he connected with one hit in four tries and scored one run. I'm sure the fans went home feeling it was money well spent. Their guys didn't beat the Yankees twice in one day very often.

6-28-31 Browns/Red Sox

Hebert Helps Browns Stretch Winning Streak to 8 Games
PREACHER WINS FOURTH VICTORY BY DOWNING SOX
Lake Charles Youth Helps Browns To Double Win Over Boston
RED SOX BOW TO 'PREACHER' IN NIGHTCAP
Score of Both Contests Is 5-4 As St. Louis Makes It Four Straight Victories Over Boston

June 28, 1931. The Browns played host to the Boston Red Sox. Surprising everyone, the Browns were riding a six-game winning streak. In fact, one sportswriter referred to them as the new phenomenon of the American League. On that Sunday afternoon in St. Louis they extended that streak to eight in a row by defeating the Boston Red Sox twice by the identical scores of 5-4.

Wally Hebert was the star of the second game — on the mound and at the plate. He found himself in trouble several times, giving up twelve hits to the foe. Those twelve hits included two home runs by the Sox right-fielder Webb, whose teammates added two more runs.

It was nail-biter of a game. St. Louis scored its first two runs in the third inning. Hebert pitched a shutout for three innings. In the top of the fourth Webb smacked his first homer into the pavilion, tying the score at two-all. The Browns came right back at them and added two more runs in the bottom of the fourth. 4-2, Browns.

For the next four innings neither team could get anything going, but in the top of the eighth Boston's bats awoke from their coma and they scored a run. 4-3. St. Louis fans got un-relaxed. They didn't have to wait long for their guys to retaliate. They obliterated Boston's run by scoring one of their own in the bottom of the eighth. 5-3. Back to a two-run lead for the Brownies. Fans relaxed again.

Top of the ninth. Sox right-fielder Webb at the plate, swinging his bat and grinning. He sent the rookie pitcher's offering soaring over the pavilion. 5-4.Not good. The Sox hopes came alive. Just one run to tie, two to take the lead. Then hold St. Louis in the bottom half, and their streak would be broken.

Hebert dashed the visitors' hopes by pitching out of yet another pickle.

He retired the side, and the game was in the rear view mirror. 5-4. The Browns had won eight in a row and four straight over Boston. It was Hebert's fourth victory against no losses.

The Red Sox had gone through three pitchers trying to pull a victory out of the hat. The Brown batters were in fine fettle, tapping Boston pitchers for fifteen hits. Hebert himself went two for four at the plate for a .500 batting percentage.

July 4, 1931

Sportscasters in St. Louis and other American League stadiums, not knowing about the Cajun culture of Louisiana, called Browns rookie Wally "Hee-bert." A baseball fan in Lake Charles wrote to the St. Louis newspapers to educate them on the correct pronunciation. Mr. O.B. Hunter told them it's not "Hee-bert," but "A-bare," with the accent on the "A."

Smart Fans Call Hebert "a bear"; Yankees, Athletics Find It's True. St. Louis fans were not technical over the pronunciation of any player's name, but those who saw Hebert's performances decided that the rookie from the bayou was something of "a bear" to opposing batters. After all, in three of his first four starts he beat the high-powered Athletics twice as well as the hard-hitting Yankees.

What had impressed baseball commentators most about the rookie was his courage in "putting 'em over" to Babe Ruth, Lou Gehrig, Jimmy Foxx, Al Simmons, and other dangerous hitters. In other words, he wasn't afraid to pitch to them—no intentional walks. The media critics decided he was "the goods," and that Brown manager Bill Killefer could dismiss the southpaw pitching problem, which would be a good thing since he had other things to worry about, such as weak hitting.

7-29-31 Browns/Athletics

Wally Hebert, Jinx in Several Games, is Chased by White Elephants

Back in July 1931 the Athletics finally broke the Hebert jinx — final score 6-3. They were playing at Shibe Park in Philadelphia. The A's were ahead of the visiting Browns by a score of 3-1.

Enter one Goose Goslin of the Browns who tied the game at three all with a homer in the top of the eighth. Then into the game came Mose (Lefty) Grove for the A's. No outs for the Browns, and a man on third. Not exactly a situation any pitcher would be happy to face. However, Grove took care of the St. Louis line-up one-two-three. The first batter popped up, the second struck out, and the third was thrown out by the shortstop.

Al Simmons, still smarting from those two previous losses to Wally, was first man up in the bottom of the eighth. He whacked the ball over the left field fence to go out in front of the Browns 4-3. Two more runs scored, bringing the score to 6-3 by the time the inning ended. All Grove had to do was get rid of three Brownies, which he did forthwith.

With this win the Athletics finally caught up with the southpaw from the Louisiana bayous who had shut them down twice before. The best Connie Mack's boys could do for seven innings was to score three runs in single doses.

Nevertheless, a win is a win, and revenge is always sweet — and best served up cold.

Pitching Statistics for 1931

Games:23

Innings Pitched: 103

Won: 6

Lost: 7

Percentage: .462

Hits: 128

Strikeouts: 26

Bases on Balls: 43

Earned Run Average: 5.07

FIVE

1932

4-5-32 Hebert and Rommel

A story about Wallace "Preacher" Hebert found its way into the American Press dated April 5, 1932. The story was printed on sports pages around the country and also made it to the radio. Eddie Rommel was one of the pitchers for Connie Mack's world champion Philadelphia Athletics. The team had trained in Athletic Park in Lake Charles, Louisiana. He remembered a youngster there chasing balls for the them during batting practice.

"Mistah Rommel, would you all mind showing me how you
all throw that air knuckle ball we uns have heered about?"

The speaker was a kid of about eight or nine years of age. He had come to the Athletics' training field in Lake Charles to watch the champs practice.

"Well, you take the ball like this," replied Eddie. "But say, kid
your hand is too small. Come around about ten years from now and
I'll show you."

"Got mighty big hands, Mistah Rommel, for a boy goin' on nine."

"I know you have, sonny, but you will have to wait a few years before you will be strong enough to throw a ball up to the plate."

"All right," replied the youngster ruefully, "but you jest remember what I'm telling you. I'm going to be a big league pitcher some day."

"The next time I saw that kid," related Rommel last summer, "was on June 11 when he stepped on the rubber at Shibe Park, let our champs down with seven hits, fanned Al Simmons with the bases filled, and beat us 8 to 2. I didn't know I ever had seen him before until he told me he was that little lad who had asked me how to throw a knuckle ball all those years ago."

Although my father always had a slight Cajun lilt to his speech, I never heard him say anything like "that air" or "we uns" or "heered about." Everything else in the story is probably true. The Athletics trained in Lake Charles, and he probably asked Eddie Rommel about his knuckleball—and he did pitch against Rommel and the Athletics, beating them 8-2 on June 11, 1931.

3-10-32 Spring Training

Killefer, Badly in Need of Good Pitchers, Is Banking on Hebert

The big question for Browns manager Killefer in 1932 was how to bring the team out of the second division. On the roster that year were five players who hit better than .300 in 1931, but not one pitcher who won more games than he lost. To get the team into the first division pitchers needed to be developed.

At the beginning of the 1931 season Wally Hebert, along with several recruits, had been added to the staff for the express purpose of pitching to Browns' batters. He was retained for the remainder of the season after making a favorable impression on Killefer.

A sweeping curve ball, plus good control, were his chief attributes. He was given a thorough trial by Killefer during the rookie season in 1931, and was making rapid progress until after a rainy day in Washington he developed a peculiar growth below his left shoulder. Several doctors ordered removal of the growth, but Hebert was having none of that. He refused any cutting, and during the off-season back home in the Louisiana oilfields the lump disappeared.

Killefer said he was banking on Wally Hebert, and was looking for some fine things from the young southpaw in the current season. Indeed, in the Browns' first exhibition game of spring training he showed well, holding Buffalo to two hits in four innings.

1932 Browns Spring Training

Manager Bill Killefer sat on the bench with a sports writer who was there to look over the current crop of Browns. The writer was there that day for an inside line on the "kid" who fanned Babe Ruth and beat the Athletics in his first major league game.

Killefer pointed to the man on the pitcher's mound and said to the writer that the one he came to see was on the hill pitching to the batters.

"Take a good look at him. He's the best prospect as a pitcher I have seen in many years."

Killefer continued, explaining in detail the fine points of the young man. "Look at those arms," he went on. "They hang below his knees. That's what a pitcher needs—long arms. Watch him when he winds up. He's like a contortionist. It doesn't seem he has a bone in his body—all muscles. I'll say "all arms."

The writer watched as Hebert hoisted his left arm and, with little exertion, burned a fast ball past the eyebrows of the batter, who took a full cut, but was a few seconds too late.

Killefer said he'd call the young man over so the writer could talk to him. "I want you to get a good look at his hands. I've never seen such mitts in my life. A baseball looks the size of a pea when he wraps his fingers around it."

Killefer's guest acknowledged the Brown's manager knew his hands. He said Hebert had the largest hands he had ever seen. One of the stories circulating says he could hold nine baseballs in one hand. Sounds kind of far-fetched—I never saw it, but he did have extra large hands.

One day in the 1990's my brother Wally brought some baseballs for Dad to autograph for his two girls. He had about six balls for signing. He asked Dad if the nine baseballs story was true, and got a demonstration. Using two of the balls, Dad put them between thumb and forefinger, one at the palm and outward. Then he took the same two balls and did the same between index and middle finger, middle and ring, and ring and little finger. "Then you put one more in the palm of your hand," he said.

The writer knew of his athletic prowess back home in Lake Charles—in track, basketball, and football. However, baseball was always number one.

Hebert remembered his first baseball game at school. "I won my first game, 3 to 1, fanned fourteen batters and allowed three hits. All the boys gave me credit for winning the game, and that's when I forgot about football, track, and basketball. Baseball was my hobby, and I had one ambition as a kid—to become a major leaguer. I'm up here, and, honestly, it seems like a dream."

6-10-32 Browns/Yankees

Yankees Shade St. Louis, 3-1
Gomez Has Edge Over Wally Hebert in Sensational Pitching Battle

Season 1932 was not a replay of 1931 for Wally Hebert, as he managed to eke out but one victory against twelve losses. On June 10 of that year the Browns hosted the Yankees in St. Louis where he pitched a game that on any other day and against any other pitcher would have been in the win column.

New York scored one run in the first inning, and St. Louis evened things up in the bottom of the second. It remained tied for the next five frames. Vernon Gomez, pitching for the Yankees, allowed the Browns but three hits, and Hebert gave up four. Four hits was usually good for a win, but St. Louis bats were in a coma, and they never got anything going after the second inning. The Yanks put two more runs on the board in the top of the seventh. That broke the tie and won the game for the boys from the Big Apple. Hebert was relieved in the eighth inning and charged with the loss.

The home town crowd went home knowing they had just seen a superb pitching duel, but unhappy the wrong team won it.

6-28-32 St. Louis Post-Dispatch

According to the sports writer, James M. Gould, all the Brownie players liked the young southpaw from Louisiana. His roommate on the road was Walter Stewart, himself quite a productive lefty pitcher, who was impressed with the ability of his young roomie. Stewart had this to say about him. "Hebert's got what most southpaws lack—control. With it, he has a real fast one and a sidearm curve which is plenty tough for any batter to hit. There is hardly a chance that he won't come through to real stardom in the majors. You can bet anything I can do to help him I will for he's a likeable chap and very willing to learn."

In Philadelphia when Hebert was told his debut start would be against the champion Athletics he didn't believe it at first. Walter Stewart told him that if he didn't win don't bother to come back to the room after the game. He thought he was in real trouble when Al Simmons came up with the bases loaded, but decided if he didn't want to sleep on the street that night he'd better dispose of one of the most dangerous hitters around—which he did with a well-placed curve for a third strike.

An interviewer asked him who he would rather pitch against—Simmons, Foxx, or Gehrig. He said it was no fun to pitch against any of them. "Of course, Ruth and Gehrig are somewhat at a disadvantage because they're left-handed hitters, but you certainly can't fool around with them. I haven't any system of pitching. They tell me I have good control, and I try to make the batters hit. I throw what Ferrell (the catcher) tells me to throw, and so far that's proven the right way. Guess I'll keep on doing it."

Hebert's stats against Simmons, Foxx, Ruth, and Gehrig were interesting, according to Mr. Gould. He had pitched against Ruth six times and the Babe hit two singles. He faced Gehrig six times and held him to one single. Simmons was hitless in four tries and Foxx got one single in four tries. So against perhaps the four best hitters in the American League the young man from the bayous had pitched them down to a .200 average for the four of them.

7-24-32 Browns/Tigers

Browns Share In Twin Bill With Detroit
Wally Hebert Gets Credit For First Victory in Second Game

Here's the account of his one and only win in 1932. On July 24 with the season in full tilt the Detroit Tigers invaded St. Louis for the second of their three double-headers. The first game was a cake walk for the Tigers. They garnered four runs in the first inning and held the lead all the way, finishing with a 6-2 victory. One down and one to go with those pesky Browns.

When they saw who was on the mound for the Browns, they relaxed. This game was in the bag, they told each other. Wally Hebert hadn't won a game all year; eight contests down the tubes. The Tigers were certainly not intimidated by a winless pitcher. They settled back in the dugout, confident, and ready to let the slaughter begin.

At the end of the top half of the first inning they knew they were on their way, grabbing the lead by two. In the bottom half of the inning their enthusiasm increased as they sent the Browns back to the diamond down 2-0.

That enthusiasm waned somewhat when Goose Goslin worked his magic and belted a four-baser in the second frame. 2-1. Hebert kept the Tigers off the board until the top of the fourth, when they managed another run. 3-1. Back to a two-run lead.

It didn't last long. After a scoreless fifth inning for the Tigers, the Browns came out of their coma and put three up in the bottom half, taking the lead 4-3.

The Browns went on a scoring spree for the next three innings. Three in the fifth, two in the sixth, and three more in the seventh, bringing the score to 9-3. In the meantime, Hebert held the foe scoreless for those three innings. The Tigers tried their best to get back into the game, tallying four times in the top of the eighth. Score, 9-7. Saint Louis fans got a bit antsy at that turn of events. Two runs was not enough of a lead for complacency. Hebert left for the showers in that eighth inning. It took two more Brown pitchers to finally retire the side, and the home town boys filed into the dugout vowing to pull that one out of the fire.

The Browns added another run in their half of the eighth. 10-7. One inning remaining. All they had to do was keep the Tigers off the scoreboard. Which they did. Three outs. No score. Game over, and Hebert got his solo win for 1932.

He pitched good ball for seven innings, and he and his teammates put the runs up to win. He was the batting star of the game, going to the plate four times. Four times he got on base. Three singles, one double. He scored three times, and got one RBI. Not bad for the bottom of the order.

That was in late July, mercifully close to the end of a season he would just as soon forget. Like that 1921 summer in the swamp, he would overcome a 1-12 baseball season and live to fight another day.

Pitching Statistics for 1932:

Games: 35

Innings Pitched: 108

Won: 1

Lost: 12

Percentage: .77

Hits: 145

Strikeouts: 29

Bases on Balls: 45

Earned Run Average: 6.50

1932 was a disappointment, to say the least, especially after his successes in 1931. There's always next year.

11-24-32 Happy Ending

The year 1932 was not a total bust for the young pitcher from Louisiana. On November 24, 1932, Wally "Preacher" Hebert married the love of his life— Nannie Locke "Bobbie" Bostick. The wedding took place in Welsh, Louisiana, a small town several miles east of Lake Charles on Highway 90. Bobbie's brother, Jadie Hollaway, stood up with them, and the wedding was officiated by the Justice of the Peace there. Thus began a sixty-seven year love affair.

They decided to tie the knot first and inform their parents later—the reason being to avoid having the event turn into a three-ring circus. They knew my grandmother well. She liked nothing better than having a big shindig to plan, and she was known throughout the family as *The General*.

She had to be satisfied with getting the word out via the newspaper. The following announcement found its way to the paper in Baytown, Texas.

> *Mr. and Mrs. M.H. Bostick of Lake Charles, Louisiana, announce the wedding of their daughter, Nannie Locke, to Wally A. Hebert. The wedding took place November 24 at Welsh, Louisiana. Mr. and Mrs. Hebert will be at home in Lake Charles.*
>
> *Mrs. Hebert is well known here, having attended school here for several years before her parents moved to Lake Charles. She is the niece of Mrs. W. T. Hobson and Mrs. Dona Townes and has many other relatives and friends here.*
>
> *Mr. Hebert is a professional ball pitcher for the St. Louis Browns.*
>
> *Mr. and Mrs. Hebert are spending their honeymoon at the Lamar Hotel in Houston and were the guests of Mrs. Hobson and Mrs. Townes here Monday.*

Bobbie and Preacher Hebert

SIX

1933

3-26-33 Pre-season Hype

As early as March 1933 the sportswriters in St. Louis were musing about the chances of the perennial second division Browns and their chances of moving up. The writer wondered if Wally Hebert could shake off the disappointments of the previous year and put 1932 behind him.

He flashed onto the scene in 1931 like a world beater, but subsided into a one-game winner in 1932. He had the excuse of a sore arm, which manifested itself in training camp and never regained its full usefulness.

His victories of 1931 over powerful opponents seemed to prove he had something. The hope seemed to be that if he was fit enough to go the distance he might be the one to help pull the Browns out of the also-rans.

5-20-33 Browns/Yankees

Hebert Pitches and Bats Browns to 4-2 Victory Over Yankees

Early in the 1933 season the St. Louis Browns traveled to New York to take on the world champion Yankees at Yankee Stadium. Southpaw Wally Hebert was on the mound for the Browns, and pitched shutout ball for six innings.

In the meantime he was not satisfied with silencing Yankee bats; he wanted to help the team at the plate. The second inning rolled around for the Browns after a scoreless first frame. Second-baseman Mellilo came to bat with one out and rapped a single into center field. Up next was third-baseman Scharein, who hit a double to right center. sending Mellilo on to third base. Up next? The pitcher, Wally Hebert. Yankee fans were not worried. Everyone knew pitchers can't hit. That's why they're always stuck at the bottom of the batting order.

The carrot-topped Yank hurler served up two strikes. Home town fans sat back in their seats and breathed easier. Hebert grabbed onto the next pitch and sent it far enough to the right of second base that second-baseman Lazerri managed to field the ball but was off balance. His throw to Gehrig on first pulled Gehrig off, and Hebert was safe on first. Both base runners scored. 2-0. Two RBIs for the pitcher. So much for taking one for granted.

Action at the plate quieted down for both teams until the top of the seventh. In the first half of the frame the Browns got to red-headed Ruffing once again for two more runs, bringing the score to four-zip. A comfortable lead for the visitors. Gloom in the bleachers.

Lazerri opened up the bottom of the seventh with a double, and a trip across the plate courtesy of two infield grounders by teammates. 4-1. Time was getting short for the home team.

After a scoreless eighth inning for both teams, the Yankees shut down the Browns in the top of the ninth. Score still 4-1. One last chance to pull it out of the fire for the hosts. Yankee fans sat forward in their seats. Much nail-biting and wringing of hands — especially when their first two big guns died at home.

Up to the plate stepped Lazerri, hero of the seventh inning. This time he smacked one into the right field bleachers for the round trip. 4-2. A glimmer of hope for the home fans. However, it was not to be. Hebert pitched out of the inning. Final score, 4-2.

The young man from the bayous of Louisiana allowed the reigning champs two runs on six hits. The big bats were largely silent. Ruth got but one single, and Gehrig got nothing at all. Lazerri was responsible for both runs and two of the six hits.

An unusual human interest side show concerning some residents of the Passaic Orphanage in New Jersey: it seems an express train with 500 passengers aboard was headed for a washed-out bridge, and six of the youngsters managed to get a warning to the crew, thus avoiding a probable tragic disaster.

The youngsters wanted a chance to see Babe Ruth, so as a reward for their heroism they got to watch the game, wearing new uniforms, in Colonel Jake Ruppert's private box . These uniforms were gifts from the Yankee organization for the orphanage baseball team.

Some *lagniappe*: just before the game Babe Ruth and the boys took the diamond for fielding practice with the Sultan of Swat brandishing the fungo bat. (Note from me to my non-baseball-savvy readers: a fungo is a fly ball hit for fielding practice by a player who tosses the ball into the air and hits it as it comes down.)

A great experience for the kids even though their idol performed below par that day.

8-15-33 Browns/Athletics

PROBLEMS MOUNT FOR HORNSBY AS BROWNS IMPROVE
New Manager Confronted With Hard Task In Selecting Regulars For 1934
BROWNS DEFEAT ATHLETICS, 7-6 IN 11 INNINGS

In late August Connie Mack's Athletics went to St. Louis to take on the Browns in a double header. It was late enough in the 1933 season for new manager, Rogers Hornsby, to be thinking ahead to 1934. He was none too pleased with several of his regulars, including southpaw Wally Hebert, who had been among those predicted to get a one way ticket out of St. Louis to some baseball backwater town.

Hebert had been turning in less than stellar performances before the arrival of Hornsby on the scene. In the first contest of the twin bill, Hornsby had sent Stiles to the mound. When the top half of the sixth inning ended the A's had jumped on the Brown's pitcher for six runs. The Browns shuffled into the dugout expecting to add a sixth goose egg to the scoreboard.

First batter up—thrown out on first. Two more to go to keep the shutout going for the A's. The next man up—Levey, the shortstop—drew a walk. No harm done. A pinch hitter went in for Brown pitcher, Stiles, and doubled, sending Levey to third. By the time the third out was recorded the Browns had scored six runs, tying the game at six-all and sending the great Lefty Grove to the showers.

Wally Hebert strolled to the mound in the top of the seventh in relief for Stiles, and proceeded to hurl a one-hit shutout for the next five innings. He allowed one single by Jimmy Foxx that went nowhere. He didn't walk a single batter and got great support from his teammates.

Bottom of the eleventh. Brown left-fielder Gullic singled to center for his third straight hit. The next batter sacrificed the base runner to second. First baseman Burns singled to center, sending Gullic across the plate for the winning run. Game over, 7-6, and Hebert added another victory to his meager string.

1933's League-Leading Batter

Better than Jimmie Foxx? Better than Al Simmons? Better than Lou Gehrig and Heinie Manush? No way. Unbelievable.

Believe it.

In 1933 Wally Hebert ended the season with a league-leading .391 batting average.

"Every time we would go up against the Philadelphia Athletics, Simmons would get all over me," Hebert recalled

Back then sports pages listed the leading hitters disregarding the number of times they faced opposing pitchers. Hebert stayed on top of the American League batting race all year long. When Simmons checked the newspaper each day for his average, whose name always appeared before his? Wally Hebert of the St. Louis Browns, the perpetual cellar dwellers.

How is this possible, you might ask. Being a pitcher he went to bat a mere twenty-three times. Nine of those times he got a hit. Do the math, folks. Nine divided by twenty-three is .391.

"Simmons always wanted me to see more action, figuring that if I went to bat more I couldn't possibly keep up that high average."

Simmons was probably right, but being bested by a pitcher must have rankled. The southpaw from the Louisiana bayous took great delight in reliving the time he beat out one of baseball's greatest hitters.

12-13-1933 Off-Season Trades

ST. LOUIS GETS ANDREWS, WILL SEND JOLLEY AND LEVEY TO COAST

The 1933 baseball season was a thing of the past. In mid-December it was nearly time to bid farewell to the year forever. Word came from Chicago that a five-player trade was in the works between the Browns, the Red Sox, and Hollywood of the Pacific Coast League.

The Browns had sent outfielder Carl Reynolds to Boston in exchange for Red Sox outfielder Smead Jolley and pitcher Ivy Andrews, a right-hander, along with some cash. Andrews would join the Browns organization, and Browns manager Hornsby would send Jolley to Hollywood along with southpaw Wally Hebert and shortstop Jim Levey. In exchange for these three the Browns would get Allen Strange, a twenty-four-year-old shortstop whom Hornsby had been watching and considered a top prospect.

As a result of these convoluted negotiations Hebert would find himself across the country tossing baseballs in the sunny climes of southern California. Turns out those seasons in the PCL were the happiest years of my parents' time in baseball.

Pitching Statistics: 1933

Games: 33

Innings Pitched: 88

Won: 4

Lost: 6

Percentage: .400

Hits: 114

Strikeouts: 19

Bases on Balls: 35

Earned Run Average: 5.32

SEVEN

1934

2-16-34 Preseason

Hebert Signs Up With Sheiks

The Hollywood club obtained southpaw Wally Hebert during the winter of 1933 from the St. Louis Browns in a deal that sent Alan Strange to the Browns. In exchange, Hebert and Jim Levey found themselves in the Pacific Coast League—known as the "best minor league." This is the league where many future hall-of-famers got their start—the DiMaggio brothers, Ted Williams, Bobby Doerr—to name a few.

The Los Angeles Times posted an article introducing the young Cajun to the coastal baseball fans. The team had received his signed contract accompanied by a note stating he found the terms highly satisfactory and would leave soon to drive to Riverside for spring training.

The article went on to say he was a smidgeon over six feet tall, weighed 186 pounds, and would be twenty-five years of age in August. He was expected by owner Bill Lane and manager Oscar Vitt to be a valuable member of the potent pitching staff they were putting together to represent the Sheiks.

For west coast fans who might be interested, the writer reported that

Hebert was of French descent and could probably trace his ancestry back to Evangeline. I don't know about that, but it was possible the Hebert forebears and Vangie may have crossed paths along the way.

When President Lane and Manager Vitt arrived at Riverside on the last day of February they found their newly acquired recruits from the Browns already there. Another former Brown, Smead Jolley, also acquired in the Alan Strange deal, was holding out and not in camp.

Hebert had driven in from his Lake Charles home and was full of enthusiasm, eager to get started on the second phase of his baseball journey.

4-16-34 Hollywood/Los Angeles

Sheiks Annex Final Game of Week's Series
Hebert Wins Own Tilt

A Sunday afternoon in April turned out to be bittersweet for the Sheiks. They got dumped on big time 11-5 by the Angels (aka Seraphs) in the first encounter of the double header, but exacted sweet revenge in the finale by a score of 5-3.

Wally Hebert, on the mound for Hollywood in the second game, allowed three hits and one run for the Angels in the second inning. The Sheiks came right back in the bottom half and tied the score 1-1. Hollywood went ahead 2-1 in their half of the third inning on three hits and one run. Hebert opened the inning with the first of his two hits of the game.

Playing tit-for-tat, the Angels took the lead again in the top of the fourth on three hits that translated into two runs. 3-2. Then Hebert settled down and pitched two more shutout innings. For the faithful Hollywood fans it looked like defeat number eight for their team. It was the bottom of the sixth—the last inning in this abbreviated game—limited to six innings to enable the Sheiks to board a train for Seattle to take on the Seattle nine in a series there.

Smead Jolley started the final round with his sixth hit of the day. With two out and two on Jolley managed to score the tying run on an Angel error. The faithful followers in the stands sat up a little straighter. The worst that could happen would be a tie since it was the last inning.

With two out and runners on second and third, Hebert strolled to the plate. The Los Angeles faithful breathed easier. It's the pitcher, after all. How hard can that be? The Angel pitcher let one fly and Hebert whacked it to deep short, managing to beat out the throw. Both base runners scored. Final score 5-3. Wally, going two for three at the plate, got credit for two runs-batted-in, thus winning the game on the mound and at the plate. A nice afternoon's work for the curly-headed Frenchman.

73

7-8-34 Hollywood/Sacramento

Two Victories on 5 Innings Work

Question: How can a pitcher work five innings and get credit for two wins in one day? Impossible, you say? Not when those wily Sheiks were trying to impress the home crowd one Sunday afternoon in July. The usual Sunday double-header was on tap for some 8,000 fans hoping for some more great baseball like what they had been treated to in the past two weeks.

They got their wish. The first game was a nail-biter—a twelve inning affair ending in a 4-3 victory for the home team. The nightcap, an abbreviated game, ended in an 8-6 win for the Sheiks. Two games that went right down to the last inning.

Back to the question. How *does* a pitcher get two wins in five innings on the same day? Read on to find out.

Hollywood had a reputation for coming from behind with rallies to win games. They did not disappoint that day in the first game. Going into the bottom of the ninth they were behind 3-2. Sheik center-fielder Carlyle tried to stretch a double to left field into a triple and got thrown out at third. Vince DiMaggio walked, and Jacobs, Sheik second-baseman, flied out. Two away.

Many disappointed fans had gone for their between-games hot dog, hoping for a better outcome in the nightcap, so they missed the excitement. As a famous Yankee catcher in later years once said; "It ain't over till it's over." Shellenback came in to pinch hit for Doerr and hit a sharp one to the second-baseman, who accidentally kicked the ball away. DiMaggio scored. All tied up 3-3.

Manager Vitt decided to send in a pinch hitter for Sheik pitcher Campbell, who had been at it for nine innings and was probably too tired to go extra innings—or so the manager thought. Vitt picked a player to go to the plate, but changed his mind and sent Wally Hebert in to bat instead. With a man on first and one on third, victory was in sight. However, Hebert made contact but was thrown out at first to retire the side. He grabbed his mitt and took Campbell's place on the mound, where he proceeded to pitch no-hit, no-run ball for three innings.

Hollywood finally won the game in the bottom of the twelfth. Third-baseman Haney's single to center sent a base runner home and the game was finally over after two hours and ten minutes. Hebert got credit for the win on three innings of work. No rest for the weary, however. A six-inning nightcap was coming up.

The Sheiks started the late game like gangbusters, scoring three runs thanks to DiMaggio's home run. Sacramento came right back in the top of the second with two runs. Then they tied things up in the third. Looked like another close one for the home town fans.

A home run in the top of the fourth gave Sacramento a temporary lead, 4-3, but Hollywood retaliated and knotted the score again in the bottom half.

With the score tied at 4-4 in the fifth inning, Sheik pitcher Densmore allowed a single to center. Manager Vitt lifted him and sent Hebert in for the second time that day. The game was his to win or lose. They managed to get out of the top of the fifth with no harm done by Sacramento bats. Score still tied at four-all.

Bottom of the fifth—next to last inning. Time for another Sheik rally. When the smoke cleared, Hollywood had scored four runs, including a homer by DiMaggio. 8-4. Jubilation reigned in the stands.

Don't forget—it ain't over till it's over. Top of the sixth. Last chance for the Senators. Surely the home team could hold on to a four run lead. The home crowd felt confident, but then, without warning the score was 8-6. The visitors had come up with two more runs. Now, all of a sudden there were two men on base and one out. More hand wringing.

Sacramento center-fielder Donovan slugged a hard one over second. Should have been good for two bases, but Sheik second-baseman Jacobs soared into the air and snagged it, robbing the batter of a double. Jacobs rushed in and stomped on second to double the base runner for out number three, robbing the Senators of a tie game. Final score, 8-6.

The home crowd went home happy and worn out. The team went home happy and worn out—eighteen innings of hard fought baseball. Wally Hebert went home happy, wondering how he could be so lucky as to get two victories the same day on only five innings of tossing a ball around.

8-1-34 Hollywood/Los Angeles

One Wednesday night in August Hollywood played host to Los Angeles and set them down in an eleven-inning heart-stopper. Sheik fans were getting used to these things and settled in for the duration, never knowing what to expect.

The skirmish began to degenerate into a free-scoring affair as early as the second inning. Dick Ward was on the mound for the Angels and Wally Hebert did the honors for the Sheiks. The bottom of the second inning saw two walks, two hits, and two runs, and the departure of Angel pitcher number one—Ward. Score: 2-0.

Hollywood first baseman Jacobs slugged the first of his homers, scoring two base runners ahead of him, bringing the score to 5-0. It was beginning to look like a Hollywood rout of their cross town rivals. However, the night was young yet.

The Angels busted loose in the top of the fourth and scored two unearned runs aided by an infield error, a wild pitch, and two hits. 5-2. Not a good inning for Hebert.

Not to be outdone, the Sheiks came roaring back with three runs in the bottom half. Jacobs whacked another homer with two men on once again. Score: 8-2. Time to go get a hot dog.

It looked like Hebert would get out of the fifth unscathed. He had two away and was going after out number three when the Angels said, "Enough already," and scored four runs to get back in the game. One walk, four singles, a wild pitch, and the score was suddenly 8-6. Say what? Those returning with hot dogs wanted to know what happened. Another bad one for Hebert.

Hebert and Angel pitcher number two, Nelson, pitched three innings of shutout ball. Top of the ninth—Hebert disposed of two Angel pinch hitters before getting into more hot water. A single and a home run over the left field wall tied the score at eight-all. In the bottom half of that inning the Sheiks banged out two hits, but couldn't do anything with them, and the game went into extra innings.

In the tenth inning the Angels threatened again with two hits but couldn't translate them into runs. The bottom half was uneventful for Hollywood. The hot dog eaters probably had heartburn by then. Score still knotted. The Angels threatened again in the top of the eleventh with one hit, but that was all.

Bottom of the eleventh—the Old Ogre of the Ozarks, big Smead Jolley was the first man to the plate for Hollywood. He was already perfect for the night—four hits and four at-bats. He latched on to one of Whitey Campbell's offerings and smacked it into the stands. Game over. 9-8.

Hebert went the distance, but was in trouble off and on all night. It wasn't pretty, but a win was a win.

Pitching Statistics: 1934

Games 37

Innings Pitched: 170

Won: 11

Lost: 11

Hits: 200

Strikeouts: 53

Bases on Balls: 49

Earned Run Average: 4.23

EIGHT

1935

4-9-35 Hollywood/Portland

SHEIKS SHELL PORTLAND DUCKS, 8 TO 1

The 1935 season got underway in April with the Sheiks sporting a new manager—Frank Shellenback, aka Shelly—who also did double duty as a pitcher. In early April Hollywood played host to the Portland Ducks and didn't treat their guests well. The Ducks scored a couple of technical knockouts, so to speak, but could only manage one run. The Sheiks, on the other hand, did things in bunches, scoring three runs in the third inning and five in the fifth. They coasted the rest of the way, admiring their handiwork on the scoreboard.

Two Sheiks were injured in freak accidents and had to leave the game early. George Myatt, young Sheik shortstop, was a base-runner on first. Levey's bunt rolled foul, but Portland catcher Cronin, fielded it and tossed it to second to head off Myatt. The second baseman attempted to throw to first and instead hit Myatt over his eye, knocking him out cold. He had a nice bump over one eye, but was expected to play the next day.

Pitcher/manager Shellenback stepped in a hole on the mound and dislocated his hip. He took his turn at bat in the third inning and hit a single. He was running to second when he took himself out of the game for fear of aggravating the injury, which turned out to be minor.

Wally Hebert replaced Shellenback at pitcher, and the southpaw from Louisiana held the Ducks to one run and five hits in the last six innings. Although Shellenback left the game with Hollywood in the lead, Hebert got credit for the win.

5-1-35 Hollywood/San Francisco Mission Reds

SHEIKS NIP REDS AGAIN
Hollywood Grabs 8-3 Triumph

The Hollywood Sheiks hosted the Mission Reds at Wrigley Field, and the Sheik infield looked like a combination of Ding-Dong School and Romper Room. At first base was George McDonald, age 17. Covering second base was Bobby Doerr, age 17. A slightly older George Myatt, 19, camped out at shortstop. Third base was covered by an oldster—Jim Levey, 26.

The author of the column, Bob Ray, said the quartet played the infield like a bunch of veterans driving for a pennant in the home stretch. The team vets had to hustle just to keep up with them.

Wally Hebert, the "good-looking Louisiana southpaw," used a sweeping curve ball to keep the Reds off balance, and let their heavy hitters down with seven scattered hits. Sheik batters helped Hebert at the plate, banging out fifteen hits off two Reds pitchers. Hebert himself did just fine offensively, going two for four and two runs-batted-in.

The first inning looked like it would be a Red rout. They smacked two hits in the first and scored one run. The Sheiks sat idly by and let them take a 1-0 lead and then did nothing to aid their cause in the bottom of the first. A home run in the top of the second and the scoreboard showed Visitors 2, Home 0.

The Sheiks said enough is enough, and got busy in the bottom of the second, getting two runs off of three hits. Score tied 2-2. Hebert settled down and pitched three scoreless innings, but got in hot water in the sixth, allowing one run. By then the score was 6-3, Hollywood. After that it was no-hit, no-run ball for the southpaw.

The Sheiks got hits in every inning after the lackluster first. DiMaggio and Jolley got home runs. Jolley ran his string to seventeen straight games in which he hit safely. As mentioned before, even the pitcher got in on the action.

5-17-35 Hollywood/Sacramento

HOLLYWOOD WINS OVER SACRAMENTO
Wally Hebert Hurls Stars to 3-to-1 Victory Over Northern Club

The Hollywood team had been in Sacramento for a three-game series in mid-May and hopped on the home-bound train with two victories under their belts. The final game of the series was played on May 16—a Thursday—with Wally Hebert keeping the Senators off the scoreboard after the first inning. He and his teammates took advantage of late-inning opportunities to eke out a 3-1 victory in the eighth and ninth innings.

The first inning did not start well for the Sheiks. Hebert gave up two hits that resulted in one run. He settled down and pitched shutout ball the remainder of the game.

A one-run lead is enough to win a game, and it looked like that was all Sacramento was going to need for another successful run. Sacramento pitcher Gregory pitched a five-hit shutout for seven innings. Their fans were sitting back on their seats, just enjoying a relaxing game of baseball with the home team ahead and zipping along with the visitors from down south at the mercy of their pitcher. Or so it seemed.

Then came the eighth inning. Gregory fell victim to an old baseball adage that said you can't walk the pitcher and get away with it. He opened the inning with a pass on the next to last man in the batting order. One on. Then pitcher Hebert was up and trying to bunt to advance the runner. He received four consecutive balls and took his place on first base. Two men on base. No outs.

Shortstop Myatt came to the plate and laid down an intended sacrifice that went for a hit when the pitcher couldn't get a handle on it in time to make the play at first. The bunt turned out to be the only hit of the inning. Three on. Center fielder Durst hit a high bouncer to second base and was thrown out at first. The third-base runner scored on that one. Levey hit a long outfield fly and Hebert scored. Score: 2-1. Home team fans leaning forward in their seats now.

No runs, no hits for Sacramento in the bottom of the eighth. In the top of the ninth Hollywood added another run on a double by DiMaggio and a single by McDonald. It was do or die for Sacramento. They got one hit, giving the fans some hope, but when the last out was called it was still eight big fat zeroes across the board for the home team. Final score, 3-1.

5-26-35 Hollywood/Los Angeles

Cherubs Held to Two Hits as Hollywood Cops Nightcap by Score of 8 to 0.

In Los Angeles, the Sheiks were hosting the Angels in a Sunday double-header. In the first game manager/pitcher Frank Shellenback was on the mound for the Sheiks and getting a royal shellacking to the tune of 8-1. He took himself out of the game after seven unproductive innings. The Sheiks weren't going to take this smack-around on their skipper sitting down. They vowed vengeance in the upcoming second game. "Ya can't kick our manager around."

In the nightcap enter Wally Hebert, Cajun pride of the Louisiana bayous. He totally avenged the defeat of his boss, allowing two hits by the shortstop and the catcher. He shut down everyone else's bat to take an 8-0 victory.

Hebert kept the Angels biting at bad balls as he mixed up a wide, sweeping curve with a snapping fast ball. Only one Angel got as far as second base. The finale was called at the end of six innings to enable the Sheiks to catch a train for Portland.

According to sportswriter Bob Ray, Hebert never pitched better ball than he did in the nightcap. He also got a little help from his friends. While making the Angels wonder why they even toted those heavy bats to the plate, the Sheiks got eleven hits off three Los Angeles pitchers and went on to win going away. Hebert helped himself out with two hits and two runs batted in.

The Angels had a second reason to be sad. Their center fielder, Jigger Statz, was enjoying a batting streak, having hit safely in twenty-four consecutive games. That came to a screeching halt when Hebert made him fly out twice— once to Jolley and once to Durst.

Shelly had been avenged.

6-18-35 Hollywood/Sacramento

STARS, SACS SPLIT EVEN

The Sheiks and the Senators squared off in a double-header to start the second half of the 1935 season and ended up splitting the prize. The Sheiks waltzed through a snoozer in the first contest, and had such an easy time of it they decided all they had to do was show up for the second meet-up.

Wally Hebert was on the mound for Hollywood in the opener and held the visitors scoreless in the first inning. The Sheik bombardment started as soon as the hosts had settled in the dugout for their turn at the plate. Myatt, DiMaggio, and Mulligan hit singles while Durst and Jolley served up doubles. This resulted in four runs in the first inning for what turned out to be enough to put the game on ice.

A base on balls by Hebert in the top of the second inning aided by a couple of errors by his teammates helped the visiting Senators to score their first run. 4-1.

Hollywood's half of the second was almost a repeat of the first. DiMaggio was the star of that one. Hebert, Myatt, and Jolley had managed to get on base. DiMaggio smacked a base-clearing double and the score was suddenly 7-1. It was time to bid farewell to Sacramento pitcher, Hartwig.

The third inning was scoreless for both teams, but the fourth inning created some excitement for the visitors when one of them homered over the right field fence. However, the Sheiks came right back in the bottom half and added another run. 8-2. Hollywood's Desautels knocked one over the left field wall, and that ended the scoring. 9-2.

Sitting on a seven-run margin, Hebert coasted to victory. He allowed eight hits over the nine innings and his teammates came through with some sensational defense, including three double plays.

It was a performance to be proud of, and the Sheiks couldn't be blamed for thinking all they had to do was take the field for a repeat. The Senators, instead of being demoralized, were fired up and ready for revenge. They allowed the overconfident Sheiks five hits and one run in the seven-inning game. The contest was tied until the last inning when the visitors scored an in-your-face run to take the game from the Sheiks

2-1. Revenge is sweet.

6-26-35 Hollywood/Oakland

Hebert's Bloomer Factor in Defeat of Hollywood 4-3 Score

"Charge defeat to Hebert."

That's what sports writer Bob Ray, writing for the Los Angeles Times, had to say about a game between Hollywood and Oakland in June 1935. No, he was not the losing pitcher—that would be Pillette, who started the game. If Pillette was the losing pitcher for Hollywood, why did the writer say "Charge defeat to Hebert?"

Oakland was leading by a score of 3-2 when Hebert relieved Pillette in the fifth inning. He pitched shutout ball the rest of the way. The outcome would be one of two things. Hollywood would get no additional runs, and Pillette would be the loser; or Hollywood would hold Oakland to four, and score two more runs themselves, making Hebert the winning pitcher. That didn't happen. Final score was 4-3, Oakland. Pillette was the loser, yet for some reason the loss was Hebert's fault— in the mind of the writer, anyway.

Here's what happened. Seventh inning. Two out. Score: 4-3, Oakland. Hebert at the plate. He smacked a double down the left field line. Safe on second. Myatt repeated with another double. The fans looked for Hebert crossing the plate—but there he was still perched on third "for some unknown reason," as the writer opined. He would have been the tying run. In the writer's mind it was all his fault that the Sheiks didn't come through. He said, "Hebert could have scored walking backward on Myatt's hit."

My question is why blame one player for a loss. What about the others who left base runners stranded or made errors allowing the opposition to put marks on the board?

Just saying.

1935: Le Grand Derangement in Reverse

The Montreal club of the International League cast covetous eyes down south to the Pacific Coast League, looking at one Wally Hebert of the Hollywood Sheiks. It seems he had been displaying such improved form during the 1935 season that Montreal took notice. However, there was something else about the left-hander that caught their attention.

Montreal had a large French-Canadian population. Hebert spoke fluent French, and he didn't learn it in school. French was his first language. Indeed, if he had gone to Montreal he would probably have encountered some distant cousins up there—those whose forefathers were not fortunate enough to find their way to Louisiana.

Bill Lane, owner of the Hollywood club, believes that was one reason— aside from his "mighty" left arm—the northern team was anxious to get him. They needed a Frenchman for a crowd attraction. Lane, however, refused to entertain an offer for Hebert.

Side note from me: I, for one, am glad my ancestor was not the one left behind. Even in January we have the occasional balmy day.

7-7-35 Hollywood/Los Angeles

July 7, 1935, was "Frank Shellenback Day" at Wrigley Field in Los Angeles, and a crowd of 12,000 fans turned out to honor the manager/pitcher. It was a double-header featuring the two local teams—Angels and Sheiks—with Hollywood playing host.

Hollywood won the opening game going away, and between games the fans presented Shelley with many fine gifts. Should have been a perfect day for the Sheik manager. Los Angeles had other plans. Shelley pitched the second game and the Angels were less than angelic, beating Shellenback by a score of 5-2.

The opener was a different story. Wally Hebert, "the good-looking Sheik from the bayou country of Louisiana, pitched good, steady ball to chalk up a win for the home team. According to the write-up, he had to pitch just hard enough to keep the Angels under control, since his teammates unloaded a thirteen-hit attack on two unfortunate Angel pitchers. Those thirteen hits included three homers—two by Desautels, aka Dezzy, and one by the ever reliable Smead Jolley.

The box score showed Hollywood scoring in all but the first and third innings. Hebert was in trouble in the fourth when he gave up three hits that resulted in the first Angel score. They added three more over the next five innings, but the Sheiks were never in danger of losing. By the eighth inning Hollywood had the game in the "W" column. Final score: 9-4.

Los Angeles got the consolation prize of ruining Frank Shellenback Day in the second game.

9-22-35 Sheiks/Missions

Joe E. Brown Stars as Sheiks and Reds Split

Wrigley Field in Los Angeles. Last two games of the 1935 season. The Sheiks and Mission Reds battling it out for—nothing, really. In the first game the Sheiks jumped out to a 7-1 lead. Then the Sheik defense decided to take a hiatus from baseball and let the Reds score four times in the sixth inning and two more times in the top of the ninth. Score tied 7-7. With one away in Hollywood's half of the inning, Sheik catcher Kerr smacked one over the right field fence. 8-7. Game over. Ball players considered extra innings on the last day of the season to be the unpardonable sin. Kerr's blast settled it for all, and everyone was happy.

Joe E. Brown was in attendance that day as usual. He acted as master of ceremonies when owner Lane presented checks to three Sheiks who had been voted most valuable players by the fans. Ced Durst, Bobby Doerr, and George Myatt finished one-two-three in the balloting.

In the second game Brown took the field and umpired third and first base. Songwriter Harry Ruby, another rabid Sheik fan, took over second base chores from Bobby Doerr for the last four innings of the seven-inning close-out round—the last hurrah of 1935.

The seventh inning rolled around, and the score was 14-7, Reds. Two outs and Ruby up to bat. Brown decided to end it all. He chased Reds pitcher off the mound and took over to pitch to Ruby. Brown took a few crazy warm-up tosses, called the Reds outfielders and infielders in, and had them sit on the grass around the mound. He proceeded to fan Ruby for the third out and the 1935 season was in the rear view mirror. The crowd loved it.

Wally Hebert had taken the mound in relief for the Sheiks and pitched the last four innings of the second game. He remembered both Joe E. Brown and Harry Ruby in his interview with Tony Salin, author of *Baseball's Forgotten Heroes.* Ruby would come to spring training and work out with the team. Hebert remembers him as a nice guy who loved to play ball, but was one of the worst ballplayers he had ever seen. Joe E. Brown, on the other hand, was a good ball handler and a competent hitter as well.

Brown, a popular movie comedian back then, was a fixture in the stands at Wrigley Field whenever the Sheiks were the home team there. He decided to make a movie based on a story by Ring Lardner—*Alibi Ike.* Brown starred as Frank Farrell, rookie pitcher on the Chicago Cubs team.

It also had William Frawley (aka Fred Mertz of "I Love Lucy" fame) and Olivia De Haviland (aka Melanie in *Gone With The Wind.)* Frawley was the long-suffering manager of the team, and De Haviland was the fiancee. Brown's character was full of alibis and excuses while trying to lead his team to a pennant.

The movie was filmed at Wrigley Field. Some eighteen Sheiks dressed up in Yankee and Cub uniforms for the cameo shots. Hebert was in a Yankee uniform, and said he guessed he was supposed to be Lefty Gomez since he was a southpaw pitcher. The wives were in the grandstand clapping and cheering. (Note from me: that was the only paying job my mother ever had.)

The players worked about fifteen days and were paid ten dollars each day. The wives received five dollars. A nice lunch was included, according to my mom and her best friend, Fay Malloy, who was visiting from Louisiana.

The scene that made it into the movie was Brown bursting through the outfield in an old Model T Ford. The ball players ran up to the car. Hebert was the one who put his foot on the running board. To anyone who wants to watch the movie: don't blink or you'll miss him.

The players pocketed $150 and got to rub shoulders with real live movie stars. The wives got $75 to blow as they pleased. Plus a nice lunch.

Pitching Statistics: 1935

Games: 39

Innings Pitched: 219

Won: 10

Lost: 17

Hits: 276

Bases on Balls: 50

Earned Run Average: 4.94

NINE

1936

HISTORY OF THE PADRES AND LANE FIELD

The Pacific Coast League has been called the "Greatest Minor League." In fact, a book by Dennis Snelling carries that title. The PCL was a stopover for professional baseball players. It was where the major leagues got many of their players, and it was a haven for those on their way down. And for those who never made it to the big leagues it was the closest they would ever come.

Padre founder Bill "Hardrock" Lane and other investors formed a club in Salt Lake City in the fledgling Union Association. This league lasted three years and Lane's group obtained the San Francisco Mission franchise, moved it to Salt Lake City, and renamed it the Bees.

In 1926 Lane abandoned Utah and headed for California. The Bees became the Hollywood Stars and were dubbed the Sheiks in honor of Hollywood heartthrob Rudolph Valentino. They were basically homeless with no ballpark of their own and had to share the new Wrigley Field with their long time rival Los Angeles Angels.

The country was in the middle of the Great Depression in 1935. Sagging attendance resulted in decreased revenue. Wrigley Field powers-that-be wanted to double the rent to $10,000 a year. In January 1936 Lane cast his eyes southward to San Diego amidst scoffing at his interest in the small border city. Lane came to a tentative agreement with city and harbor officials to relocate the club there. All he asked was for a suitable ballpark and rent that wouldn't break the bank. March 31 was set for the season opener—two months away. Could they make it?

Construction began immediately in January for an 8,000 seat stadium at a cost of $25,000. The public was invited to rename the team. Dons, Flyers, Gobs, Blues, Balboas, Friars, Tars, Skippers, Gaels, Tunas, Gorillas, Vaqueros, Pilots, Aviators, Twilers, Giants, Don Juans, and Sandies were submitted. Eight people suggested Padres, and it was an immediate hit with fans and sports writers alike.

Today Lane Field is a nondescript tract on the corner of Broadway and Pacific Highway. It echoes with a ghostly silence. Gone is the crack of wood on horsehide and the roar of the crowd. Gone are the bleachers and the diamond and the dugouts.

My younger brother Stephen visited the place where our dad had his best years. He called our mother and told her he was standing on the pitcher's mound at Lane Field—the very spot where Wally Hebert spent his working days facing down the best batters in the Pacific Coast League. Stephen said he was surrounded by cars. The place where so many Hall of Famers—Ted Williams, Bobby Doerr, the DiMaggios—got their starts was a parking lot. Bill Swank, local baseball historian and author, had to show Stephen exactly where the pitcher's mound had been. This was the birthplace of the Padres, and Wally Hebert had been there from the beginning.

One-Pitch Wonder

San Diego versus Seattle in Seattle. Bottom of the ninth—bases loaded, no outs. San Diego ahead 3-2. Pitcher in trouble. Bring in a reliever—this time it was southpaw Wally Hebert. After warming up he tossed the batter an inside curve, the batter made contact, and the game was over. Chalk up another win for the Padres.

What's that, you say? Bases loaded, no outs, one pitch and it's over? No way. Well, yes. Way. Here's how. The batter hit a soft liner to shortstop Jimmy Levy. Out # 1. Levy stepped on second base. Out # 2. Tossed the ball to first. Out # 3. Levy, the fastest sprinter in the league, probably could have outrun the batter and had an unassisted triple play.

Hebert said he had a lot of interesting moments during his baseball years, such as striking out the Bambino but that's another story. He always said the unique triple play was the most unforgettable thing he ever saw in his baseball career.

3-29-36 San Diego/Los Angeles

San Diego Takes Opener, 9-2
Six-Run Uprising Gives Cherubs 9-6 Finale
Hebert Hurls Five-Hit Ball

The first double-header of the 1936 season saw the San Diego Padres go up against their former field mates, the Los Angeles Angels, at Wrigley Field on March 29. The Angels found themselves with the short end of the stick in the first game, losing to their rivals 9-2. They decided to return the favor in the nightcap, pounding out a 9-6 victory over the Padres.

Shellenback's charges had an easy time of it behind the five-hit pitching of Wally Hebert, the "Cajun portsider from the bayou country of Louisiana." He had a 6-0 shutout going by the time he got to the sixth inning. He gave up two hits which became two runs in the bottom of the sixth. That was the only noise coming from the Angels. Zeroes bloomed across the home team's column on the board except for that sixth inning. A single and a walk gave them their lone tally.

Hebert's teammates did their part in the march to victory along with a little help from their foes. Vince DiMaaggio started it off, slugging a home run with one on for the first two Padre runs in the top of the fourth inning. DiMaggio's homer landed in the trees on the far side of 39th Street in Los Angeles. Angel errors gifted the Padres with four unearned markers of the hapless Angel pitcher in the fifth.

While Hebert coasted along to his win, Padre batters added three more scores in their last three at-bats. Final score: 9-2.

In the second game the Padres and Angels were tied at 3-3 in the top of the sixth. The Padres added three runs to take the lead 6-3. Victory seemed to be on the horizon. Just hold them two more innings and the boys from down south could go back to San Diego with a double victory on their belts. However, their baseball muse had left the ball park. The Angels tied it up, 6-6. Then they loaded the bases and Gudat, Los Angeles left-fielder, clouted a double to right center, scoring all three base runners. Score: 9-6 with one inning left. One more chance for the Padres to snatch a victory.

Like Yogi Berra said—"It ain't over till it's over." This time it was over when that seventh run crossed the plate.

4-12-36 San Diego/San Francisco Seals

SAN DIEGO COPS A PAIR
Padres Annex Series From Seals by Double Win, 6-5 and 3-2

San Diego's Padres took two nail-biters from San Francisco's Seals one Sunday afternoon in early April. They played host to the Seals at Lane Field, but weren't very hospitable to their guests. The two wins gave the Padres their first Coast League series of the season—four games to three.

Wally Hebert went the distance for the Padres in the first contest. In spite of allowing ten hits to the San Francisco nine, he managed to pull this one out of the fire. He shut them down when it counted.

He pitched a one-hit shutout for three innings before getting into hot water in the fourth and fifth innings. San Diego had a 2-0 lead since the third inning, but Seal bats woke up to snag three hits that turned into two runs, tying the score at two-all. The Padres came up short in the bottom half of the fourth. The Seals rattled the cages again in the fifth with three runs on three hits. Score: 5-2, San Francisco.

Ten-thousand fans had turned out for Navy day, and they were getting restless at this turn of events. San Diego bats came right back and added two more runs in the bottom half of the fifth. 5-4, Seals still on top.

Hebert settled down and pitched four innings of shutout ball, while scattering three more hits that went nowhere. In the meantime, his teammates came through for him and added a run in the sixth and another in the seventh, bringing the score to 6-5, San Diego. Hebert held the Seals scoreless in the top of the ninth and that was the ball game. The faithful sat back in the their seats, breathing a sigh of relief and hoping for a little less stress in the second game.

It was not to be, however. The Padres squeaked by on a score of 3-2. The score was tied until the bottom of the sixth inning when Ernie Holman, Padre third baseman, cranked one out of the park to give the Padres a one-run advantage. Then all Pillette, Padre pitcher, had to do was keep more numbers from appearing on the visitors' "run" column. He came through, and everyone went home happy—except the Seals.

5-8-36 Padres/Missions

Padres Blank Missions 4-0

The Padres traveled north to San Francisco and took on one of the local teams, the Mission Reds. They weren't very nice to their hosts, blanking them 4-0 in a game that entertained the crowd with a fine pitching duel between Wally Hebert, San Diego ace, and Otho Nitcholas of the Reds.

After four scoreless innings the Padres broke into the run column on a pair of Texas Leaguers by right-fielder Wirthman and pitcher Hebert. A long fly by shortstop Berkowitz scored one of the runners. 1-0.

There followed three more innings of ho-hum scoreless play on both sides. Top of the ninth — the last inning — and the Padres woke up and decided to put their bats to work. Mission relief pitcher, Stitzel, walked Padres Jacobs and DiMaggio, and was sent to the showers, making way for yet another reliever — Gallison. The new guy gave up two doubles to Wirthman and Desautels, and when the inning ended three more Padres had stepped on home plate. 4-0. That would be the ball game.

Hebert got credit for a five-hit shutout, and the boys from down south were satisfied with a job well done.

6-3-36 Padres/Angels

HEBERT'S HURLING TOO MUCH FOR LOS ANGELES
PADRES SMASH LOSING STREAK WITH 5-1 WIN
San Diego Triumphs Over Angels, 5 to 1, Behind Five Hit Hurling of Hebert

If the Los Angeles Angels had a guardian angel, he must have taken the day off on Wednesday, June 3, 1936. He was nowhere to be found at Lane Field in San Diego that day. Maybe he simply missed the train. Or perhaps he had another client who needed him more.

At any rate, he wasn't around during his team's hours of need when the San Diego Padres took his charges apart by the score of 5-1. I guess he thought since they were enjoying a three-game winning streak and their opponents, the Padres, were slogging their way through four straight defeats, his darlings could do without his help for one day. Wrong thinking—especially since Wally Hebert was on the mound that day.

Hebert had his foes eating out of his hand throughout most of the afternoon. The Angels caught a break in the fifth inning—the only stanza where they put a lone run on the scoreboard and denied Hebert a shutout. The Angel catcher hit a long fly to left field, which dropped safely at the fielder's feet due to a miscalculation of where the ball was headed. The batter made it to third base and came home when a teammate hit a grounder to first.

After that, it was smooth sailing for the Padre southpaw, silencing Angel bats the last three innings. He allowed five stingy hits over nine innings and registered six strikeouts. The game was his second straight win over the Angels, whom he beat during the opening week of season 1936.

On the offensive side Hebert's teammates came through for him, but he also helped his own cause in the third inning with a double and a run-batted-in. His mates added two more in the fourth and sixth innings as they coasted to a 5-1 victory.

It would seem even if said guardian angel had made it to the game he would have had to work overtime to help his charges along to victory.

6-4-36 Sports X-Ray Column by Bob Ray

"Who's the most improved pitcher in the Pacific Coast League this season?"

This was the question sportswriter Bob Ray put to his readers on June 4, 1936, in his column—The Sports X-Ray. He had three hurlers in mind: Lou Koupal, Seattle; Wally Hebert, San Diego; and Kenny Sheehan, San Francisco Seals.

Ray pointed out that none of the three was a .500 pitcher during the previous year. Hebert's record was ten victories against seventeen defeats while pitching for Hollywood in 1935—hardly anything to write home about.

Ray had this to say about Hebert. "Hebert's improvement is remarkable." The pitcher had put on weight over the off-season and weighed more than he ever had. The added weight seemed to have generated more speed. Ray said it was a treat to watch the southpaw work on the Angel batters in the previous day's contest. He had perfect control with his curve, fanning six batters and allowing a mere five hits.

Ray went on to say he thought it was a safe bet that all three of the aforementioned hurlers would finish up among the leaders in both percentage and earned run average in 1936.

Turned out he was right—at least as far as Hebert was concerned. I'm not aware of how the other two fared. His won-lost record was eighteen wins, twelve losses. He registered a percentage of .600, and his earned-run-average was 3.03. All of these stats added up to his best year since starting his professional career in 1930.

6-7-36 Padre/Angels

SERAPHS IN EVEN SPLIT
Padres Divide Double Bill
Salveson Hurls Win in Open but Hebert Takes Second

The Los Angeles Angels had been in San Diego for a week of games, and had been fairly successful, taking the series five games to two. On Sunday, June 7, the series wrapped up with the Angels taking the opener and the Padres successful in the nightcap. Some 7,500 fans saw the twin bill.

The mood was somber at the end of the first game, but the ever-faithful San Diego fans stayed on, hoping for better luck in the next endeavor. Turns out they were rewarded for their patience.

Hebert asserted his dominance over the Angels with his southpaw slants. He had pitched both San Diego wins in the current series, and it marked the third time that season he had taken down the boys from Tinsel Town.

The Angel pitcher was having control problems, and his wildness helped the Padres score their first two runs. With one out in the second inning, he walked the next two batters. Shortstop Berkowitz beat out a bunt and the bases were loaded. Hebert struck out, but the next Padre, Myatt, knocked one just over third base to score two base-runners. The score remained 2-0 until inning number four.

With one out in the bottom of the fourth, Berkowitz slammed a triple to right center. Before the Angel fielders had recovered their breaths from chasing the Padre triple, Hebert whacked one to deep center, and before center-fielder Statz could get the ball back to the infield Hebert had made it home for an inside-the-park homer. That was it for the Angel pitcher. Score 6-0.

The fifth inning saw the final scoring for San Diego, thanks to McDonald, Hebert, and Doerr. They all banged out singles, scoring one run. 7-0.

Los Angeles, scoreless for four innings, managed to put a run in the fifth and sixth innings on the scoreboard, and that was it for them. Final score, 7-2.

Some *lagniappe* for Hebert—$15.00 for his trip around the bases.

6-11-36 Padres vs Seals

Padres Beat Seals Again

The Padres were up north making life miserable for the San Francisco Seals in early June. Their victory on June 11 was win number three in the series, even though the outcome wouldn't be known until the last inning.

The visiting Padres got first bat and struck early, scoring three runs off of four hits in the top of the second. Then Seal pitcher Campbell shut them down until the sixth. In the meantime, San Francisco put one on the board in the bottom of the fourth bringing the score to 3-1.

Hebert's shaky inning reared its ugly head in the bottom of the fifth when the home town boys smacked him with four hits that turned into three runs. The scoreboard lit up. 4-3 San Francisco.

Not to be outdone, the Padres came right back in the top of the sixth with another run All tied up. 4-4. And there it stayed until the last inning. Home town fans stayed in their seats.

In the top of the ninth Hebert got one of his three base hits. He was forced out on second base when Myatt got his hit. Myatt stole second and scored on Doerr's single. 5-4. Still half an inning to go Remember—it's not over till it's over.

The Seals couldn't get anything started in their half of the inning thanks to Hebert and the final numbers on the scoreboard showed Visitors-5, Home-4.

6-17-36 Padres/Oaks

PADRES ROUT ACORNS, 16-0
Hebert Registers Eleventh Win of Season as Mates Ruin League Leaders

The headlines delivered the synopsis, but the clipping from the Los Angeles Times related the details. Oakland, sitting atop the standings, visited Lane Field on June 16 in San Diego, and looked nothing like the first-place team they bragged about being. The Oaks went through four pitchers trying to quiet Padre batters. The home team took advantage of seventeen hits served up by the unfortunate quartet, as well as the four errors by Oakland fielders.

Wally Hebert, on the other hand, was the lone hurler the Padres put on the mound. He pitched shutout ball for nine innings, scattering nine hits sparsely throughout, and posted his eleventh victory of the 1936 season. Since he did so well on the mound, he can be forgiven for being the only Padre to post goose eggs at the plate. All eight remaining Padres banged out at least one hit. Three batters—Myatt, Durst, and McDonald, hit safely three times, and another three—Holman, Desautels, and Wirthman—got two hits apiece.

Vince DiMaggio started the rally in the bottom of the second inning with a home run. San Diego hitters batted around, scoring five runs on the way. DiMaggio came to bat on the second time around and was fanned to end the frame. The Oaks, I'm sure, were thankful for a chance to rest.

The Padres went on to score once in the third, and twice in the fourth. Another five-run rout took place in the sixth, and two more scored in the seventh. The home team couldn't resist twisting the knife one more time, and in the eighth inning they put another one in the run column. 16-0. Oakland had one more chance to do something in the top of the ninth and managed to get two hits off the southpaw. The runners died on base, and the game, mercifully for Oakland, was in the books.

6-21-36 Padres/Oakland

Padres Drub Oakland in Twin Bill, 20-4, 3-2

Another double header against Oakland at Lane Field yielded two more victories over the boys from up north. After this series with the Padres, Oakland fell from leading the league to just barely being in the first division, hanging on to fourth place. The two games could not have been more different.

The first game was much like the game played by the two teams on June 16 when Wally Hebert and the Padres handed Oakland their collective *derrieres* by a score of 16-0. Hebert was again on the mound for the first game, coasting to his twelfth win of the season by a top heavy score of 20-4. The nightcap packed all the thrills the opener lacked. The score was knotted at 2-2 until inning number seven – the last inning of the abbreviated late game.

George Myatt, Padre shortstop, was on base, courtesy of a base on balls by the Oakland pitcher. Cedric Durst, hot-hitting Padre center fielder, smashed a screamer to right field, scoring Myatt and ending the game, 3-2. A nail-biter of the first order.

Back to the opener with Hebert on the mound. He served up sixteen hits – surely enough for victory. Not so here. The Oaks could only squeeze four runs out of that. The Padres, on the other hand, smacked out twenty-two hits and were able to put twenty runs on the scoreboard, due mostly to the expert base running of the hometown boys.

This time all the San Diego starters got at least one hit – even pitcher Hebert. George Myatt got greedy and cranked out five hits in six times to the plate. Everyone else had to be satisfied with one, two, or three.

San Diego was relentless in its march to victory, scoring in every inning except the first and seventh. A batting session in the bottom of the ninth was unnecessary. The big inning for San Diego was the fourth, when they scored six runs and ran the score up to 10-1.

The mighty Oaks were down, but not out, as they proved in the second game They lost again but made the Padres work for it.

6-30-36 LA Angels Bulletin

The Bulletin reported the Padres under Shellenback were clicking in every segment of the game, showed by increases in the batting averages of Bobby Doerr, Holman, DiMaggio, Durst, and other members of the club.

The team had benefitted from excellent pitching by Hebert, Horne, and Shellenback. Howard Craghead, a recent recruit, had also been turning in fine performances. The star of the staff was Hebert, whose work had been stellar all season. Shellenback would have liked to start him three times against the Angels since he had been their nemesis so far in the '36 season. In the first series played in Los Angeles he had beaten them in one game, and put them down twice in the series played in San Diego.

Hebert Scores Five Shutouts For New Mark

At some point in the 1936 season Wally Hebert established a modern shutout record when he blanked Sacramento 10-0. That win was the fifth time during the season that he had held the opposition scoreless. Mound record: Missions 4-0; Oakland 16-0; Los Angeles 2-0; Portland 10-0; Sacramento 10-0.

7-28-36 Padres/Angels

POLICE HELP UMPIRE PUT DOWN ANGEL RIOT
PADRES WIN OPENER, 2-0
Seraphs Blanked by Hebert
San Diego: Umpire Runs Belligerents Off Diamond

Some things never change. Even back in the 1930s the boys of summer would take on the umpires only to find out who really ruled the diamond. One July day at Lane Field in San Diego three ill-fated Angels discovered who was still in charge.

In the main attraction of the day—the game—the Padres, behind the great southpaw hurling of Wally Hebert and timely hitting of Ivey Shiver, bested their rivals from Tinsel Town, by a score of 2-0. This gave Hebert his fourteenth triumph—a five-hit shutout.

If the game was the main attraction that delighted the San Diego faithful, the side show that occurred in the third and fourth innings was just as entertaining. The first inning was uneventful, with neither team doing anything. By the end of the second frame San Diego had one run on the board. Hollis Leake—a 220-pound former policeman—was calling the shots behind the plate, and enjoying what looked like might be a calm, uneventful ball game on a sunny afternoon in July.

Top of the third. Angels at bat. One out. Statz, Angel center fielder, drew a walk from Hebert. The next batter dropped a single into short left, and Statz made it into third with no trouble. Padre second baseman, Bobby Doerr, bobbled the ball for a second, and Statz headed for home. Doerr's throw to the Padre catcher was spot-on, and Umpire Leake called Statz out as he slid into the plate.

Statz jumped up and confronted Leake. "He never tagged me. Can't you see anything?" he yelled.

Leake, in no mood for arguments, yelled back. "You're out of the ball game."

111

Angel manager Lelivelt, coaching on third base, joined the fray and jerked Leake's face protector half off. Leake answered by banishing Lelivelt. This brought the remainder of the Angels rushing into the fracas. The protesting Angels refused to leave the field, and Leake, whose last nerve had just left the ball park, called the four policemen to the battlefield. They escorted the manager out first and returned for Statz.

The visitors rearranged their team positions and the game resumed after the comic relief for the home town crowd. After the Padres had batted in the bottom of the third inning the score remained 1-0. Everyone settled down and the fourth inning got underway. Umpire Leake could only hope for six uneventful innings. He had quite enough for one day. It was not to be.

Top of the fourth. Angel second baseman Reese at the plate. Two out. Angel first-baseman Russell on first. Hebert sent a perfect strike to the batter — Reese — and then made him hit four or five foul balls. After that Hebert tossed a fast one inside. It either hit Reese's bat or ticked his sleeve. Padre catcher Desautels caught the ball and Leake called Reese out, having decided it had hit the bat. This would retire the side.

To say Reese was angry would be like referring to World War II as "the late unpleasantness." There is some confusion about what happened next. After Desautels caught the ball Reese turned to Leake and yelled, "That ball hit me on the arm. Are you blind today?" Reese lost the last of his temper, grabbed Leake with both hands and shook him, almost knocking him off his feet. The Four Horsemen of the Apocalypse descended, and Reese was on his way to join his manager and teammate in Never-Never Land.

Here's how the Los Angeles Times reported the incident. Reese whirled on Leake and gave him a vigorous shove, still yelling. Leake told him he was out of the game. That was the final straw for the batter. He ripped off his cap and slapped it across the umpire's face. For a few seconds the onlookers held their collective breaths. It looked like Leake might retaliate physically, but he kept his cool and called for the *gendarmes* once again. However, Reese joined his teammates without the escort.

Not knowing which writer was correct, I decided to report both and let the reader decide. To me, the slap across the face was the more egregious of the two. Either way, he had probably received a heavy fine and could have been suspended for the remainder of the season.

Back to the ball game. The Angels couldn't blame the umpire for losing it. Hebert pitched one of the best games of his career. The "handsome left-hander" gave up a mere five hits, and eleven Angels went to the dugout after getting a third strike. The game was his fourteenth victory of the season, his third shutout, and the fourth time he had stymied the Angels.

And the Kings of the Diamond? They still rule—even when some irate man-child kicks dirt on home plate or on the umpire's shoes. They still reign.

9-6-36 Padres/Sacramento

San Diego Sweeps Double-Header From Sacramento Ball Club, 15-3, 1-0.
Pillette and Hebert Nab Wins

Sacramento had been in San Diego for a nine-game series. The Padres were comfortably ahead in the series, having won six out of seven games—two of them won in a double header on September 6. If scores were any indication of the type of games that ensued, the first one was a yawner and the second one a nail-biter.

Wally Hebert started things off in the opener, notching victory number seventeen. However, Sacramento started off like gangbusters for four innings, getting all six hits and all three runs in those innings. After that, zeroes across the board. At the end of the first inning the score was 1-0, Senators. The San Diego faithful were no doubt somewhat apprehensive.

Not to worry. The Padres answered with five runs on five hits in the bottom of the second inning. 5-1. Everyone relaxed. By the end of the fourth inning the score was 6-1. Hebert settled down after a somewhat shaky start that had fans worried, and pitched no-hit, no-run ball the last five innings.

The home town boys didn't give the bats a rest. They added four runs in the seventh and five more in the eighth. Final score, 15-3. Offensive hero was Joe Berkowitz, who had four hits and four runs-batted-in. Defensive star was teenager Ted Williams, who robbed the Senators of three hits by fantastic catches.

The Padres did their part at the plate. All but one player hit safely at least once, with four responsible for extra bases, including the pitcher. Hebert went three for four and got two RBIs. He also registered seven strikeouts on the mound.

The second game was as tense as the first game was a free-wheeling slug fest and lasted only seven innings. The Padres were out-hit three to two, but the game was a shutout for Herman Pillette, right-handed Padre pitcher. He allowed the Angels three hits, but his teammates came through in the fourth inning with the run that won the game. Padre fans went home knowing they got their moneys' worth.

9-14-36 Playoffs   San Diego/Oakland

Mid-September saw the end of regular play in the 1936 season of the Pacific Coast League. In their first year as San Diego Padres, the team formerly known as the Hollywood Sheiks did quite well. They finished in third place and qualified for the Shaugnessy playoffs and a share in the prize money thereof.

Final standings for 1936: Portland, Oakland, San Diego, and Seattle finished in the first division and would play for the championship. The bottom four—Missions, Los Angeles, San Francisco, and Sacramento—stowed their gear and headed for home, hoping for better luck in 1937.

Playoff games were scheduled for September 15 with San Diego traveling to Oakland, and Portland hosting Seattle. The best four out of seven would take home the bacon.

The playoffs were a disappointment for the Padres. They lost out to Oakland in five games, winning only one by a score of 7-1. Wally Hebert started the second game, but was relieved in the seventh inning when the Oaks scored what would be the winning tally. The game was a squeaker. 3-2. A miss is as good as a mile, so they say.

Then on September 21 Oakland won their fourth game 7-6 in San Diego, sewing up the series and the right to meet Portland in the finals. Hebert pitched part of the ninth inning in that game, the last of four mounds men to try to keep the dream alive. The boys from northern California packed up and went back, ready to fight another day. The San Diegans cleaned out their lockers and left for their off-season lives.

"Wait till next year," was the rallying cry.

Hebert headed back to Louisiana to see his new baby daughter, who was born in Lake Charles three days before his twenty-ninth birthday in August. (That would be me—Linda Fay.)

Bobbie, Wally & Linda Fay

Pitching Statistics: 1936

Games: 35

Innings Pitched: 229

Won: 18

Lost: 12

Percentage: .600

Hits: 240

Strikeouts: 87

Bases on Balls: 51

Earned Run Average: 3.03

TEN

1937

2-28-37 Spring Training

Padres Open Spring Drills

Spring training for the 1937 Padres was due to get underway on February 28. Shellenback brought his charges to nearby Navy Field to train until March 7, when they were scheduled to play their first exhibition game. Lane Field was undergoing improvements.

Some 500 fans showed up to watch the Padres in practice on March 6. They were especially impressed with the long range bombardments of catcher George Detore and Ted Williams, eighteen-year-old outfielder in his second year with the Padres. Detore was knocking the ball to all corners of the field and one of his drives to center field carried more than 400 feet in the air. Williams, a native San Diegan, pounded out several smashing drives to deep right and center field.

Manager Shellenback spent a lot of time drilling the pitchers on running to first and covering the bag on rollers down the first base line. Hebert, Craghead, and Shellenback took to the mound for batting practice.

The Padres were scheduled to take on the San Diego County All-Stars the next day in the first exhibition game of the new season.

Conventional wisdom seemed to be that San Diego might be the team to beat for the 1937 Pacific Coast League pennant.

LANE'S PADRES LOOM ONE OF THE BEST TEAMS.

The article beneath that headline went on to say that the team appeared far stronger in early 1937 than they did at the same time the previous year. They had gathered momentum later in the season and got into the 1936 playoffs.

The team had an excellent pitching staff going into 1937—maybe the league's best, the writer said. Right-handers Craghead, Ward, Salvo, and Pillette with southpaws Hebert and Horne, would carry the burden. They also waited for Jim "Tiny" Chaplin, an excellent acquisition, to report. Manager Shellenback—a fine pinch-hitter—could be counted on for occasional work in starting and relief roles.

They had lost DiMaggio to the Boston Bees and Bobby Doerr to the Boston Red Sox, but picked up capable replacements. Ted Williams was one of the best prospects to make it to the majors, but for 1937 he would be manning the outfield along with Durst, Patchett, and Thompson.

Sounded like an exciting year for the San Diego faithful. We shall see.

3-15-37 Exhibition: Padres/Portland

Padres Beat Portland
Williams Leads San Diego Attack in 12-1 Victory

San Diego routed Portland, 12-1, in an exhibition game on March 14, and eighteen-year-old Ted Williams led the assault. He drove in four runs, hit a homer and three singles to get four of the Padre twelve hits. Helping Williams was Jimmy Reese, second baseman, who smacked two singles, sent three RBIs across the plate, and lit up the infield with his defensive moves.

The 1936 champion Beavers could manage but four hits from the three Padre pitchers—Wally Hebert, Berly Horne, and Manuel Salvo.

San Diego scored four runs in the second, three in the third, three in the fifth, and two more in the ninth. The Padre pitchers held the league champs to one run in the sixth inning.

An omen of things to come?

3-18-37 The Sports X-Ray

Bob Ray, sports writer for the Los Angeles Times, used his column, "The Sports X-Ray," to report on San Diego's outlook for the 1937 season. The team finished second in the final 1936 standings, but lost out to Oakland in the Shaughnessy Playoffs.

If manager Shellenback had any worries about his 1937 charges, it wasn't about the pitching staff. Eight of the Padre pitchers, including Shelly himself, were considered starting pitchers. His only headache was to decide which ones to put in the regular rotation.

The pitching staff was headed by Wally Hebert, Howard Craghead, Dick Ward, Manuel Salvo, Herman Pillette, and Berly Horne, as well as Shelly. Newcomer Jim "Tiny" Chaplin, a fireballer, came to the club from the Boston Bees. Also added was Bud Tuttle and Hec Carroll.

If Shellenback didn't have to waste time worrying about his mounds men, he did have some worries elsewhere. Three regulars from the 1936 second-place team had left for the majors. Being good enough to make it to the majors meant they might prove hard to replace.

Bobby Doerr, eighteen-year-old second baseman, ended the season with a .342 batting average, and was picked up by the Boston Red Sox. Gene Desautels, catcher, with a .319 average, joined Doerr on the Red Sox team. Vince DiMaggio was also headed to Boston, but for the other team—the Bees. He batted .293 but led the club in RBIs and extra-base hits. These three also came through for the team defensively.

Preseason predictions in 1936 didn't give San Diego any kind of chance to finish in second place. Fans hoped owner Bill Lane and manager Shellenback could come up with another surprise for 1937. Lane obtained George Detore and Bill Starr from the International League, and Hughie McMullen, a free agent, to shore up catcher after Desautel's departure.

Jimmie Reese stepped into Doerr's shoes at second base, and having a veteran's baseball wisdom, was expected to be a help to George Myatt, a young shortstop and fastest man in the league. Myatt, recovering from a lame arm, was expected to hit better than the previous year.

Another teenager, George McDonald, took over at first base, and was sporting a .317 average. Ernie Holman was back at third base.

The outfield looked good. Cedric Durst, who batted .306 in 1936, was a popular and efficient veteran. Ted Williams was eighteen years old and fresh out of high school. Mr. Ray had this to say about the youngster: "The kid looks like a future star and may blossom into a sensation this year." A spot-on prediction.

Another youngster, Van Worthman, was a holdover from 1936. Lane obtained newcomers Rupert (Tommy) Thompson and Harold Patchett to round out the outfield.

Ray saw a probable weakness when the Padres would come to bat. There were only five right-handed hitters on the squad. That meant possible problems against southpaw pitching. However, whether they hit or not, they would still be tough to beat because of the pitchers.

Mr. Ray was right. 1937 turned out to be a good year.

3-20-37 Pre-Opening Day

COAST LEAGUE OPENING NEARS, CLUBS ALL BUSY

Pacific Coast clubs were busy looking forward to opening day on April 3 of the 1937 season. Managers hoped for ideal weather to compensate for a wet week that hampered practice down in the California camps.

The schedule called for Seattle to play in Sacramento, the Missions to meet the Seals at San Francisco, Portland at Oakland, and—last, but not least—San Diego would open in Los Angeles.

The most improved teams appeared to be San Diego, Missions, San Francisco Seals, and Sacramento. San Diego and the Missions showed strong pitching staffs and good all-around balance. In fact, according to the writer in the Press Democrat, San Diego's pitching staff of Craghead, Ward, Salvo, Chaplin, Pillette, Horne, and Hebert appeared to be one of the strongest in the whole league. If it was strictly up to the pitchers the Padres would be counting the pennant as theirs before the first "Play ball" was shouted. A rosy future indeed.

3-27-37 San Diego/Valley All-Stars

Hebert Hurls No-Hit Game
Only Two Men Reach First as Padre Ace Blanks Team, 8-0

San Diego's only southpaw pitcher—Wally Hebert—hurled a no-hit, no-run triumph against the Imperial Valley All-Stars in an exhibition game, taking it 8-0.

Hebert faced twenty-eight batters and only two reached first base—one on a walk and one on an error. Eight batters went down swinging. His teammates, in the meantime, were lighting up the scoreboard with eight runs as they went through two pitchers for the foes.

As if his pitching wasn't enough, he showed off at the plate, going two for four. His teammate George Myatt was the other big gun, going three for five.

The Padres had their way with the same team the next night, although the second encounter was much closer at 7-2. Jim Chaplin and Tony Salvo shared pitching honors in the second tilt. No doubt manager Shellenback's mind was resting easier after he saw Hebert, Chaplin, and Salvo work. They seemed ready for the grueling 179-game Coast grind slated to start the following weekend.

The Padres were scheduled to meet San Diego State in a postponed charity game. Admission charge was twenty-five cents with all proceeds going toward a fund to pay hospital bills of injured sandlot players. One more exhibition game against the Pittsburgh Pirates and on to Los Angeles for opening day of the Pacific Coast regular season.

4-3-1937 Opening Day Padres/Angels

PRIM, HEBERT HURL IN COAST OPENER TODAY
Southpaw Duel on Tap as Angels Meet San Diego at Wrigley Field

Excitement always ran high on opening day, and April 3, 1937, was no different from every opening day since the first umpire yelled "Play ball." Sunny weather was expected for Los Angeles as their Angel squad was primed to welcome the San Diego Padres on this, the thirty-fifth season opener, to Wrigley Field.

A southpaw duel was planned by Angel manager Truck Hannah and Padre head honcho Frank Shellenback. Hannah sent Ray Prim, a thirteen-game winner in 1936, to the mound for the Angels. Shelly tapped Wally Hebert, 1936 eighteen-game winner, for Padre pitcher honors.

The weatherman promised to do his part and a turnout of 35,000 fans up and down the coast was expected to see the 1937 season get going.

Opening day ceremonies were short and sweet. Los Angeles mayor Frank Shaw threw out the first pitch with Sheriff Gene Biscalluz, whose business was catching criminals, attempted to catch Hizzoner's toss. Five of Uncle Sam's marines handled the flag-raising ceremony. After the flag went up the game was slightly delayed while the mayor tossed the "first ball" three times before the sheriff finally caught it.

Both teams, whose bitter rivalry dated back to San Diego's Sheik days in Hollywood, had high hopes for a pennant win since both teams seemed much improved over the 1936 season. On to the game.

Rally Beats San Diego
Seraphs Score Five Runs in Sixth to Nip Padres in Thriller

As the headlines revealed, things did not go well for the boys from down south. Any Angel fans among the 11,223 spectators went home delirious after their idols put the hurt on their rivals by a score of 9-7. Their victory was not a walk in the park, however. It was nip and tuck most of the way. Hebert was on the mound for the Padres.

The Angels started the scoring in the bottom of the first inning, turning three hits into two runs. The Padres came right back at them in the top of the second with a four-run spree that lifted Padre fans' spirits.

They had confidence in their pitcher. After all, he had eighteen victories in 1936. And hadn't the batters just charged ahead 4-2? It would be okay, they decided. Just settle down and pitch shut-out ball for the next seven innings. How hard was that?

The Angels weren't going along with that. They put another run on the board in the bottom half of the second. 4-3 Padres. That was okay with Padre fans. Their guys were still ahead. Their team added a run in both the third and fourth innings. A 6-3 lead. On top of that, Hebert was humming along with no-hit ball for the next three innings. The San Diego faithful began to relax. Then came the bottom of the sixth with the Angels at bat.

By the time the third out had been called Hebert and reliever Tiny Chaplin had given out four hits between them. That, coupled with an infield error, resulted in a five-run rally. Now the score sat at 8-6, Los Angeles. Hand-wringing time for the San Diegans.

Both teams added runs after the disastrous San Diego sixth inning. Los Angeles scored in the bottom of the eighth, bringing the score to 9-6. San Diego kept hope alive when they tallied once more in the top of the ninth. Once was not enough. Final score: 9-7. The Angels and their fans blew the stadium up with their celebration. The Padres, in a blue funk, made themselves feel better by saying, "One game does not a season make."

4-8-37 Padres/Missions (SF)

San Diego Wins Over Missions

A night contest at Lane Field saw the Padres reward their fans for coming out late to watch them beat the Mission Reds for the third straight time. Final score 4-1.

Wally Hebert was on the mound, giving up ten hits but keeping numbers off the board with much help from his mateys. It was shutout ball for seven innings until San Francisco managed to light up their side of the board with a solo score.

The Padres were already ahead by a score of 4-0, having done all their damage in the fourth, fifth, and sixth innings. The Missions out-hit the Padres — ten to seven — but Hebert was more effective in the clinches and got better support than Mission right-hander Walter Beck.

This victory set the Padres into a first place tie with Sacramento and Seattle. So far, so good for the southern lads.

4-19-37 PCL Race

SAN DIEGO IS PACE-SETTER IN PCL RACE

A pair of major league veterans—Wally Hebert and Jim Chaplin—had helped the Padres set the Pacific Coast League pace by the time mid-April rolled around. The club advanced from third place to first during the second week of play. They defeated Oakland four games to three in the series that ended on the 17th.

The two veterans hurled San Diego to a double win over Oakland on Sunday. Right-hander Chaplin passed out six hits to the Oaks, beating them in a squeaker 2-1. Lefty Hebert took the mound in the night cap. A Padre five run rally in the sixth offset a four run uprising in the seventh by Oakland. San Diego ended up with an 8-5 victory.

4-27-37 Padres/Oakland

Padres Crack Oaks, 18-3
Hebert Breezes Home on Mound; McDonald, Williams Hit Homers
PADRES TROUNCE OAKS TO RETAIN LEAGUE LEAD

It was the Hebert, McDonald, Williams show at Lane Field one afternoon in 1937, according to San Diego sportswriter Earl Keller. What Frank Shellenback found to his delight was that Wally Hebert was in great shape, that George McDonald had developed a taste for home runs, and that Ted Williams really did know what to do with a bat. These three were the heroes of the 18-3 shellacking the Padres laid on the unfortunate boys from Oakland. With this win the Padres dug themselves somewhat deeper into first place in PCL standings as of April 27.

The heavy-hitting Padres took it to a pair of Oakland pitchers, hammering out seventeen hits that became eighteen runs. In addition to his home run, McDonald slugged a double and three singles. Williams added two singles to his homer, going three for four at the plate. The rest of the squad did their part, as well. All but two got on base at least once, including the pitcher, who went one for three and sent two base runners across home plate.

Hebert's mound work was top flight as well, according to Keller. He sent six batters back to the dugout with their bats on their shoulders. He allowed eleven hits but only three made it home. Oakland scored once in innings one, two, and three. After that it was six innings of shutout ball for the gentleman from the Pelican State. He issued no bases on balls, but did hit one batter. Bet that smarted.

Hebert didn't have to work very hard for this victory, his third of the season, because of the rainstorm of hits and runs pelting down on Lane Field. All San Diegan players and fans went home happy.

5-8-37 Padres/Seals (SF)

PADRES BATTER SEALS, 7 TO 0
Padres Shut Out Seals
Hebert Hurls Two-Hit Ball as San Diego Scores 7-0 Victory

The San Diego squad visited the San Francisco rival Seals and were not well-behaved guests, pounding them 7-0. Southpaw Wally Hebert tossed a two-hit shutout to move the Padres into a second-place tie with the boys from up north.

Hebert went the nine-inning distance, pitching a no-hitter for six innings. The Seals finally put some numbers on the board in the seventh and eighth innings when the shortstop and the catcher managed to get on base. They went nowhere, however, and when the last out was called the only numbers in the run column were big fat zeroes.

Once again every player except one — the pitcher — got at least one hit. Cedric Durst, Padre right fielder, starred at the plate, getting four hits in five trips. They scattered their scores throughout the game, getting one run in the second and another in the sixth. The score remained 2-0 until the eighth inning. The game was won in the second inning, but they just couldn't resist twisting the knife two more times. Two more runs scored in the eighth, and then a little *lagniappe* for their fans back home in San Diego — a three run rally in the ninth. Then a no-hit, no-run ninth and that was that.

6-6-37 Padres/Portland

PADRES ROUT DUCKS TWICE
Hebert Turns 12-1 Victory in Opener; Second Won, 8-5, San Diego

The Padres came off a four-game losing streak with a vengeance on June 6. The unfortunate recipients of their awakening were the Portland Ducks, crushing them 12-1 and 8-5 in a Sunday double-header. To make matters worse, the insult was in front of the home crowd in Portland. The first game was Batters Heaven.

The Padres blew through two Portland hurlers on their way to victory in the first game. Every San Diego player on the team hit safely at least once, including pitcher Wally Hebert, who helped himself to a double. Center fielder Hal Patchett smacked a first inning home run. Eighteen hits fell like stars over Oregon. Inning number three was the only one with a zero.

The game stayed close until the fourth inning. San Diego tallied once in the first, second, and fourth innings, showing a score of 3-0. Then came the top of the fifth—the *coup de grace*—putting the game out of reach for Portland. The Padres bombarded the place with a seven-run spree and ran the opposing pitcher off the mound.

Wally Hebert, on the other hand, had things under control from the beginning. He handed out seven hits but only one made it home. Portland fans were puzzled. What had happened to their defending champions? They scratched their heads and wondered which team would show up for the nightcap.

It was a somewhat better team than the one who had just taken a good, old-fashioned drubbing, but still not good enough to put a "W" in the books. They lost that one 8-5. Not as bad as before, but a loss is a loss. The Padres could be forgiven for feeling somewhat smug. It's always fun to embarrass the home team.

6-10-37 Padres/Seals

SHATTERED BY PADRES

At Lane Field on June 10 the San Diego fans were treated to a nail-biter by their idols. San Francisco Seals ace Sad Sam Gibson had ample reason to be gloomy. The Padres were unimpressed by Gibson's winning streak and smacked him down in a 3-2 decision. Wally Hebert, on the mound for San Diego, turned in a stellar performance, and his teammates did their part at the plate.

San Diego put two runs up in the bottom of the second inning. Hebert pitched a shutout for three innings, and San Francisco tied things up in the top of the fourth. Then the Padres came to bat and scored another run, taking the lead 3-2. Hebert came through with a shutout for the last five innings.

Not content to keep the foe off balance with his pitches, he did his part at the plate in the second inning. Detore knocked a single into right field. McDonald hit another into left. Durst moved both runners ahead with a sacrifice — a runner on third and another on second. Who's up next? The last man in the batting order — the pitcher. Wally Hebert. He rapped a sharp single into the outfield and sent both runners home. Chalk up two RBIs for the guy from Louisiana.

Hebert got into hot water in the top of the eighth. The bases were full with one out. (This is when wife Bobbie would make her way to the ladies room.) Third baseman George Detore executed a brilliant double-play to retire the side. Final score: 3-2. Padres fans were happy to hear the last out called, and Bobbie knew it was okay to leave the ladies room.

6-19-37 Padres/Angels

HEBERT'S HURLING CHECKS ANGELS; PADRES WIN, 5-1

According to Bob Ray, writing in the Los Angeles Times, his Angels had been traipsing down the winning primrose path the last few days. They were hosting the San Diego Padres out at Wrigley Field, and feeling a bit over-confident since the Padres were riding a four-game losing streak.

The home team came down to earth with a bang when Padre Wally Hebert took the mound and held them to six hits and one run. This was not a good day for the 6,000 Angel fans who had come out on a Saturday afternoon hoping to watch their team put it to the Padres. Among those in attendance were almost 3,000 kid members of the knothole gang.

It was a game that could have gone either way, but the Padres took advantage of Los Angeles errors to put four unearned runs on the scoreboard. They drew first blood in the top of the first inning, scoring two runs on two hits. A long, dry spell followed with neither team showing signs of life. Then the Angels woke up momentarily and got two hits in the bottom of the seventh, one being a home run by right fielder Carlyle. Score: 2-1 Padres.

The Angels threatened again in the bottom of the eighth, attempting to tie the score with one hit that went nowhere, so the 2-1 score still stood. Top of the ninth saw the Padres put three runs on the board, starting with an error by Jigger Statz, Angel center fielder. With the score sitting at 5-1, the Angels came to the plate hoping to make it five in a row themselves. Hebert was having none of that and put them down with no activity from Angel bats. Final score: 5-1, Padres.

In addition to a five-hit, one-run game, Hebert fanned three, and helped out at the plate with one RBI, getting one hit in three at-bats.

In Los Angeles' scoring inning—the seventh—the spectators were treated to some side entertainment between the home team and the umpire. First baseman Hurst rapped a Texas Leaguer to short center and tried to stretch it to a double. Umpire Steengrafe called him out on second and received a stomach bump by Hurst for his call. Hurst was sent packing by Steengrafe, bringing manager Hannah and center fielder Statz into the fray. They skipped the stomach bumps and were allowed to remain in the game. Umpire Steengrafe remained adamant. The decision stood.

6-23-37 Padres/Portland Beavers

Thompson Hit Ruins Beavers
Eighth Inning Homer Gives Padres 3-2 Win Over Portland

On June 23 at Lane Field it was *deja-vu* all over again. Tuesday, June 22. Bottom of the eighth. Ted Williams at the plate. Big blast over the fence. Final score 3-2, San Diego.

Fast forward to Wednesday, June 23. The Beavers struck in the top of the second inning with a home run, but the Padres came right back in their half of the inning with a run. 1-1. Portland scored again in the top of the third. 2-1, Beavers. Neither team did anything until San Diego's half of the sixth. Two singles, a sacrifice, and a fly brought a run in to tie the score at two-all. After much biting of nails and wringing of hands, Padre fans settled down since their team was no longer behind — not winning but not losing.

After holding Portland hitless and runless for two innings the Padres came to bat in the bottom of the eighth. Right fielder Tommy Thompson stepped to the plate and took a couple of practice swings. The Beaver pitcher's offering sailed over the right field wall and all at once the score was 3-2, Padres. A repeat of the day before. Game won in the eighth inning by a score of 3-2.

Wally Hebert pitched that day for San Diego, limiting the Beavers to five hits. Four of those hits fell in the first four innings when Portland scored their runs. After that Hebert was in complete control, hurling a five-inning one-hit shutout. San Diego fans went home happy but minus a few fingernails.

7-16-37 Padres/SF Mission Reds

Wally Hebert Stops Reds With 3-0 Mound Win

It was lefty versus lefty one July night in San Diego. Brilliant southpaw pitching was the dish served to some 6,000 fans at Lane Field. Wally Hebert, "stellar" San Diego southpaw had things go his way as he led his team to a 3-0 win over their San Francisco rivals. On the mound for the Reds was another fine southpaw—Lew Tost.

It was a pitcher's duel for three innings. The Reds tried to make a go of it in the third inning when two singles put two men on base, but Hebert struck out three to neutralize those singles.

San Diego drew first blood in the fourth. Right fielder Thompson slammed a single into right field. First baseman McDonald hit safely, but Thompson was forced at second. McDonald made it to second on a catcher's error. Ted Williams got hit by a pitched ball. Two on. Next up came Reese— second baseman—who knocked a single into left field to score McDonald. 1-0.

Both pitchers seemed to get better as the game rolled on. After six innings the score books showed two hits off Hebert and four off Tost. Strikeouts: Hebert-five; Tost-seven.

In the bottom of the seventh the Padres got out of hand even though the Missions nearly got out of hot water due to fine pitching and fielding by Tost. Padre third baseman Mulligan started the fireworks with a single into left field followed by catcher Starr, who knocked one into the same spot. Two on. Hebert laid down a nice bunt, but Tost picked off the runner going to third. Still two on. Then center fielder Patchett was safe on an error. Bases loaded.

Next up—shortstop Myatt hit a weak grounder to Tost, who got the man out at home. San Francisco thought they might be out of the woods until Thompson lifted a floating fly over second base scoring Hebert and Patchett for the last two scores. 3-0. That's how it ended. A nail-biter but great baseball for the home crowd.

7-18-37 Padres/Mission Reds

Hebert Twirls 1-0 Victory in Second Tilt

A double-header was on tap Sunday, July 18, at Lane Field. The Padres were sailing along in Pacific Coast League first place, and the fans arrived expecting to see two more wins to solidify their position. The Mission Reds had other plans. The opening game resulted in a 9 6 defeat for the league-leading Padres who were all of a sudden league leaders no longer.

The home team jumped to a 5-0 lead in the first three innings, so the home town fans sat back, satisfied their idols had everything under control. Along came the fourth inning and before they knew it their guys trailed by a score of 6-5. The Reds went on to score three more runs in the late innings, and San Diego added one more in the sixth. Final score: 9-6. The fans' sense of invincibility vanished, and they wondered what the second game held in store.

Not to worry. Wally Hebert took the mound for the pitching detail in the seven-inning nightcap. With a helping hand from the Los Angeles Angels and the fine pitching by Hebert, the Padres came back in the second game to retake the lead in the standings, squeaking by with a 1-0 win.

The nightcap kept everyone on edge and needed some great fielding on the part of the home team to keep the visitors off the scoreboard. In the second inning with two on and two out Thompson made a long run and diving catch to stop a liner that appeared destined for extra bases. He came to the rescue again in the fourth when he grabbed a single and made a perfect throw to cut the runner off at home plate.

San Diego scored one run in the bottom of the first inning and kept the Missions runless for seven innings in spite of being out-hit by the Reds. Hebert had three strikeouts, and helped at the plate with a base hit on two trips. Only three of his teammates hit safely. It was one of those games where fans were afraid to go to the concession stand. Who knew what would happen next?

The win in the final game of the series gave the Padres six out of the seven games and put them back in first place, a half-game over Sacramento, who had split with the Angels.

7-25-37 Padres/Oakland

Padres Drop Twin Bill
Oakland Takes Both End of Double Header From Foes

A double-header was on the docket in Oakland on a sunny Sunday afternoon between the league-leading Padres and Oakland. Not a good day for the Padres, who were the recipients of a double defeat at the hands of the host team.

The Oaks squeaked by 2-1 in the first game at the expense of Wally Hebert, who was on the mound for the visitors. Hebert gave up both Oakland runs in the first and second innings, but settled town to pitch shutout ball the rest of the way. Unfortunately, Padre bats were mostly silent as they tallied their lone run in the sixth inning.

Jim Chaplin came in to bat for Hebert in the top of the ninth inning and was thrown out at first base on a close call. This was the last play of the game, and the Padre players took umbrage at umpire Mitt Steengrafe. What followed was a sidebar of entertainment for the ecstatic Oakland fans.

Padre players emptied the dugout and charged Steengrafe. Police rushed in to rescue the beleaguered umpire. Oakland fans retaliated by tossing pop bottles at the San Diego players. Shortstop George Myatt issued a challenge to a fan, who started to make his way down and accept the dare. Myatt's teammates stepped in to prevent a confrontation.

The authorities calmed things down and the nightcap started. This time the score was 6-1 with no resulting hostilities. All was quiet on the northern front.

8-28-37 Padres/Portland

Padres Nose Out Portland
Hebert Checks Duck Uprising in Ninth to Win, 3-2

The San Diego Padres treated their fans to another nail-biter of a game on a Saturday afternoon at Lane Field in August. The Portland squad had been in town all week, and led the series three games to one.

The first two innings were unexciting for both teams. In the bottom of the third San Diego scored two unearned runs on three hits which came after the side should have been retired. A dropped ball in the Portland outfield sent the Padre batter to second base. Myatt singled and Thompson followed with another. Two base runners scored. 2-0, Padres.

The third Padre tally came in the sixth inning when Ted Williams smacked his seventeenth homer of the year over the right centerfield wall some 390 feet away. 3-0. San Diego fans breathed easier. Their team was ahead, and Wally Hebert was on the mound pitching a shutout.

That ended in the top of the ninth. Beavers at bat. First man up—a pinch hitter who led off with a double. Next man up grounded out. Next batter was good for another double, scoring the lead runner. 3-1. Padre faithful leaned forward in their seats.

Hebert issued two walks. Bases full, one out. Fans worried. (Trip to the ladies room for Bobbie.) The next batter was out at first, but a run scored. 3-2. Base runners on second and third with two outs. Still in danger of more runs. One more out and the game would be over. Hebert came through and forced the batter to ground out.

9-1-37 Padres/San Francisco Seals

Padres Sink Seals, 10-5
San Diego Pounds Three Pitchers; Williams Bat Star

September came to Lane Field with a bang as the Padres uncorked power while taking on the San Francisco Seals, beating up on three Seal pitchers on their way to a 10-5 victory — the second straight win over the visitors.

Wally Hebert took the mound and the Seals started right in on him in the top of the first inning. He walked the first batter and gave up a double to the next man up. Two on. Dom DiMaggio — younger brother of Vince and Joe — came up next and slugged a triple into the outfield, scoring two base runners. After that first little flurry Hebert pitched out of that hole without further damage.

The activity in the top half of the inning seemed to energize the home team. Not wanting to let their fans down, they went to work and kept the base paths hot until five batters had stepped on home plate. Seal pitcher Sheehan started his half of the inning by loading the bases with two walks and a single. Manager O'Doul sent him to the showers and called in Sad Sam Gibson, the league's leading pitcher, to protect the lead of 2-0. By the time the last out had been called the score was 5-2, Padres.

The second inning for the Seals was unproductive since Hebert kept them shut down. No so for the Padres in their half. George Myatt singled and Ted Williams socked his nineteenth homer of the year, scoring Myatt. 7-2.

The fourth inning saw the Seals add one run and two more in the sixth. That was it for them. Hebert pitched one-hit shutout ball for the next three innings. San Diego scored once in the fifth inning — Ted Williams' twentieth home run. By then the score was 8-3.

When the Seals added their two tallies in the sixth it brought the score to 8-5. Still not out of reach for them. Don't forget: "It ain't over till it's over." The Padres decided to twist the knife one more time and sent two more men across the plate, bringing the final score to 10-5. Hebert allowed the only hit in the last three innings and no runs. This was his fifteenth victory of 1937.

San Diego fans were grateful for two hours of relative peace.

9-12-37 Padres/Los Angeles

Wally Hebert Shuts Out Seraphs, 5-0

The Angels had been in San Diego for a week and were ahead in the series three games to two. The Padres didn't want the Angels to make it four games to two so they came to Lane Field ready to play ball on September 12.

They put Wally Hebert on the mound, and he responded with a two-hit shutout, tying the series three games to three. Hebert's teammates came through with five runs on eleven hits.

With both teams and Padre fans on edge for four innings of airtight baseball the home team finally got one on the board when McDonald got himself a double. Catcher Starr tagged a slow rolling single, allowing McDonald to move to third. A single by third baseman Holman sent McDonald home for the first score of the game.

The Padres got to Angel pitcher Prim in the seventh inning when they added three runs on five straight hits. This included a single by Hebert that resulted in a run batted in for the pitcher, aiding his cause. San Diego's final tally came in the eighth inning—a kind of in your face, catch me if you can challenge to the hapless Angels.

Hebert had been humming along, putting batters down in short order. He held them to one hit in the fourth for the first eight innings, but loosened up somewhat and let them have one more in the ninth.

Everyone went home happy. The fans were enjoying a winning afternoon. All the batters except one had hit safely at least once. The pitcher added another notch in the victory column. Management was glad the team was still in the first division. The pennant was on the horizon.

9-27-37 Playoffs

San Diego, Portland Open Coast Playoff

Late September meant it was time for the Shaughnessy playoffs once again. The final standings in the regular season play showed Sacramento in first place, San Francisco Seals in second place, San Diego holding down third, and Portland squeezing its way into fourth place by nosing out Los Angeles.

When the dust had settled after the semi-final games, first place Sacramento and second place San Francisco went home. Third place San Diego and fourth place Portland advanced to the finals. Portland had taken care of San Francisco in four straight games, and San Diego took four in a row from Sacramento.

The opening game was scheduled for Wednesday, September 28 with Wally Hebert, San Diego's lone southpaw, getting the nod for mound work. The first three games were played in San Diego, and then the two teams headed north for the concluding games of the best four of seven games. At stake was $5,000 in prize money — the winner to take $3,000 and the loser receiving $2,000. That was the amount to be split by the players, not for each player individually. A lot different from today's monetary prizes.

9-28-37 Padres/Portland

Padres Nip Portland, 4-3
Thompson's Second Homer of Game Wins in Tenth
Rupert Thompson Has Field Day, Hits Two Homers

Lane Field was abuzz with playoff fever as the opening game of the Shaugnessy finals got underway on Wednesday, the twenty-eighth of September. Wally Hebert went the ten-inning distance for the Padres, and the Beavers used two pitchers—Liska and Thomas—in their quest for the elusive "W."

The first two innings were uneventful; no hits, no runs for either team. In the top of the third Portland got to Hebert for two hits, and one of them made it across the plate. 1-0, Portland. San Diego fans grew somewhat restless, but decided it was too early to get worried. Better to see what their team would do with the bat. Turns out they weren't to be disappointed.

Hebert and shortstop George Myatt hit safely off Liska. Two on, one away. Right fielder Rupert "Tommy" Thompson took his place at home plate and promptly uncorked one that cleared the fence and brought Hebert and Myatt home with Thompson hot on their heels. A collective sigh of relief went up from Padre faithful. Now just sit back and watch their guys finish off those pesky Beavers.

Not so fast, people. Still six innings to go. A lot could happen in six innings, as they would soon find out. Hebert hummed along for three scoreless innings, and complacency set in among the folks in the bleachers. The Beavers put one on the board in the seventh and all of a sudden it was 3-2. A one-run lead was not enough. In their half of the inning the Padres got one hit that went nowhere.

In the top of the eighth Beaver bats came to life as they got to Hebert for three hits. One of them made it home. Score tied at three-all. Uh-oh. Now what? The ninth inning ended with no activity for either team. Extra innings.

Hebert kept Beaver bats hitless in their half of the tenth. After the Padres had retired to the dugout, Thompson came to bat with one out. He sent the ball sailing over the fence for his second homer, sending any Portland fans there filing toward the exit. Padre devotees, of course, were anything but calm.

One down, three (hopefully) to go.

10-3-37 Padres/Portland

PADRES ANNEX LEAGUE CROWN
PORTLAND NINE IS TURNED BACK BY SAN DIEGO
Rupert Thompson's Big Bat and Hebert's Steady Twirling Decide Final Contest
San Diegans Whip Portland 6 to 4, for Sweep in Playoff

The Padres took it to the Portland Beavers in three straight games at Lane Field. Both teams grabbed their cleats and bats and headed north to Portland. The Beavers hoped to get something started so they could show off for the home crowd. The Padres, on the other hand, were looking for victory number four so they could go south with the prize money and the adulation of their faithful fans waiting back home.

They hoped for a repeat of the semi-finals against Sacramento, who were the recipients of a good, old fashioned trip to the woodshed in four straight games at the hands of the southern boys. The championship meant a $3,000 bonus for the winners. Losers would receive $2,000.

The baseball angels were smiling on the Padres that Sunday afternoon in early October. The game had been delayed from the day before because of rain. Wally Hebert got the nod for mound work, having had a five-day rest. That was all he needed to finish off the Beavers in game number four and bring the championship home to San Diego.

The Padres came out of the gate swinging and promptly put three runs on the board. Hebert went to work and pitched three innings of no hit, no run ball. The score remained at 3-0 until the bottom of the fourth inning. Hebert gave up three hits that turned into two runs, bringing the score to 3-2—a one-run game. Not what San Diego wanted to see—or hear.

The baseball angels smiled again when the Padres came to bat in the top of the fifth. Rupert Thompson came to the plate with one teammate on base. He swung for the fences and put one over, scoring the runner. Two runs crossed the plate. 5-2, Padres. That effectively put the game out of sight for the Beavers since from then on Hebert was stingy with base hits. Portland scored again in the bottom of the seventh with one run on two hits. 5-3.

The Padres answered with another tally in the eighth. 6-3. Portland threatened again in the bottom of the ninth giving hope to the home crowd with two hits and one run, but that was all they could muster. Final score: 6-4. The 1937 season was over and a new champion reigned.

Even though they were in somewhat of a slump during the last few days of regular play, the Padres came through in the playoffs like the champions they were. The Lane Field pitchers set a unique record. San Diego steamrolled over Sacrameto and Portland to win the pennant. Manager Shellenback utilized only four pitchers to put the quietus on their foes — Tiny Chaplin, Manuel Salvo, Dick Ward, and Wally Hebert. Each scored two victories apiece. To top it off, not one of them needed to be relieved in any game. Every one of them went the distance.

A satisfying season indeed.

Pitching Statistics: 1937

Games: 39

Innings Pitched: 244

Won: 17

Lost: 14

Percentage: .549

Hits: 257

Strikeouts: 90

Bases on Balls: 42

Earned Run Average: 3.02

ELEVEN

1938

1-19-38 The Sports Parade/LA Times

San Diego Fans Expecting Another Strong Coast League Club Despite Loss of Williams, Thompson, and Myatt

Braven Dyer, writing for the Los Angeles Times, reported that San Diego baseball fans were confident their Padres would be in the thick of the playoff race once again in 1938. Even though they finished regular play in third place in 1937, what they did in the playoffs was nothing short of spectacular—eight consecutive victories without changing one single starting pitcher.

Boss Bill Lane sent three of his better young players up to the majors—Ted Williams, Rupert Thompson, and George Myatt. They would be missed, to be sure, but Lane made the necessary replacements, and if the pitching was as good as 1937, the boys from the south should be good to go for the 1938 pennant.

George Detore, who led the Coast League at bat in '37, returned to handle catching assignments along with Bill Starr. Young George McDonald was back at first base. Veteran infielder Jimmie Reese decided he could squeeze out at least one more campaign on his aging legs. Lane procured Al Niemic to fill in at second and John "Bunny" Griffeths to step into the shortstop spot. (Note from me—I remember Bunny and Marie visiting us in Westlake after we had moved there.)

Another newcomer, Johnnie Williams, from Washington State, would be at third. Outfielders included Cedric Durst and Hal Patchette from 1937. Joining them were Dominic Dallasandro from the Red Sox, and Spencer Harris, a good prospect from Seattle.

The pitching staff was in essence unchanged. Hebert, Chaplin, Salvo, and Ward—the winning 1937 pitchers—were joined by veterans Craghead and Pillette as well as newcomer Pat Tobin of Washington.

Looked good on paper. Time would tell.

2-22-38 Spring Training-Carlsbad

The headline in a newspaper article by Earl Keller dated February 22, 1938, shouted "TUMMIES HINDER PADRES." It seems the 1938 Padres had more to do than just getting their arms and legs into shape for the upcoming season. A bigger job might be getting rid of bulging mid-sections.

Several of the Padres "looked more like brewery owners than ball players," according to Keller. Manager Shellenback came close to mistaking pitcher Dick Ward for "a circus fat man." Shelly, however, was somewhat impressed with the condition of his players in spite of the obvious weight gain. They all seemed ready and willing to get down to the training necessary to successfully defend the title they won in 1937.

The morning saw the manager put them through two hours of pepper games, fly chasing, and laps around the school field where they were training in Carlsbad. The pitchers were allowed to toss around a few balls, but nothing like the velocity one might see in a regular season game.

Next, they returned to the hotel for sulphur baths. That afternoon there was a five-mile walk into the hills. The next day a three-mile walk along the beach at Oceanside was scheduled. Shellenback followed the same training plan for the rest of the week, and felt certain those mid-sections would be streamlined. Regular training at Lane Field was set to begin the following Monday, and the entire Padres roster was under orders to report to Lane Field then.

Most of the players at Carlsbad complained of sore joints and stiff legs, but their gripes fell on deaf ears, and Shelly took no mercy on them. He told them to hang in there, that the soreness and stiffness would go away in a day or two. Cold comfort for the sufferers.

Although training had just begun, the talk turned to pennant races. Team members were confidant they could take the Coast flag again. The pitchers all said they felt great and expected to improve on their 1937 records.

Wally Hebert told Shellenback he had been throwing rocks all winter and didn't know how it would feel handling a baseball. Keller went on to say, "Wally looks as if he's in tip-top shape already." Guess he wasn't one who looked like a brewery owner.

Unfortunately, 1938 was not a repeat of 1937, but that's another story.

5-2-38 Padres/Seals

Padres Take Pair From Seals at 16 to 1

The San Diego Padres went to San Francisco to take on the Seals and found themselves in the Twilight Zone, or so it appeared. It seemed the Seals opted to forego regular baseball for the day, and decided to be batting practice for the visitors from down south.

The San Francisco fans came to the ball park, eager for two exhilarating games of baseball — a nine-inning game, and a seven-inning nightcap. What they got was four hours and two minutes of what looked to be two games of croquet, with Padre mallets executing all the knocks.

Wally Hebert offered up six scattered hits to the Seals, and Manuel Salvo gave up four, limiting the home team to one run in each game. In the meantime, the Padres were running amok at the plate, hitting everything the parade of Seal pitchers threw at them.

In the first game, with Hebert on the mound, San Diego basically won the game in the first inning with a four hit, four run barrage. They added four tallies in the third and again in the fourth. Score, 12-0. San Francisco put their lone run on the board in the fifth, ending Hebert's shutout. 12-1. Then it was shutout time again for the rest of the game. San Diego couldn't resist and put another run up in the seventh. They added three more in the eighth. 16-1. The Padres decided to rest on their laurels in the ninth with one hit. No runs.

San Francisco fans were no doubt in shock. There was still another game. Right? It couldn't be as bad as this. Not two games in a row. Right? Actually, it was. The Padres took the field, and Salvo held the home team to four hits and one run. Another drubbing at the plate with sixteen runs scored. *Deja vu* all over again. Right? It was enough to put a fan off baseball forever.

The next day Braven Dyer, writing in his Los Angeles Times column, "Sports Parade," had this to say. "Frank Howe says Wally Hebert has the last laugh on me . . .I no sooner get through saying that Wally has lost his stuff than he comes through with a six-hit game against the Seals . . . Howe thinks Dick Ward will probably bob up with a no-hit game now that I also included him among the has-beens."

I suppose Mr. Dyer had said some less than complimentary things in earlier columns.

5-6-38 Padres/Portland

PADRES DEFEAT PORTLAND FOR SEVENTH STRAIGHT WIN

On Saturday, the sixth of May, Padre players arrived at home park Lane Field riding a six-game winning streak, hoping to stretch it to seven. The Portland Beavers were visiting, hoping to stop said winning streak.

The Padres went right to work and started their half of the first inning with a run after holding the Beavers hitless and scoreless. The second inning rolled around and after a fruitless run by Portland in the top half, the Padres uncorked four hits and converted them into four runs in their half of the inning. Things looked good for win number seven.

After three futile innings served up by Padre pitcher Wally Hebert, Portland hit pay dirt and scored three runs on three hits in the fourth. All of a sudden things weren't looking quite as rosy. 5-3 was not nearly as comforting as 5-0.

But wait. San Diego hadn't been to bat yet. When the fourth inning was over and the Padres took the field for the start of the fifth, the scoreboard showed two more runs for the home team. 7-3. Better.

Hebert hummed along with things seemingly under control for the next two innings, but the Beavers scored two more times in their half of the seventh after Hebert gave up two more hits. Padre half of the seventh proved unproductive for them but they headed into the eighth still leading 7-5. Hebert gave up two hits, and Shellenback was afraid the lead might be in danger so he sent Craghead in to try to protect it. Craghead pitched the Padres out of the hole and shut the Beavers down in the last two innings. Hebert got credit for the win since the Padres were ahead when he exited the game.

5-30-38 Padres/Stars

Stars Drop Double Bill
Hebert and Humphries Hurl San Diego Club to Twin Win
Stars Drop Double-Header to Padres, 5-1 and 3-0

Memorial Day 1938 found the Padres visiting Wrigley Field where they had played when they were known as the Sheiks. Now the new Hollywood team—aka the Stars—were playing host to the team that formerly shared Wrigley Field with the Los Angeles Angels. Since it was Memorial Day it was only fitting the Padres would give the Stars something to remember them by, taking both games of a twin-bill 5-1 and 3-0. When it was all over the Padres had taken the series six games to three.

The Stars showed no punch at all, scoring one lone run in the bottom of the sixth inning because of an error. Wally Hebert had drawn pitching duties for San Diego in the first game after a week's layoff due to an ailing shoulder. He was back in form, however, and zinged along with a three-hit shutout for five innings. Then came the sixth, and Hebert found himself facing one tally, one out, and loaded bases. (If Bobbie was there, she was probably checking out the facilities in the ladies' room at Wrigley Field.) The next batter hit into a double play, and Hebert no longer found himself in hot water. The next three innings were a cake walk for him with a one-hit shutout.

On the offensive side of the ledger Hebert started things off in the top of the third with a single that got by the Stars left fielder. The San Diego hurler scampered on to second base while the fielders chased the ball around the outfield. The Padre center fielder came to bat and smacked a double, scoring Hebert. By the time the inning was over, three Padres had crossed the plate, having gotten to the Stars pitcher for five hits. The boys from the border city scored again in the sixth and seventh innings. They held on to that, and the final score was 5-1.

Byron Humphries pitched a four-hit shutout in the second game—a seven inning affair. All in all, a productive Memorial Day for the Padres. Almost compensated for missing the barbeque.

6-7-38 Padres/Oakland

Wally Hebert Twirls Padres to 8-1 Victory Over Oaks
Lowly Acorns Humbled in Series Opener

Lane Field. June 7. The Oakland Oaks came south to visit the Padres of San Diego, hoping to solve the puzzle of why Wally Hebert seemed to get to them on the diamond. The Oaks were scheduled to be in the border city a week or so, but when they got back to their hotel that first night they would still be in the dark about his strange hold over them.

Hope springs eternal, and they took to the dugout ready to give the southpaw a run for his money. By the end of the first inning the score was 0-0, neither team having put anything in the "Run" column. Oakland had managed to get a hit and San Diego hadn't. Maybe this would be their night.

The hope grew stronger in the second inning when they laced three singles off the lefty from Louisiana. When the first batter crossed the plate they just knew this was their day. They were leading their nemesis 1-0.

The next inning—the third—was uneventful for Oakland. Not so San Diego. The Padres notched three runs on two hits and went ahead 3-1. How did they get three runs on only two hits? Two bases on balls and one error did the trick. They added two more runs in the seventh and *lagniappe* of three more runs in the eighth. Final score. 8-1. Hebert went one for three at the plate, donated two RBIs to the cause, and struck out seven Oaks.

After Oakland's lone tally in the second it was shutout ball for the next seven innings. Hebert did give up nine hits, but they were so well scattered the Oaks were never able to mount any kind of offense. They returned to their hotel, still puzzled, and hoped for better luck the next day.

The Padres went home, satisfied with a good day's work.

6-29-38 Padres/Portland

PADRES BLANK PORTLAND, 6-0
Beavers Shut Out 6-0 By Padres

The San Diego Padres made their way up the coast to take on the Portland Beavers in Oregon. The Beavers were generous hosts while on the field. They ran around committing four errors which constituted a giveaway of four runs to their guests. Wally Hebert, pitching for the guests, brandished a whitewash brush by allowing only four hits and no runs.

On his way to a 6-0 victory, Hebert completed the game with a mere seventy-four pitches. The only time he had to throw more often than ten times was the ninth inning—fourteen tosses. Up until that last inning he had used up only sixty windups in a game lasting one hour and twenty-six minutes.

This was his fifth victory of the year and he did a lot to help himself at the plate as well as on the mound. He went two for four at bat, rapping a double and a single, and sent two Padres across the plate for two RBIs. The Beavers were no doubt happy to see the caboose of the train carrying their visitors homeward.

7-17-38 Padres/San Francisco Seals

PADRES ANNEX DOUBLEHEADER

The San Francisco Seals traveled down the coast to take on the Padres in a seven-game series in mid-July. San Diego had been in third place in the standings when the series began. The victories on the Sunday double-header ensconced them even tighter into third place. Wally Hebert and Jim Chaplin were the two hurlers who worked their magic against the Seals to take the victories on the last day, winning the series six games out of seven. Playoff status was still within reach.

Hebert pitched the first game, and it was not one of his better performances in spite of it being his eighth win of the season. He gave up nine hits while striking out only one. He committed one error and gave three Seal batters a free pass to first base. Even so, the Padres still managed to pull out a 7-3 victory.

Hebert more than made up for it at the plate, along with a little help from his friends. Only two Padres failed to hit safely. Hebert himself got on base twice in four trips to the plate. He belted a single and a double to send three Padre base runners home. A win is a win even if it's not pretty.

8-28-38 Padres/Beavers

San Diego Triumphs in Double Header by Scores of 6-1, 5-1

Lane Field had a double-header scheduled for Sunday afternoon and early evening. Wally Hebert was to be on the mound for the opener and Manuel Salvo was set for the seven-inning nightcap.

"Oh dang. That Frenchie guy from Louisiana's up for the first game. Bad news." This was probably the sentiment from the opposing dugout. Hebert was almost always bad news for the Beavers, and things didn't get any better for the visitors. If they were holding out any hope for a victory in the second game they were in for another disappointment.

The first three innings of the opener were quiet for both teams—zeroes across. Things started going the home team's way in the bottom half of the fourth inning. They managed to collect two hits off Portland's pitcher, and ended up with five runs. Portland aided San Diego's cause by muffing three balls, something that surely caused Beaver pitcher Darrow to grind his teeth in frustration. That was all the Padres needed to win that game, but they added another tally in the next inning. 6-0.

It looked like Hebert might be headed for a shutout on his way to victory number ten. The Beavers came out of their coma and scratched out two hits in the top of the sixth, managing to send one base runner across the plate, but that was all for them. The last three innings were hitless and scoreless. Final score: 6-1.

Hebert ended up with a three-hit one-run game, and was credited with one run-batted-in even though he didn't hit safely. Still—a good days work.

Portland's fears of Hebert were realized in game one, but the Beavers still held out hope for the nightcap before they caught the northbound train. Their luck didn't change with Padre pitcher Salvo, who held them to three hits and one run just like his predecessor. The Beavers were no doubt glad to leave the lights of San Diego behind them.

9-18-38 Padres/Seattle

Padres Bow Out of Play-Offs

Lane Field. Mid-September. The 1937 PCL champions would not be taking the field for the playoffs in 1938. They met their Waterloo in Seattle at a Sunday double-header. They needed to win both games to stay in the hunt for the elusive prize.

The first game was the bugaboo. Seattle took the game—a 9-8 nail-biter in eleven innings. It's not that Seattle played a great game. They just didn't play quite as badly as the Padres. San Diego went through two pitchers, and Seattle used up three. Both teams rang up fifteen hits each—a pitcher's nightmare.

In the field the game looked more like a modern-day Wee Ball contest as spectators watched while players from both teams booted the ball around for seven errors between them. Seattle won it in the eleventh inning, thus eliminating the Padres from playoff competition.

On to the nightcap, a game that meant absolutely nothing—to the Padres, at any rate. It was Wally Hebert's turn on the mound, and the boys from the border city redeemed themselves, even though they would be going home earlier than all the pre-season conventional wisdom predictions. With nothing left to lose, they relaxed and had fun taking it to the enemy.

San Diego opened up the second inning with two hits and one run. They added two runs in the fourth and again in the seventh. 5-0. They collected eight hits from two Seattle pitchers. Hebert was responsible for one RBI even though he didn't get any hits.

Seattle batters couldn't figure Hebert out. He gave up one hit to them in the second inning, but he silenced their bats for the rest of a game that took a mere one hour to complete. A one-hit shutout was cause for rejoicing, but it still didn't compensate for missing the playoffs.

Pitching Statistics:1938

Games: 37

Innings Pitched: 243

Won: 12

Lost: 16

Percentage: .429

Hits: 244

Bases on Balls: 58

Earned Run Average:: 3.11`

TWELVE

1939

3-8-39 Preseason

Season 1938 was in the rear view mirror. The 1937 champs disappointed their fans with a fifth place finish and no trip to the playoffs. A new king was crowned—the Sacramento Solons. A new day dawned as the Pacific Coast League geared up for the 1939 season. Hope springs eternal, so they say, and the Padres once again had high hopes and a new manager. Popular outfielder Cedric Durst, a twenty-year veteran, took over the managerial mantle from Frank Shellenback.

The off-season saw the departure of pitcher Manuel Salvo—twenty-two game winner in 1938—who was taken by the New York Giants. Others who would not take the field for the Padres were catcher Frank Hogan, infielder Jimmy Reese, and outfielder Spencer Harris. Salvo was the main loss. Twenty-two game winners don't show up that often.

In the pitching department manager Durst still had Wally Hebert, Dick Ward, Jim Chaplin, Howard Craghead, Byron Humphreys, Herman Pillette, and Pat Tobin. Durst was also looking at a few rookies.

George Detore and Bill Starr returned at catcher. Also returning were George McDonald, Al Niemic, and Bunny Griffiths. They were joined by newcomer Mickey Haslin. Outfielders Hal Patchette and Dominic Dallesandro were joined by Fred Berger, late of St. Paul. Three talented rookies were battling for outfield positions.

On paper the Padres looked to be competitive. Only time and action would tell, but a few days before opening day the team received devastating news. Jim "Tiny" Chaplin—twenty-one game winner—had lost his life in an automobile accident. The burden of hope was on Howard Craghead and Wally Hebert. Could they come through for the team? A lot could happen in six months. Read on.

3-21-39 Intra-squad game

San Diego Padres are ready!

New manager Cedric Durst oversaw a sizzling seven-inning intra-squad game at the El Centro training camp. After watching the team performance he pronounced the 1939 squad, outside of three or four players, ready to take on the foes of Pacific Coast league competition.

Durst was the most pleased with his two veteran pitchers—Howard Craghead and Wally Hebert. Durst said he believed they would be the best in the league. No rest for the weary, however, since the manager ordered another seven-inning tilt for the next morning.

The team returned to San Diego for two exhibition games with Portland before opening day on April 2 where they would take on Oakland for the beginning of the 1939 season.

Hebert was one of the hardest workers in spring training preps and said he was ready for the start of the '39 games. He had come off the 1938 season with a mediocre record of twelve wins to sixteen losses, and was anxious to improve on that year's endeavor.

4-6-39 Padres/Seattle

Padres Wallop Rainiers, 9-5

Lane Field on April 6 saw the home team Padres unleash a fourteen-hit assault on three Seattle pitchers. Seattle had just arrived for a seven-game series, with the first game being played on Thursday the sixth of April.

Wally Hebert, who drew pitching honors for San Diego, gave up seven hits but managed to put the game in the "W" column for the home team. He must have been feeling somewhat generous that day, giving free passes to five Rainiers, but he did strike out four of them.

San Diego struck first, putting two runs on the board in the second inning and added another in the third. 3-0. Hebert held the visitors scoreless for three innings, but the next two proved productive for Seattle—scoring twice in the fourth and twice again in the fifth, taking the lead 4-3. Oops. Home fans not happy.

San Diego didn't stay behind for long. They came roaring back in their half of the fifth and tied things up four-all. Not wanting to disappoint the home crowd, they proceeded to add one run in each of the next two innings and twisted the knife a bit with three big ones in the bottom of the eighth. 9-4. The faithful celebrated in the stands.

Seattle struck one more time in their half of the ninth, eking out one more run on two hits, but that was all they could muster, and the Padres shut them down after that. Game over. 9-5.

Hebert's teammates gave him plenty of support—all but one got at least one hit, and three of them hit safely three times. Hebert himself aided his cause, smashing a triple in the seventh, sending one run across the plate. He got greedy and tried to turn the triple into a home run and got called out at home plate. Hare relieved Hebert in the seventh but it was still the Cajun gent's game.

4-15-39 Padres/Seals

Seals Beaten by San Diego
Wally Hebert Again Proves Nemesis by Score of 2 to 1

Lefty O'Doul's hard-hitting Seals were in San Diego in mid-April, tied with San Diego at two games each in the series. Dismay set in when they saw who was up for mound duty in Saturday's contest. Wally Hebert knew how to get to them over the years. They could only hope things would be different for the Saturday game.

It was a pitcher's fight from the get-go. Hebert allowed six hits and San Francisco pitcher Shores gave up eight. Final score was a nerve-wracking 2-1. Hebert got into hot water three times—in the first, fourth, and sixth innings—when Seal batters made it to third base with only one out. (Bobbie Hebert undoubtedly set the path to the ladies room afire on her three excursions there.) Hebert was in top form and pitched his way out of trouble all three times. Both pitchers went the distance, not needing relief.

O'Doul was probably grinding his teeth, wondering how the heck his guys could be so close and still fail to make it that last ninety or so feet to cross home plate. San Diego put runs on the board in the fourth and again in the seventh. By then the Padres led 2-0, but no one was feeling the least bit confident. There were still two innings to go and everyone at Lane Field knew that a lead could disappear faster than it would take the umpire to yell "Play ball."

The home crowd wrung their hands when the visitors got two hits in the top of the eighth. Niggling turned to consternation when a run scored. A one-run game was no cause for celebration with one inning left.

The Padres got a hit in the bottom of the eighth and the gang in the stands felt better. We need more runs, they said, but nothing happened. The home team had to take the field again. Just hold them, the faithful prayed. Just three outs and it's over. We can go home.

And that's what happened. No activity at all in the ninth. No hits. No runs. The home team scattered to their respective homes. The visitors made their way back to their hotel to lick their wounds. The fans left happy but worn out.

5-4-39 Padres/Angels

ANGELS DROP ANOTHER TILT AS PADRES RALLY TO WIN
Angels Drop Third Game to Padres, 3-2

Lane Field. May 4. Another hand wringer for the fans. Wally Hebert took the mound for the Padres and had things going his way for three no-hit shutout innings. It was three up, three down for the southpaw from the bayou. In fact, it was going so good it was almost boring. The fans were lounging in their seats gossiping, having such a good time they weren't even worried about their team's lack of activity at the plate. At the end of the third inning the score was 0-0. The Padres had managed one hit in their half of the second inning but had nothing to show for it. The fans weren't worried—not as long as Hebert was in the zone.

The Padres took the field in the top of the fourth. Hebert took his warm-up tosses and got to work. He started the inning with a strikeout. Next man up—Angel's second baseman—slashed a single into center. Third baseman, English, whacked a triple down the third base line, scoring the base runner. 1-0, Angels. English crossed the plate on the next batter's softie over second base. 2-0. That got the crowd's attention.

The home crowd started to fret as the innings marched on, and the Padres appeared to be in a coma. Hebert had calmed down and continued to pitch shutout ball until the eighth inning. San Diego shut the visitors down in the top half and ceded the field to Los Angeles.

First man up was a pinch-hitter—Stewart hitting for Hebert. He led off with a single. Center fielder Patchett got to first on an error by the Los Angeles shortstop. The next batter, Berkowitz, hit safely but forced Patchett at second. Base runner Stewart scored and cut the lead to one run. 2-1.

Most of those in the stands were on their feet. By the time the eighth inning was in the record book the Padres had scored two more times bringing the tally to 3-2. Tobin came in to pitch the bottom of the ninth inning for San Diego. The Angels couldn't get anything started, and the game ended with a victory for the boys from the border city. Hebert was credited with another win, and the fans left in a jubilant mood.

5-14-39 Padres/Hollywood

HOLLYWOOD DROPS OPENER TO PADRES, 5-4

The Hollywood Stars visited the border city for a seven game series and enjoyed a one-game advantage at three games to two. They hoped for a sweep of the double-header to take the series five games to three, and for the first three innings it looked like their dream might come true.

Wally Hebert had drawn pitching duties and gave up seven hits and three runs in the first three innings. Not an auspicious start for the home team. San Diego's bats finally came to life in the bottom of the third when they put one tally on the board on one hit. 3-1, Stars. Not looking good for the Padres. Fans not too worried though. The game was young, and their heroes had been there before.

Hebert shook it off and pitched shutout ball the next six innings. In the meantime, Padre bats added a run in the fifth, bringing the score to 3-2, Stars. Better and better for the fans. One run would be easy to overcome.

The eighth inning brought Padre fans to their feet. A base on balls, a sacrifice, and two singles resulted in the tying run added to the scoreboard. 3-3. New game. Both teams had an unproductive ninth inning with one hit apiece but zero on the scoreboard. Extra innings.

Things quieted down in the stands when the Stars took the 4-3 lead in the top of the tenth, scoring one run on one hit. After their half of the inning Hollywood players swaggered on to the field, confidence oozing from every pore. We'll show these border guys how to play the game. The Padres filed into the dugout—not much conversation going on. This was it. The last hurrah.

Hollywood hubris evaporated when the Stars relief pitcher—Moncrief— found himself facing loaded bases and the ever-dangerous Cedric Durst swinging the bat and grinning. Moncrief let it fly and Durst smacked it into the outfield for a single. The first runner crossed the plate: tying run—four all. Second runner close behind. Go-ahead run: 5-4, Padres.

I'm pretty sure I wasn't there—I was only three years old, but I've seen games like that in later years. The stands no doubt looked like an anthill someone had stirred with a stick. Just another day at Lane Field.

6-2-39 Padres/Portland

San Diego Blanks Portland, 9-0

The boys from the border city were way up north in Oregon taking on the home team in Portland. They were ready to exact revenge on the Beavers, who had a series lead of four games to two.

Manager Durst sent Wally Hebert to the mound, and he came through for the team big time. The Oakland "run" column on the scoreboard showed big fat zeroes all the way across. The five hits he gave up were well-spaced throughout the nine innings. He gave one Beaver a free pass to first base, but sent four back to the dugout with their bats on their shoulders.

In the meantime Hebert and his colleagues ran two Portland pitchers to the showers with a deluge of nineteen hits and belted out a 9-0 victory in the fifth game of the series. Everyone—*everyone*—who batted got at least one hit. Left-fielder Dallassandro went five for five and center-fielder Patchette made it to first base four times. Hebert himself smacked a double, sending a base-runner across home plate. Remember—pitchers are at the bottom of the batting order. They get no respect at the plate.

6-6-39 Padres/Oakland

Hebert Gives Padres Split
Veteran Southpaw Hurls Four-Hitter to Annex 3-0 Nightcap

Oakland was in San Diego for the start of a nine-game series against the Padres. The Oaks had made up their minds they could win at least six of those games. After the first game of Tuesday's double bill they felt more confident than ever. At the end of a game lasting an interminable two hours and twenty-two minutes they had eked out a closely fought 8-6 victory. Ten of those minutes were taken up by a sixth-inning brou-ha-ha that finally ended with young Padre first-baseman George McDonald being asked none too politely to leave the field by umpire Wally Hood.

Oakland bats sent two San Diego pitchers to the showers. All of this was enough to get the home team's collective back up, and egged on by the raucous cheering squad in the stands they vowed vengeance on the visitors later in the nightcap.

Second game. The Oaks swaggered into the dugout, ready to shellac the border city boys a second time. They watched the home team take the field and start tossing the ball around, yelling and slapping their gloves. Not demoralized at all, it would seem. Wally Hebert stepped on the mound and took his practice throws. The same Wally Hebert with eight notches on his victory belt. Hmm. *Might not be so easy after all.* Turns out they had reason to worry.

Hebert, on his way to victory number nine, dished out only four hits. However, one of them was a gift from umpire Hood to Oakland in the second inning. The Oakland batter hit a drive down the right field line, and it was obvious to all that the Padre fielder was almost to the bleacher fence when he reached out for the ball. He got his hands on it but couldn't hold on. The umpire called a fair ball, and the batter got credit for a triple. Mickey Haslin raised such a ruckus and called the umpire so many bad names he was tossed out. He was also fined a whopping ten dollars.

While Hebert had silenced Oakland bats, San Diego's sticks came alive enough to give the Padres three runs on six hits to take the contest 3-0. Not only did he do his part on the mound he was also involved in the two times the Padres put runs up. In the third inning catcher Bill Starr doubled, and Hebert belted a single. A bad throw by Oakland's center-fielder resulted in Starr crossing the plate. 1-0.

After an uneventful fourth inning the Padres struck again. Hebert drew a walk and became a base runner. George McDonald smashed a triple, scoring Hebert. Bunny Griffiths laid down a perfect bunt, and McDonald scored for the second run. 3-0. One more inning to go in the short nightcap. The gentleman from the bayou applied the finishing touches and retired the side.

The Oakland defeat brought Hebert's record to nine victories and two defeats with a percentage of .818. This put him in second place among Pacific Coast hurlers. He who laughs last laughs best.

6-27-39 Padres/Portland

Hebert Stops Portland, 4-0

The Portland Beavers blew into town ready to hand the home team Padres seven—count 'em—seven defeats in a seven game series to be played at Lane Field in late June and early July. A collective groan went up when the visitors saw who stepped on the pitcher's mound and started throwing practice tosses.

Wally Hebert, San Diego's leading hurler, was warming up. Not that guy again, the guests moaned. He had already shut them out not too many days in the past. As the sports writer noted, Hebert was always at his best against the usually hard-hitting Beavers. Not only that, he was coasting along with ten triumphs to his credit

The home town boys didn't disappoint their fans. Hebert shut the visitors out while allowing them five puny hits in the third, fourth, and ninth innings. He chalked up seven strikeouts on his way to victory.

While Beaver bats were somewhat silent, Padre bats did what they needed to do. Nine hits resulted in four players crossing the plate. Hebert went one for three and notched a run batted in to help his cause. Dominic Dallessandro, one of the league's leading hitters, socked a home run in the eighth inning.

Final score was 4-0, and Hebert added another win, bringing his total to eleven. So much for seven wins for the visitors.

7-1-39 Padres/Portland

PADRE RALLY FATAL FOR DUCKS

On July 1 the Beavers found themselves tied with their hosts two games to two. They had given up hoping for a seven-game triumph. Just win the last three and they could take five goodies back to Portland after Sunday's double-header. They filed into the dugout, ready to take their turn at the plate—laughing, joking, high-fiving. Ready to take it to the southerners. They quieted down when they saw who stood on the pitcher's mound. Not him again.

Wally Hebert. The guy who had shut them out four days previously.

Hope springs eternal, so they say, and the Beavers had good reason to celebrate after their half of the first inning. They tapped Hebert for three hits and turned them into two runs. Joy reigned in the visitor dugout. Today would be their day. Scoreboard showed Visitors-2, Home-0.

The inning wasn't over, though. San Diego still had to bat. The visitors took the field, vowing to show no mercy. But you know what they say about good intentions. By the time the Padres turned in out number three the score was 2-1, visitors. No big deal, according to the Portland nine. Still eight innings to play. It ain't over till it's over.

Turns out it was over for the Beavers. For the next eight innings Hebert pitched a five-hit shutout. The Padres added two runs in the third, and coasted on to a 3-2 win over the unhappy boys from up north. On his way to a twelfth victory Hebert got one hit, struck out four, and donated two free passes to Beaver batters. The Padres were ahead in the series three games to two. I have no information on the Sunday double-header since Hebert didn't play.

According to the San Bernardino County Sun dated July 4, 1939, two Padre sluggers were leading the league in batting. Dominic Dallesandro, left fielder, was in first place with a .390 average, and catcher Gene Detore followed him with an average of .372. An interesting side note: Dominic DiMaggio, youngest of the clan DiMaggio, held down third place with a .369 average while playing for the San Francisco Seals.

Wally Hebert was in third place among the PCL pitchers with twelve wins against four losses. In spite of having the top two sluggers and a pitcher near the top the Padres found themselves in fifth place in league standings.

7-16-39 Padres/Angels

Angels Split With Padres

Wrigley Field. Los Angeles. Sunday, July 16. The Padres and the Angels were at it again, trying to come out on top in the final two games of the seven game series. The Angels were ahead three games to two, and hoped to take the double bill to finish up at five to two. The Padres had their own agenda, aiming for four games to three. They each got half a wish.

A fired-up Los Angeles team stormed over the visitors by a score of 14-5 in the first game. They scored ten of their runs in the first inning, signaling they were ready to kick butt.

The frustrated Padres decided to wage a bean ball war, resulting with an Angel (I use the term loosely) attempting to spike pitcher Olson and first baseman McDonald as he slid into first base. The Angel failed to make contact and got called out.

Padre catcher Starr got ejected from the game by umpire Fanning when he decided to avoid an incoming pitch. He stepped aside and the ball whizzed by him, thumping into the umpire's chest protector. I guess Starr hadn't gotten the memo. "Don't mess around with the umpire." He found himself headed for the showers.

The 15,000 or so fans there certainly got their money's worth. A fine shellacking by their favorite team and an entertaining side show by the "boys" of summer. They couldn't wait for the second game to commence.

The triumphant Angels were raring for the second game to start. They were pumped. They wanted to get started on their next rout and took the field with Stine on the mound. The Padres got nowhere in the first inning—no hits, no runs. One down and six innings to go. The hosts filed into the dugout, confident they were on their way to victory number two for the night. Charley English, Angel right-fielder, blasted a home run. 1-0, Los Angeles. Jubilation in the dugout. No stopping them now.

Wally Hebert was on the mound, and stopped the Angels cold for the next three innings, allowing only two hits. In the top of the fourth the Padres evened things up with one run on three hits. Dallessandro and Detore hit successive singles to tie the score.

A four run rally in the fifth frame broke the deadlock and set Angels fans back on their heels. This couldn't be happening, they said. The team shuffled into the dugout, finding themselves behind 5-1. Hebert gave up two hits, and the Angels managed to add another run to the board. 5-2. Better, but still not looking good.

San Diego scored again in the top of the sixth, adding to Los Angeles misery. 6-2. The misery increased when Hebert put the kibosh on their half of the inning. Score still 6-2.

The Padres were not through adding to Angel distress. They tallied two more times on two hits, bringing the score to 8-2 in the seventh frame. By now Los Angeles was on pitcher number three.

Angel bats woke up in the last half of the ninth. This was it. They had a flurry of four hits and three runs, giving the faithful hope. Score 8-5, San Diego. Humphreys came in to relieve Hebert and finished off the hosts, saving the game for Hebert, who got credit for the win.

That would be the last time the two teams faced each other in 1939 unless they met again in the playoffs.

7-26-39 Padres/Portland

San Diego Padres on Hitting Spree, Win

Late July. Lane Field. The folks who showed up for the game with Portland that night were the truly dyed-in-the-wool fans who braved any kind of weather or hardship to watch their beloved boys of summer take the field. Only 1,000 more or less were in attendance for the contest. A six-game losing streak might have been the reason for so many empty seats. Some people are just fair weather fans.

Those who opted to stay home were the losers. The faithful few enjoyed a wild ride as their idols came through for them 8-3. Wally Hebert was designated hurler for the night—he with thirteen wins to his credit. And he did not disappoint. It was shutout ball for the most part, with Portland managing runs in the fourth, seventh, and ninth innings.

In the meantime San Diego batters were having a high old time knocking two Portland hurlers around for fourteen hits. In fact, all Padres except one got on base at least once, including pitcher Hebert who went one for four. The home team scored two in the third inning, three in the fifth, two in the seventh, and a twist of the knife for one more in the eighth. The bottom of the ninth was unnecessary since the Padres had already stashed the game into the record book. A good time was had by all, and those who showed up were treated to Hebert's fourteenth victory of the season.

7-30-39 Padres/Portland

Padres Divide With Beavers As Wally Hebert Wins Again
SOUTHPAW STAR SCORES BOTH S.D. VICTORIES OF SERIES

The Beavers had handed San Diego one loss after another since they had been in town for the series against the Padres. The only game they had lost was earlier in the week when Wally Hebert had taken the mound and walloped them 8-3. Portland was on a sugar-high of victories and looking forward to another two in the double-header coming up.

After all, hadn't they been on a roll since that opening loss to the old crooked arm from the Louisiana swamps. Imagine their dismay when they saw who was on the mound taking practice pitches. Old Crooked Arm himself.

The first three innings proved unproductive for both teams. No runs and only one hit apiece. Then came the top of the fourth with Portland in the dugout. One Beaver was on base, courtesy of a base on balls donated by Hebert. Up to the plate stepped manager and first-baseman Bill Sweeney. Hebert let one fly and Sweeney popped it over the right-field fence, scoring himself and the base runner. 2-0, Beavers. Much joy in the dugout. They were on their way.

The Padres were shut down for the next two innings, and it looked like Portland might pull it off, even though they, too, seemed to be sleep-walking through the game. San Diego gave the visitors something to think about when the sixth inning rolled around. The hosts loaded the bases. George Detore was deliberately walked. Al Niemeic, second-baseman, socked a big one into center, scoring two base runners. Score tied 2-2.

Hebert continued on his merry way, pitching shutout ball to the frustrated Beavers who had seen their lead obliterated and couldn't seem to get around Hebert's curves. The bottom half of the seventh inning was lucky number seven for San Diego, and Hebert himself was the jackpot winner. A single to center by shortstop Berkowitz started them off. Catcher Starr moved him to second on a bunt. Up to the plate stepped pitcher Hebert. No worry, opined the

Beavers. Pitchers can't hit, can they? This one whacked one into center, scoring Berkowitz. 3-2, Padres. Hebert and his teammates combined brilliant fielding and stingy pitching to keep zeroes on the scoreboard for the remainder of the game. This was Hebert's fifteenth win of the season.

Portland caught a break in the nightcap, taking the game by a 3-0 score. They considered themselves fortunate not having to face Hebert again in that one. They took the series five games to two — the two losses coming from the left arm of Hebert. In fact, one sportswriter in the Los Angeles Times had this to say about the curly-haired Cajun: "Hebert has the Indian sign on the Beavers, whom he can beat by tossing his glove out on the field."

The San Bernardino County Sun reported on Pacific Coast League leaders in batting and pitching as of August 1. Dominic Dallessandro, San Diego outfielder, was perched atop the sluggers with a batting average of .378. San Diego catcher, Gene Detore was right behind him in second place with .361. Wally Hebert held down fourth place in the hurling department with a record of fifteen wins against five losses.

One would think a team with those assets would be sitting atop everyone else in the standings. *Au contraire.* The Padres were one and one-half games out of last place. Sitting there in seventh place that late in the season there was no way they would ever make it into the first division and playoff hopes. Of course, they could always get lucky and win the rest of their games. Nothing is impossible.

8-24-39 Padres/Stars

PADRES CONQUER HOLLYWOOD, 7-6
Three-Run Rally in Ninth Wins Game

The Cardiac Kids were at it again. This time they were battling it out with the Stars from Hollywood—the baseball team, not the movie idols. San Diego fans sat scratching their heads for six innings, wondering if their money would have been better spent at a darkened theater watching the other stars.

They weren't expecting a hand-wringer. Hebert was on the mound—the winningest pitcher on the Padre team. Most of the San Diego faithful had barely taken their seats when he gave up three straight hits. All of a sudden the Stars had a two-run lead. No big deal. They had been behind before; it was just the first inning. Their heroes would undoubtedly catch up in their half of the inning. Not this time.

Both teams decided to take a sabbatical from scoring for the next four innings. Hebert was still serving up hits, but nothing came of them. The Padres weren't even doing that. One hit in five innings was all they could muster.

The top of the sixth rolled around. The Padres took the field, hoping to shut the Stars down once again. The first two Hollywood batters didn't make it to first base. Those in the bleachers settled down, feeling better. Two out, one to go. The Stars third-baseman belted a double into the outfield. The next batter sent a single to center, and the base-runner scored. 3-0, Hollywood. More hand-wringing for the home fans.

The Padres registered their second hit of the game in their half of the sixth. Still no runs, though, after the third out was called. The home crowd was debating on whether to leave early to avoid traffic.

Top of the seventh—all quiet on the Hollywood front. Bottom of the seventh—Padre bats awoke from their coma. Dallessandro led off with a double. Niemiec grounded out, moving Dallessandro to third. Durst knocked a fly into right field, scoring McDonald. 3-2, Hollywood.

Top of the eighth. Elation turned to despair. Hollywood belted four hits and added three runs. 6-2, Stars. Joy in the visitors' dugout. Sweet revenge. Gloom on the diamond.

The home team shuffled into the dugout for their turn at bat and watched the celebration going on around the field.

Bottom of the eighth coming up. San Diego surprised everyone with three hits and two runs. 6-4. Hollywood still ahead. Ninth inning coming up. Was this game winnable? Long shot.

The die-hards decided to stay and ride it out. Hebert bore down and denied the Stars additional tallies. One hit, no runs. Score still 6-4. (Bobbie had probably decided to camp out in the ladies' room.)

Pinch hitter Berkowitz started things off for the home boys with a single to center. Pitcher Hebert's single sent Berkowitz to third, and he then scored on a sacrifice fly. 6-5, Hollywood. Third-baseman Stewart got to first on a single and center-fielder Carlyle singled to center, scoring Stewart for the tie. 6-6. The stands erupted.

Dallassandro beat out an infield hit to fill the bases. More joy in the bleachers. Second-baseman Al Niemeic stepped to the plate. He fooled the Stars by laying down a squeeze bunt and beat it out. Stewart, on third, crossed the plate with the winning run. 7-6, San Diego.

Now if I was there I don't remember. I was only three, and even if I could have remembered I would have been in the ladies' room with my mother. I can only imagine what was going on in the stands and on the field. One could almost — *almost* — feel sorry for the Stars. And if any San Diego fans left when the score was 6-2, I'm sure they were kicking themselves the next day.

It was certainly not Hebert's prettiest game, but a win is a win is a win.

9-3-39 Padres/Sacramento

HEBERT AND NEWSOME HURL TRIUMPHS FOR SAN DIEGO

Lane Field was the scene of a double-header between the Padres and the Hollywood Stars one Sunday in September. The 1939 season was drawing to a close and the playoffs were on the horizon. Every game counted for San Diego if they wanted to end their Shaughnessy drought and make it into the post season.

The opener was another one of those squeakers San Diego fans had become accustomed to. When the Padres took their places on the field fans breathed a little easier. Wally Hebert was taking warm-up tosses. After all, didn't he have eighteen victories to his credit? Wasn't he sitting near the top in PCL pitcher standing? This should be no worries.

First batter up—no problem. Going to be a long night for Sacramento. Next batter, outfielder Marshall, belted one out of the park. 1-0, Sacramento. It didn't take long to quiet the bleachers down.

Hebert settled down and denied the Solons anything else, but the Padres couldn't seem to get their game legs moving for the next two innings. It remained 1-0 until the bottom of the fourth inning. San Diego's bats awoke, and they managed to send one run across the plate. Score tied 1-1.

Hebert kept zinging away, pitching no-hit shutout ball until the ninth inning. The Solons were frustrated every time their half of the innings ended since they still had nothing to show for their labor. They eked out another hit in the eighth, but the run column showed a zero when the side retired.

San Diego was having no better luck in the run department although they were hitting the Solon pitcher consistently. They just couldn't seem to send anyone home. At the end of nine full innings the score remained at 1-1. Extra innings.

Top of the tenth. No luck for Sacramento—no hits, no runs. The visitors took the field, and the Padres filed into the dugout. Center-fielder Hal Patchette was first up; he opened the inning with a single. The fans weren't too hopeful.

Their guys already had eight hits to their credit but only one run. They just couldn't seem to break away with anything. Next up was young Ed Stewart, right-fielder, who had two hits under his belt but nothing else.

The Sacramento pitcher let one fly. Stewart connected and sent it soaring over the fence, scoring Patchette. 3-1, Padres. Game over. Hebert had his nineteenth win, a two hitter, on his victory belt.

9-12-39 Padres/Hollywood

Padres Pelt Twinks, 6-2
Dallessandro Batting Star; Slim Crowd Sees Gilmore Field Game

Gilmore Field in Hollywood. September 12. The Padres wanted to keep their hopes alive and stick around for post-season play. They needed this win. Hollywood took the field, and San Diego filled the dugout. Neither team scored in the first inning, although Wally Hebert gave the home team a couple of hits.

Hollywood's half of the second inning gave home fans encouragement. The first batter socked a homer over the left-field fence. 1-0, Stars. Up next, a double followed by a single scored the second run. 2-0, Stars. Hebert decided enough was enough and kept Hollywood off the board for the remainder of the game.

Top of the third. Padres at bat. Pitcher Hebert, right-fielder Stewart, and second-baseman Berkowitz bunched three singles for one run before a double play put an end to the uprising. 2-1. Still the Stars.

The Padres rallied again in the fifth. With two outs, Patchette doubled. He was on third when Dallassandro beat out a hit and scored Patchette. Hollywood manager Killefer protested the decision at first, and was politely asked to head for the showers. Seems he got a little too close to umpire Widner. Umpires don't like their space invaded. Score tied, 2-2.

The sixth and seventh innings were quiet for both teams. Hollywood fans were frustrated because their team had blown a two run lead. Now it was like starting over. They were also antsy because the team couldn't seem to do anything with what Hebert was serving up.

Top of the eighth. Padres at bat. Dallessandro at the plate. He whacked a hard one to left center and ended up on third base. Haslin, up next, singled, scoring Dallassandro. 3-2. San Diego took the lead. Collective groan rose from the bleachers.

Same inning. Detore and McDonald each hit safely, scoring Haslin. 4-2.

San Diego increased their lead. Home town fans dismayed. Praying for something—anything—to happen to wake their guys up. It was not to be.

When Hollywood's turn at bat rolled around Hebert gave up one hit—and that was it. Another zero in the run column. Score still sitting at 4-2.

Top of the ninth. Just hold the visitors to no runs, no hits. Then they would have one more chance to make something happen. Padre right-fielder Stewart got on base with a single. Mighty mite Dallessandro stepped to the plate. Not him again. He already had two hits—a single and a triple. No singles or triples this time up. Instead, he sent one over the right center fence and followed Stewart across home plate. 6-2, San Diego. Not a lot of activity in the bleachers.

Despite home town hope that the ninth would be their big inning, it was another no hit, no run frame for them, and the boys from the border city ruined everyone's evening with a score of 6-2. Every Padre got at least one hit for a total of seventeen. The only inning they failed to get anyone on base was the seventh.

A good night for the visitors. The batters had a field day, and Hebert registered his twentieth win of the season. Every pitcher's dream.

REDS SEEKING HEBERT, RUMOR
Want Southpaw To Bolster Staff In Title Drive

What was the going rate for a ball player back in the thirties? $7,500. Sounds a bit ridiculous when compared with the million dollar transactions of today. That's the price tag placed on Wally Hebert, ace pitcher, and George Detore, San Diego's prize batter, during the 1939 draft. The midnight deadline for deals passed, and certain Pacific Coast League players became eligible for the draft, of which Hebert and Detore were considered the most likely prospects.

Some well-founded last minute reports circulated that the sale of Hebert was about to be completed. San Diego officials, however, all denied any definite negotiations were being attempted, but rumors in the north hinted the Cincinnati Reds had made an offer for Hebert.

The Reds, it seemed, were in need of support for their pitching staff, which had but two reliable hurlers in Paul Derringer and Bucky Walters. The Reds were in the closing drive to the National League pennant. They needed help right away. Cincinnati was insisting on immediate delivery, hoping to get the southpaw east in time to take on some of the pitching load before the end of the week.

Padre manager, Cedric Durst, however, announced Hebert would be his mound selection when the Padres took on the Hollywood Stars in the final week of the season. San Diego was in the middle of a winning streak which was carrying them closer to their own first division. They weren't about to let their ace go anywhere.

Hebert himself held little hope he would ever return to the majors. In his early thirties, he considered himself too old for consideration from major league teams. "They want young fellows that throw a blazing fast ball." He said he used his head more than his arm, but that he threw harder than some of the younger pitchers in the circuit. "I don't believe I'll go up to the big time, however."

He was wrong about that, but it would be another three years.

9-17-39 Padres/Stars

STARS MISS BID FOR FIFTH BY DIVIDING WITH PADRES

Gilmore Field in Hollywood. September 17. Double header — last two games in regular play for the 1939 season. A crowd of 5,000 came to see if their Stars could beat San Diego in two games to take over fifth place in PCL standings. At stake was nothing, really. Neither team would be heading to the playoffs. The Stars had to win both games to take over fifth place. A split would have them holding down sixth place. Nothing to celebrate here.

San Diego got things going in the first inning. Mickey Haslin, third-baseman, clouted a homer, scoring the two base runners. 3-0 right away for the visitors. Wally Hebert was on the mound for the visitors, and gave up one hit and one run to the hosts in the bottom of the first. Both pitchers held things down for two scoreless innings, but the Padres got to Stars pitcher Osborne for one hit and one run. 4-1, Padres. An unproductive bottom half of the fourth ensued for Hollywood, but they came back with a vengeance in the next inning. After shutting the visitors out in the top of the fifth, the Stars came roaring back when they had their turn at bat. They tied the score, sending three runners across the plate. 4-4. New game.

The eighth inning provided a side show — how not to endear yourself to an umpire. The Padres scored two runs and came close to starting a riot when umpire Widner called the third out before the third run crossed the plate. No score. No less than four Padre uniforms charged the umpire — pitcher Hebert, manager Ced Durst, third base Haslin, and second Niemiec. It was four against one with much abuse, some verbal and some physical. The umpire prevailed, and manager Durst was invited to vacate the diamond. The scoreboard showed 6-4, visitors. Home town fans were not happy, and it got worse when their team failed to answer the foe.

San Diego scored again in the top of the ninth to increase their lead 7-4. Many of the hometown fans thought it was all over even though the Stars had at least three more players to bat. They'd been burned before.

With one out the next batter doubled. Manager Durst replaced Hebert. The reliever loaded the bases, and the home team thrilled the home crowd by scoring four runs and winning the game 8-7. One down and one to go to send those pesky Padres down to sixth place. The boys from down south won the night cap, however, and everything stayed the same. San Diego—fifth place, Hollywood—sixth.

It was Hebert's last game of the 1939 season. He wasn't the loser in the game since he was ahead when he left the mound. The reliever was charged with the loss. Hebert ended the season with twenty victories against ten defeats. Not bad for someone who spent his childhood running barefoot through the marshes and swamps of Louisiana.

Both the Padres and the Stars stowed their gear and headed home to wherever, along with Portland and Oakland—the other teams sitting in the second division. Hebert had a good year. Twenty wins is what every pitcher dreams of, but he hoped for a better year in 1940 for the team.

Pitching Statistics for 1939

Games: 39

Innings Pitched: 299

Won: 20

Lost: 10

Percentage: .667

Hits: 295

Strikeouts: 104

Bases on Balls: 64

Earned Run Average: 3.13

THIRTEEN

1940

Padre Pilot Expects Hebert to Pass 20-Mark in Victories This Season

Cedric Durst, Padre manager, had high hopes for the 1940 season after he got a letter from Hebert, who reported he had picked up some weight over the winter and was in fighting condition for the upcoming season. Durst said the hard-working left-hander would pass the 20-mark. "There's no reason to believe Wally won't improve off 1939," Durst told the writer.

To refresh the memory, one would recall Hebert rang up twenty wins against ten losses in 1939. He had some bad breaks in some of those losses or he might have chalked up more victories.

Durst had more to say. According to him Wally was the hardest worker he had ever managed. "He takes orders without talking back, and I'm telling you if there were twenty-five players like him on a team a manager wouldn't even be needed." He was always in the best of condition, but was always the first one out for spring training preps each day.

Hebert had not signed his 1940 contract, but he was on his way, and the Padres had never had any trouble in the past getting him to sign on the dotted line. Since his 1940 contract called for a nice raise, there was no reason to be concerned he would start beefing then.

Angels Invade San Diego
Gene Lillard to Face Wally Hebert Today

The Pacific Coast League got the jump on the rest of organized baseball circuits by scheduling their opening day games two weeks ahead of everyone else. Four games were scheduled for March 30 with much fanfare and hoopla on tap for this, their 38th season.

The San Diego Padres were to play host to the hard-hitting Los Angeles Angels at Lane Field. San Diego—youngest city in the PCL—feted its baseball team on the day before the big game. The Angels rolled into town and took one last workout at Lane Field while their game foes were living it up at a banquet. A big parade had been planned to lead 6,000 rabid fans into Lane Field where they hoped to see their heroes hand those pesky Angels their collective *derrieres* in the contest.

Manager Cedric Durst planned to do just that and named Wally Hebert, 1939 twenty-game winner, as starting pitcher. The Padres hadn't won an opener against the Angels since their entry into the league, and were hungry for an opening day success. They would be without the services of third-baseman Mickey Haslin, who was at odds with the front office over his contract, and first-baseman George McDonald who was on the mend from surgery.

What they lacked in manpower would be made up for in zeal. The entire town was talking baseball, and weren't intimidated by the Angel sluggers. They had faith in Hebert's curve ball.

Opening day ceremonies were a bit unusual. Normally the mayor of the city would toss out the first ball. Not that year. This time the home team pitcher—that would be Hebert—was scheduled to throw it out. Pacific Coast League president Wilbur Tuttle was the guest of honor at the San Diego-Los Angeles game, where he witnessed the pitching duel between southpaw Hebert and Angel right-hander Gene Lillard.

3-30-40 Padres/Angels

7,000 Fans See Padres Humble Angels in Opener
Wally Hebert Stymies L.A.
Angels Upset by Padres, 5-1
Hebert Tames Angel Hitters

Lane Field. March 30, 1940. Opening Day. San Diego Padres versus their old nemesis, the Los Angeles Angels. The bitter taste of opening day defeats at the hands of the Angels still lingered from years gone by. The border city boys had yet to hand the Tinsel Town troops a loss. To say the Padres were looking forward to pounding their foes into the dust of Lane Field would be an understatement—sort of like referring to a World War as the late unpleasantness.

Seven-thousand raucous fans filed into Lane Field with hope in their hearts and fire in their eyes, ready for their guys to take it to the visitors from Tinsel Town. They had just come from a rousing parade through downtown San Diego and a flag-raising ceremony in the park. Adrenaline was running rampant, and they couldn't wait for the slaughter to begin. Normally they wouldn't want to hurt an angel, but this was different. This was war. It mattered not that the Angels were favored to take the contest. As far as Padre fans were concerned, this would be their day.

Hebert finished his practice tosses, and the umpire yelled "Play ball." The game began. Hebert dispatched the lead-off Angel, and the crowd went wild. Next batter up—Eddie Mayo, Angel third-baseman, who latched on to one of Hebert's offerings and sent it soaring over the right field fence where it cleared the railroad tracks on Pacific Boulevard—340 feet from home plate. This quieted the crowd down a bit, but not for long.

Hebert decided he wasn't putting up with any more enemy hits, and pitched shutout ball for the next eight innings, with a lot of help from his fielders. At the same time Angel pitcher Gene Lillard held the hosts scoreless for six innings. This didn't silence Padre fans, and by the time the seventh inning rolled around, they were at full throat, screaming for some action.

Padre left-fielder Jensen sent a single into center field. Lillard walked the next batter, and Detore bunted to advance both runners to second and third base. Ed Stewart, right-fielder, sent a hard grounder through second base, and both runners scored. 2-1, Padres. The fans smelled blood, and there was no keeping them quiet from then on.

After another scoreless inning for the Angels—they got one hit—the Padres headed for the dugout. Egged on by the rowdy crowd, they got three hits and scored three runs, bringing the score to 5-1. The top half of the ninth inning saw the Angels collect three hits off of Hebert, but great fielding kept them off the scoreboard, so the Angels' half of the ninth inning was the end of a game that lasted an hour and a half.

Except for Mayo's homer in the first inning, it was a fine pitching endeavor on Hebert's part, but he was well-supported by the brilliant fielding of his teammates. Berkowitz was perfect at third, handling all six of the zingers that came his way. Third base is called the hot corner for good reason.

Left-fielder Jensen robbed one heavy-hitting Angel of a sure double with an electrifying running catch. Two double plays by infielders Berkowitz, Sperry, Stinson, and Mesner cut short the Angel's attempts to send base runners home.

San Diego was one happy city. The opening day Angel jinx had finally been broken. Next leg of the journey? Get back in the first division.

Opening day March 30, 1940 at Lane Field
Padres/Angels
Wally Hebert On The Pitcher's Mound
Book Cover: *Echoes From Lane Field* by Bill Swank

4-5-40 Padres/Stars

HEBERT HURLS TODAY
Hebert Wins Own Battle

Early in the 1940 season it looked like Wally Hebert was well on his way to the outstanding season of his career. After defeating the Angels 5-1 a week earlier, he took it to the Hollywood Stars by a score of 1-0. Sportswriter Keller pointed out that Padre pitchers seemed to be in the best of condition. Hebert had not been scored on in seventeen innings and was tied with pitcher Dick Newsome in shutout wins.

What made the victory over the over the Stars better than ever for Hebert? He drove in the winning run, which was the only score in the game for either team. Hollywood's pitcher, Ardizola, had effectively shut down San Diego's bats for seven innings. Hebert decided to take matters into his own hands when Padre first baseman, Frank Stinson, got to first on an error and second on a sacrifice fly. Wally zinged a single over shortstop, and Stinson crossed the plate for the lone score of the game.

This was not a game for the faint of heart. Hebert was in several tight spots, but his spot-on hurling aided by the great fielding of his teammates got him out of trouble every time.

Take the fourth inning, for example. The Hollywood batter started it off with a double. Hebert settled down to get the next three on fly balls. Fifth inning was nearly identical. With one out Hollywood's catcher doubled, but Hebert got the next two batters in a row to end the inning. However, it was the seventh and eighth innings that offered up the most scares.

The seventh inning started off with a single by Hollywood's right fielder, who then made it to second on a bunt. Two of Hollywood's better hitters were up next. The first one hit to the Padre shortstop, who threw high to first, but the first baseman leaped high enough for out number two. The next batter knocked one past Hebert, and for a second or two it looked like a base hit. However, shortstop Mesner came from out of nowhere to get it to first for out number three.

The fireworks weren't over, though. Hebert started the eighth inning off by walking the first batter, who made it to second on a sacrifice fly. One out. Another base on balls. Two on. One out. Top of the Stars' batting order was up and raring to go. The Hollywood second baseman hit into a fast double play to end the top of the inning. Hebert got his RBI in the bottom half. 1-0, Padres.

When the Padres took the field in the top of the ninth, all they had to do was hold fast. Easier said than done. The Padres and their fans started to breathe easier when the Stars had two outs. A double by the Hollywood batter caused everyone to sit back down. Babe Herman, always dangerous, was up for Hollywood. He got on base with a single. Two out. Two on. More nail biting. The next batter up was an easy out, however, and all was well again at Lane Field.

Among the San Diego fans in the stands that day was Wally Hebert's wife, Bobbie. She made several trips to the ladies' room. "There goes Mrs. Wally," the sportscaster would say.

4-10-40 Padres/Oakland

Wally Hebert Hurls Victory
San Diego Tightens Grip on Loop Lead With Another Win

Lane Field. April 10. San Diego had surprised everyone by taking the lead in the Pacific Coast League standings. They would have a chance to lengthen that lead by defeating Oakland for the second straight time. Fan enthusiasm was running high as Wally Hebert took the mound for the Padres.

Not much happened for either team during the first four innings. Both pitchers pitched shutout ball — big zeroes across the scoreboard. Both teams got four hits along the way with nothing to show for it. Both teams woke up in the fifth.

The Oaks broke through first since they got first bat because they were the visiting team. They got two runs on two hits given up by Hebert. This broke up his string of twenty-one scoreless innings. 2-0, Oakland. Not to be outdone, the Padres came right back at them with the same thing — two runs on two hits. Tit for tat. 2-2. Hebert settled down and pitched four innings of shutout ball, allowing three more Oakland hits.

The home team, however, was not finished. They added another run in the bottom of the sixth, courtesy of pitcher Hebert. He smacked a fly into left field. It was caught but it sent Detore across the plate. 3-2, Padres. That turned out to be the winning run. Hebert wasn't through at the plate, however.

The eighth inning provided some *lagniappe* for the home crowd. Catcher Detore and right-fielder Ed Stewart were on base. Hebert sent them home with a stinging double into the outfield. Three RBIs for the pitcher — one in the sixth and two in the eighth. 5-2. Home team wins it.

Hebert's pitching was anything but flawless that game, though. He allowed Oakland nine hits, issued a base on balls, hit one batter, and registered but one strikeout. He did assist in a double play and starred at the plate. He could be forgiven for the other stuff. I'm sure the fans couldn't care less.

San Diego sportswriter Earl Keller wrote that if Hebert's left arm ever lost its punch he wouldn't have to quit baseball. He would simply transfer to center field and give the ball a ride whenever it was needed.

4-28-40 Padres/Oakland

OAKLAND BREAKS EVEN WITH PADRES, KEEPS LEAGUE LEAD

The Padres were up north in Oakland taking on the league-leading Oaks in a Sunday doubleheader. The boys from down at the border lost a heart-breaker by the score of 2-1 in the first game. Things went a little better in the seven-inning night cap.

Wally Hebert pitched for the Padres and met no less than four Oakland pitchers in their attempt to pull the game out of the fire. The first inning saw the Padres get to Oakland's starting pitcher for four hits. They ended their half of the inning with two runs on the board. First inning for the Oaks was unproductive. Score: 2-0, San Diego.

The situation was reversed in the second frame. San Diego got two hits but couldn't do anything with them. In the bottom of the second Oakland got to Hebert for two hits which turned into two runs. Score tied: 2-2.

San Diego continued on their merry way. They scored a run in the fourth and another in the sixth, and made life miserable for four Oakland pitchers who just couldn't get it together.

After that two-run second inning, Hebert settled down and kept Oakland off the scoreboard for the next three innings. He relented a bit and let them score once more—in the sixth. The last inning was unfruitful for both teams. No hits, no runs. Padres took it 4-3.

5-2-40 Padres/Sacramento

PADRES TRIP SACS IN 12TH TO RECAPTURE LEAGUE LEAD

The border city boys had traveled north to take on Sacramento in an attempt to regain the PCL lead. San Diego opened the action in the first inning by putting three men on base. This quieted the home crowd down a bit. They were most unhappy when one of those base-runners made it across home plate. 1-0, visitors.

The Padres struck again in the top of the fourth — another run on two hits. 2-0, San Diego. The Solons had so far been shut out by Wally Hebert, who was on the mound for the Padres. That changed in Sacramento's half of the fifth when four batters got to Hebert and put three runs on the board for the home team, giving them the lead 3-2. The crowd reacted as expected, making enough noise to alert the stay-at-homes that something momentous was going on at the ball park.

Sixth inning up. San Diego answered with a run in their half. Score tied, 3-3. Home crowd subdued. Hebert shut Sacramento down in the bottom half and the Padres filed into the dugout for their turn at bat in the seventh inning. The crowd reminded one another their guys just had to hold the Padres scoreless and get at least one more run.

The Padres answered with two hits, sending one run home. 4-3, Padres. A collective groan went up in the stands. Anyone back in San Diego listening on the radio broke into the happy dance.

Then followed two innings of no action from either team. Ninth inning coming up. Sacramento held the visitors to one hit, no runs. Padres still ahead. This was it for the home team in their half. Do or die. They took their places in the dugout. The Padres took the field. Just hold them for three outs and the game, along with first place, was theirs.

Two Solons out. One on base. One out away from victory for the visitors. The Sacramento manager sent a pinch-hitter in for the pitcher. Two out, one on. The batter sent a hot one into center field for a double. The base runner scored. 4-

4. The home crowd was on its feet again. They could win this game. But Hebert bore down and retired the side. Extra innings.

Starting pitcher for Sacramento, Tony Frietas, was replaced by Rolland Van Slate. Hebert stayed on for San Diego. Innings ten and eleven were uneventful. The game had gone on for over two hours. It was the top of the twelfth, but no one was leaving.

Padre catcher Detore opened the inning with a double. McDonald belted a single and sent Detore to third. Next batter up—pitcher Hebert. The crowd breathed easier. He had been pitching over two hours. He was bound to be tired. Besides, pitchers can't hit, can they? One could only hope.

Hebert fooled them all and whacked a single into the outfield, scoring Detore. 5-4.

The home town fans didn't give up. Still half an inning to go. They did it once; they could do it again. Just not this time, though. Hebert was ready to get out of there. He shut Sacramento down—no hits, no runs. Game over. Another win for the curly-headed Cajun, and the Padres were once again in first place.

5-12-40 Padres/Portland

Padres Split With Ducks, Retain Lead
Wally Hebert's Spell Broken

The league-leading Padres hosted the team from Portland in a Sunday afternoon double header hoping to hang on to their first place position in the PCL standings. Wally Hebert took the mound in the opener seeking his seventh straight victory over the boys from Oregon. This time the magic wasn't there for the southpaw from the bayou.

It started out looking like more of the same. The first three innings were a barren desert island for Portland — no hits, no runs. Home town fans settled back for same song, second verse. Especially since the Padres were leading 1-0, having put a run on the board in the bottom of the first. All of that changed in Portland's half of the fourth inning.

Hebert gave up three hits — his first of the day. Unfortunately those three hits turned into three runs. 3-1, visitors. The home-towners were not too worried. Their guys still had to bat in the bottom of the inning. They had been in that situation before. Turns out their faith was in the right place. The Padres scored two runs off of four hits, tying the score at three-all.

Hebert pitched two more innings of shutout ball and the Padres pulled ahead in the fifth. 4-3. The fans were feeling good.

Top of the seventh. *Deja vu*. Hebert gave up three hits, and Portland took advantage scoring three more runs — a duplication of the fourth inning. 6-4. That's when manager Durst tried to save the game and sent his starting pitcher to the showers. Portland scored again in the eighth, increasing their lead to 7-4. They shut the Padres down in the bottom of the eighth.

Top of the ninth. Portland players were elated. It looked like they had finally put one over on that pesky lefty from Louisiana. They tried their best to lengthen their lead, but when they took the field at the end of their stint the score was still 7-4. Now it was San Diego's turn.

The home town boys gave their fans some hope when they scored a run, bringing the score to 7-5. The fans had been here before, and their guys had come through for them then, so why not now? *It ain't over till it's over.*

But this time it was over. Portland 7, San Diego 5. The Hebert jinx had been broken. Portland players looked forward to doing it again in the second game and knocking San Diego out of first place.

Didn't happen. San Diego walloped them good, 6-0. Home town fans were happy. Their guys were still in first place, and they knew Wally Hebert would live to fight another day.

7-4-40 Padres/Sacramento

Padres Move to Third Spot

Lane Field. Independence Day. For the country—not the Padres. It may have seemed so for the Padres, what with their double win sending them out of fourth place in the Pacific Coast League standings to third place. Excitement ran high in the border city at the prospect. Hadn't they finished up in fifth place in 1939? They had missed the playoffs for two years. Players and fans alike longed for a repeat of 1937.

The first game of the double bill was another of those nail-biters the fans had gotten used to. Sacramento started out like they were going to deny their hosts a chance to get out of fourth place. Wally Hebert, on the mound for the Padres, gave up one hit in the top of the first inning which resulted in a run for the visitors. 1-0, Sacramento. The Padres came up empty in their half of the inning. Sacramento's half of the second inning looked to be a repeat of the first— two more hits, one more run. 2-0, visitors. San Diego decided to wake up and scored one run on one hit in the bottom of the second. 2-1, still Sacramento.

Then both teams opted to rest on their laurels for the next four innings. Both pitchers—Hebert for the Padres and Kleinke for Sacramento—pitched four innings of shutout ball. Both teams were hitting the ball, but neither could seem to make it across the plate. That is, until the seventh inning.

Hebert gave up two runs on four hits, extending the visitors' lead to 4-1. Activity in the bullpen, and Bobbie Hebert's usual trek to the restroom. Fans were not worried; their guys had yet to bat. Bottom of the seventh was a no-go for the home team. One hit, no runs—fans worried.

Top of the eighth. *Nada f*or the visitors, but they didn't mind. They were ahead 4-1 with one and a half innings to go. It was in the bag. They were nonchalant as they took their places around the diamond—laughing, joking, high-fiving all over the place. What is it they say about pride going before a fall?

The pitcher finished warming up, and the bottom of the eighth commenced. The Padres' baseball angel finally showed up. Mickey Haslin, George McDonald, and Ed Stewart all got on base with a one-baser apiece. Stan Perry belted a double. Hebert and Hal Patchette each added triples. Five runs scored on six hits. 6-4, San Diego. Pandemonium in the stands; glee in the dugout; Sacramento pitcher headed to the showers.

Top of the ninth. This time the situations were reversed when the teams changed places. The visitors shuffled into the dugout, heads down, mitts tossed into the corner. The home team danced around the field. Both teams got the message. "Still an inning to go. Anything can happen. "

To the Padres: *Don't get too cocky.*

To Sacramento: *It ain't over till it's over.*

Hebert settled down, and he and his teammates retired the side. No hits, no runs. Game over. 6-4. Joy in San Diego.

7-20-40 Padres/Hollywood

Wally Hebert Downs Twinks
PADRES DEFEAT HOLLYWOOD, 3-2

The Lane Field denizens were playing host to the Hollywood Stars the third week in July down at Lane Field. The home team had already dropped the first three games to their visitors from Tinsel Town against one game won. Home town fans were hungry for a victory. They saw Wally Hebert warming up. They hoped he was ready to return to his winning form.

The umpire yelled "play ball," and the game commenced. The visiting Stars batted first and got one hit. The side was retired with nothing on the scoreboard. Hebert pitched a four inning no-hit shutout. In the meantime the Hollywood pitcher did the same to the Padres for the first two innings—no hits, no runs.

In the bottom of the third a Padre bat woke up, and its owner made it to first base, but not for long. The home team failed to launch, and the score remained 0-0. San Diego joined the Stars with nothing doing in the fourth and fifth. At the end of five innings the score was still 0-0. Frustration was building in the stands.

Sixth inning coming up. Padres took the field. Stars filled the dugout. The serenity of the California day was shattered with the cracking of horsehide on wood. Stars shortstop Hoover got things started with a double. He was sacrificed to third and scored when third-baseman Kahle sent a long fly to deep right field. 1-0, Stars. Home crowd getting antsy. Three successive singles sent another run home. 2-0, visitors.

After an ill-fated sixth inning fans and players alike were somewhat dismayed. But they knew it wasn't over until the last out had been called. The jubilant Stars scattered onto the field, and the subdued Padres stomped into the dugout.

First batter up—Hebert, who singled to start things off. Second-baseman

Sperry smacked a double to right field and scored Hebert. 2-1, Stars still ahead. Sperry on base. Right-fielder Stewart belted a long fly to the fence, which was caught, but it allowed Sperry to take third safely. Catcher Salkeld drew a walk. One on first, one on third. Up next—shortstop Haslin, who singled to score Sperry. Game tied, 2-2. Fans feeling better.

First baseman McDonald sent one over second base and Salkeld scored. 3-2. The Stars changed pitchers, and the side was retired, but not before the game changed leaders. Elation in the dugout, pandemonium in the stands.

Then it was like the baseball angels for both teams decided to take the rest of the afternoon off. The whole game had been condensed down to one inning. Hebert pitched three more innings of shutout ball, allowing one hit. San Diego could do nothing against the new pitcher. The game ended after eight and a half innings with the score still 3-2, Padres.

The fans left wondering if they really got their money's worth. They paid for nine innings of baseball and they got one.

8-2-40 Padres/Stars

Wally Hebert Blanks Stars in Series Opener, 5-0
Padres Score Easy Victory

Sportswriter Bob Ray, writing for the Los Angeles Times, said San Diego's Louisiana lefty Wally Hebert pitched strictly his "nothing ball" at Gilmore Field one night in early August, and that's just what the Hollywood Stars ended up with—a big fat nothing. This was not what the Hollywood fans had paid their hard-earned cash to see.

The first and second innings came up empty for both teams. The Padres got one hit in the second inning, but the batter stayed put. The Padres decided to get going when their half of the third inning rolled around.

They went on a batting rampage for the next three innings—the third, fourth, and fifth. In the third frame they tapped the Stars pitcher, Bithorn, for three hits. Two of those base runners crossed home plate. 2-0, visitors. When the Padres took the field after their productive time in the dugout, Hebert and his teammates worked their magic in the bottom of the third, and denied their hosts anything. No hits, no runs.

When the Stars took the field in the top of the fourth they hoped they would accord the Padres the same thing—big nothing. Not this time. San Diego got to Bithorn for three more hits which added another run. 3-0, Padres.

Top of the fifth. More misery for Bithorn. Two bases on balls and two singles raised the score to 5-0. That was all for the starting pitcher. Hollywood threw two more pitchers into the fray, and they did quite well shutting the Padres down for the remaining four innings. However, the hosts were unable to break through the pitching and fielding of the San Diego boys.

August 2, 1940, was a good night for the border city cadre. Hebert did a brilliant job of keeping the Stars off the scoreboard, hurling a four-hit shutout. He also had a rather nice night at the plate, going three for four—a double and two singles, registering one run batted in. He and his teammates made out like bandits, knocking twelve hits around on the way to their 5-0 victory.

An interesting side note—Stars first-baseman Gray was the only Hollywooder to make it past second base. He drew a walk and made it to third when a teammate sent a single into center field.

8-10-40 Padres/San Francisco

Padres Thump Seals Again
Hebert Hurls Mates to 5-3 Victory Over San Francisco Club

The Padres of San Diego were up north in San Francisco taking it to the Seals. They had already won two games in the series and were hoping to make it three in a row in the Saturday game. Wally Hebert had drawn pitching honors, so the team had high hopes for victory.

The game started out somewhat slow, with both pitchers sending their foes back to the dugout with nothing to show for their labor in the first inning. No hits, no runs. It wasn't until the third inning that action commenced.

The Padres started things off in the top of the fourth frame with hits by second-baseman Sperry, and left-fielder Garibaldi. Those turned into two runs with the help of two Seal errors. 2-0, Padres. When San Francisco got their turn at the plate they came up empty on the scoreboard. They did manage one hit off of Hebert.

Up next—inning number five. Both teams' baseball angels decided to drop in. San Diego batted first and tapped San Francisco pitcher Guay for five hits, including a two-bagger by third-baseman Haslin. Four runs scored, bringing the total to 6-0.

San Francisco fans were frustrated, to say the least. The players must have felt that frustration because they answered the Padres in the bottom of the fifth with three hits and two runs. Score: 6-2, visitors. San Diego's angel bowed out, and the last four innings were zilch for them.

San Francisco, on the other hand, was not quite finished. In their half of the seventh they added another run on two hits. 6-3. Their angel took the rest of the day off, and the score remained 6-3.

San Diego won their third straight. Hebert got his victory in spite of allowing ten hits. He was seldom in serious trouble except for that wild and wooly fifth inning. Things were looking good for first division and a playoff spot.

8-20-40 Padres/Portland Beavers

Padres Whip Ducks, 8 to 3

Lane Field. San Diego. August 20. Wally Hebert got a birthday victory a day early with an 8-3 shellacking of the Portland team. The Padres were in the thick of the war for a first division place in the Pacific Coast League standings. Hebert was in fine form, handing out seven hits to the Beavers, who couldn't seem to get anything going at home plate. San Diego, on the other hand, spent the evening knocking the ball around Lane Field for fourteen blows. In fact, every Padre who took their place at the plate that day got at least one safety. Stewart connected four times; Mesner got two; and Salkeld hit twice, one of them being a homer.

Hebert pitched five innings of shutout ball until a flurry of Portland activity in the sixth and seventh innings when they added two runs in the sixth and one in the seventh. That was all the Beavers could manage off of Hebert — three runs.

San Diego failed to put runs on the board in the first, second, and fourth innings. The home fans got their money's worth that night in late August. Two runs in the third, fifth, sixth, seventh, and eighth frames. Final score: 8-3.

Hebert had a good night at the plate and on the mound. He batted one for three and sent one runner home for a run-batted-in. He sent six Beavers back to the dugout with their bats still on their shoulders. On the down side he gave six Beavers a free pass to first base. He also hit one batter, resulting in another freebie.

The evening ended with San Diego still in the race for a playoff spot.

9-16-40 The Final Four

The run for the Governor's Cup in the Shaughnessy playoffs was set to begin on September 17—a Tuesday. At the close of 1940 regular season play the last four still in the hunt for the elusive cup were Seattle in first, Los Angeles in second, Oakland in third, and San Diego in fourth. Seattle was set to square off against Oakland on September 17. Los Angeles and San Diego were to meet in Los Angeles on the 18th.

9-17-40 Pre-Playoff Info

Padres Power Feared by Jigger's Angels
San Diego Club Tops Coast League in Team Batting at .291

The San Diego Padres, who finished in fourth place, were set to take on the Angels of Los Angeles, PCL second place finisher, at Wrigley Field in Los Angeles. The opening game was set for Wednesday, September 18, with games two and three set for Thursday and Friday nights. If neither team won three straight the fourth game would be at Lane Field in San Diego on Saturday. If one of the teams won three in a row the fourth game was set for Sunday afternoon to take advantage of a large Sunday gate.

Manager Jigger Statz of the Angels knew his pitchers would be facing the number one hitting team in the league. The Padres led the circuit with a .291 team batting average. Six Padre regulars sported .300 or better batting averages. Leading the pack was Steve Mesner at .341 — second only to Angel Novikoff with .363.

The other five Padres in that elite group were: Mickey Haslin, .321; George Detore, .321; Ed Stewart, .320; Stan Sperry, .303; and Swede Jensen, .301. Three other Padres were close behind, in the high .280s — Salkeld, McDonald, and Patchette. Statz had reason to worry.

Padre pitchers also had their work cut out for them. Los Angeles sported six .300 plus batsmen. The big advantage the Angels had was in home run hitters. They racked up a total of 116 to the Padres thirty-eight.

Padre pitcher Dick Newsome, a twenty-three game winner, was scheduled to pitch the first game. Bill Thomas and Wally Hebert were on tap for games two and three.

9-18-40 Padres/Angels Games 1 and 2

Game one was played at Wrigley Field on September 18 — Wednesday night. It was a less than stellar performance by the border city boys. For the first six innings it was a pitcher's duel with neither team's batters doing anything — goose eggs across the board. With two out in the bottom of the seventh the roof caved in on Padre pitcher Newsome when the Tinsel Town team scored three runs. Manager Durst replaced Newsome on the mound with Craghead, who allowed two more runs. 5-0, Angels. The Angels brought the final score to 9-0 in the bottom of the eighth by adding four more runs. Most of the 5,000 fans went home happy, but there was still a pocket of die-hand Padre fans left over from their Hollywood Sheik days.

The two teams met again the next night — Thursday — for game two. Bill Thomas was on the mound for the Padres, and it was a different scene from the embarrassment of the previous night. San Diego scored two runs in the first inning. The five-run fourth inning turned into a Padre stampede, saddling the Angels with a 7-0 deficit. The southern boys added another tally in the seventh — icing on the cake. The Angels managed a two-run homer in the bottom of the sixth, but it was too little too late. Final score, 8-2. Ah, sweet revenge.

Game three was set for Friday night, still at Wrigley Field. Wally Hebert was prepared to do the hurling honors.

9-20-40 Padres/Angels Game 3

Four-Run Uprising Gives Seraphs Play-off Victory Over Padres, 5-2

Wrigley Field. Los Angeles. Friday, September 20. Game number three. The Angels and the Padres were locked in mortal combat, aiming for a cut of the $10,000 prize money. They were deadlocked at one game apiece. Angel fans were hungry for that second win that would give them a one-up over their rivals from down south. The Padres were just as anxious to deny them their wish.

The game got started amidst pandemonium in the stands. The Padres, being the visitors, batted first and came up empty in the first inning—one hit, no tally. The Angels took their turn against Wally Hebert, on the mound for San Diego. Same song, second verse—one hit, no runs. The second inning was a repeat of the first—more zeroes on the board.

Third inning up. The Padres' bats seemed to be in a coma. Not so the Angels. The third inning was theirs. Hebert couldn't seem to get things together as he gave up five hits, and four of them crossed the plate. He settled down and pitched three more innings of shutout ball. At the same time two Angel pitchers kept San Diego off the scoreboard until the seventh inning.

Hebert helped his own cause when he knocked a single to right field and sent base runner Sperry home for the first Padre run. 4-1, Angels. McDonald made it to third on that play and scored on a long fly to center by Padre outfielder Jensen. 4-2. The Padres' spirits rose as they closed the gap. Hebert had made it to third but remained there when the Angels retired the side.

The Angels got one run back in their half of the seventh inning where Hebert gave up two hits. Final score, 5-2, Angels. If San Diego could have erased that disastrous third inning they would have won the game 2-1. *If wishes were horses beggars would ride.*

Lane Field, here we come.

9-21-40 Game 4

The two teams boarded trains for the trek south. The Padres were anxious to get back on home turf. The Angels were feeling a bit smug, sitting on a two games to one advantage. Just two more to go and they're halfway there. San Diego was just as determined to thwart them.

Four-thousand rowdy fans showed up to urge their guys on. They went wild when center-fielder Jensen opened the first inning with a triple and scored when the next batter grounded out. They kept it up until inning number four when the Angels scored a run, tying the game. They quieted down even more in the top of the fifth when the Angels went ahead 2-1.

The blue funk lasted until the bottom of the sixth when the Padres tied it up 2-2. The Angels scored no more from then on. San Diego tallied the winning run in their half of the seventh.

The top of the ninth saw a pugilistic side show for entertainment. Jigger Statz, Angel manager and center-fielder, was trying to break up a double play and slid into Padre short-stop Steve Mesner. They had been teammates in Los Angeles during the years 1937-1939. Mesner was having none of that, and a fight ensued. Just a little *lagniappe* for the fans. That pretty well ended things since the bottom of the ninth was not needed.

Padre fans left happy. Their team had tied things up with the rivals from Tinsel Town. The series was knotted at two-all. Games five and six were set for the next day—Sunday—in a double header that could decide who would move on if either team could take both contests. A big day coming up.

9-22-40 Padres/Angels   Games 5 & 6

Angels Split With Padres
Angels, Padres split, Stay Even in Series

Excitement was rampant in the stands at Lane Field Sunday afternoon where 6,000 fans—most of them San Diegans—had come out hoping to see their team take two games and head out to Seattle to take on the Rainiers and a share of the big money.

Game five was a roller-coaster of a game that was basically over by the end of the fourth inning. San Diego scored a run on three hits in the bottom of the second frame. The fans reacted typically. Six-thousand people can make a lot of noise.

The top of the third quieted things down. Los Angeles evened the score at one-all. Then the racket in the bleachers erupted again in the bottom half of the third. The Padres sent two men to the bases and one crossed the plate. 2-1, Padres.

The Angels put another goose egg on the scoreboard in the top of the fourth. The Padres came back in the bottom half and scored one more run. The game, for all practical purposes, was over by then. No one knew that, of course, and the game went on as usual. Neither team could send anyone home. Big fat zeroes across the board for the remainder of play. Final score, 3-1, Padres. Three games to two.

Hope springs eternal. One game down, seven innings to go in the second game. Some players were no doubt already spending that prize money. The fans were on fire. I doubt anyone left the stadium that day. They couldn't wait for the next "Play ball" shout.

The best laid schemes o' mice and men go often awry according to the poet Robert Burns. A young Mexican pitcher—"Chuey" Flores—held the Padres scoreless, limiting them to four hits. Angel batsmen pounded three Padre pitchers for eleven hits and eight runs.

Game seven, the last contest, would be played Monday, September 23 with Wally Hebert on the mound for the Padres.

9-23-40 Padres/Angels Game 7

Padres Held to One Hit

Lane Field. San Diego. September 23. 1:30 p.m. Game number seven. The Shaughnessy playoff semi-finals. The teams were tied at three games apiece. The winner would take the 4:05 train to Seattle and the championship series. Hence the early start time of 1:30.

LA started the game in the first inning with two hits and a run, taking an early lead. The San Diego faithful weren't too worried. They still had eight and a half innings to go. Just wait for the bottom half.

Swede Jensen, Padre center-fielder, didn't let them down. He smacked a single to third base and beat the throw to first. "See," the fans told each other. "We're on our way." Right-fielder Stewart bunted Jensen to second, and there was a mini-celebration in the stands. However, the next two batters were retired forthwith, and the runner died on second base.

The second inning was quiet for both teams — no hits, no runs, for either. But the third inning was another story. Angel batsmen got to Hebert for three hits — one of them a homer, bringing the score to 2-0. That would be the final score.

Normally a six-hit, two-run game would win nine times out of ten. Hebert had pitched quite a few games like that and came away the winner. But when the opposing pitcher, Bob Weiland, delivered up a one-hit shutout all bets were off. The box score showed Hebert's stats from the fourth inning on as a one-hit shutout. That pesky third inning.

The game lasted an hour and thirty-five minutes, giving the Angels plenty of time to catch their train to Seattle. So the Angels boarded the train for Seattle, and the Padres packed up their equipment until the spring of 1941.

The Hebert family went back to the rivers and bayous of Louisiana and the oil field job awaiting Hebert in Jeanerette. I was anxious to see if Blackie

Nose, the cat, would remember me.

A post-script. Seattle took the championship in five games. The Padres split $1,250 of the prize money. That came to $55 per player. It was worth about $357 in 2000 — probably more today in 2019.

Hebert didn't surpass his 1939 twenty game performance. In fact, he ended the 1940 season with a less than stellar fifteen wins to eighteen losses. But just wait till next year.

Pitching Statistics: 1940

Games: 38

Innings Pitched: 280

Won: 15

Lost: 18

Percentage: .455

Hits: 316

Strikeouts: 106

Bases on Balls: 100

Earned Run Average: 3.91

FOURTEEN

1941

1941 Pre-Season

At the beginning of the 1941 PCL season, many thought the Padres were going to be MOA—Mediocre On Arrival. The particular three sportswriters, whom we will call Curly, Larry, and Mo, so as not to offend their descendants or successors, declared that San Diego was clearly a team destined for the lower tiers of the league. We'll see about that.

Curly had a formula for the '41 Padres. Take a 1940 fourth place finisher, subtract their best pitcher and two .300 hitters. Add a handful of inexperienced youngsters, and make your own guess where San Diego would finish out the 1941 season.

The most obvious conclusion was that San Diego was headed for the second division. Starting pitchers and powerful hitters were essential for successful ball clubs, and the 1941 Padres were facing a drought in both areas.

Twenty-three game winner Newsome and two heavy hitters—Mesner and Stewart—were taken by major league clubs. Other than that, the 1940 club was intact, but the loss of those three generated a huge problem for second-year manager Cedric Durst. The pitching staff boasted only three hurlers who could be called veteran — Wally Hebert, Bill Thomas, and Byron Humphreys.

In another column Larry added his two cents. He said the Padres appeared headed for a second division berth in the PCL. The team needed batting power and pitching strength.

He said manager Cedric Durst did not have a sure-fire twenty-game winner to depend on. He went on to point out that Hebert, Humphreys, and Thomas should be good for fifteen victories — and about twelve losses. He did say that Hebert was a crafty fellow, who slid the ball inside and outside with varied changes of pace — but still good for only fifteen wins.

Finally, Mo wrote about an early game between Oakland and San Diego — neither team was given much chance of making it into the first division.

To see if these "experts" knew whereof they spoke — read on.

BULLETIN: Attention: Curly, Larry, and Mo

As of May 14 the San Diego Padres were in undisputed possession of second place in the PCL after beating Los Angeles 2-0. Wally Hebert blanked the Angels with a seven-hit shutout. He aided his hurling effort with one hit and one run.

5/25/41 San Diego/San Francisco

San Diego Uses Four Hurlers for Slow, Sloppy Game

If baseball games had names like stage productions or movies, this one could be billed as "Parade of the Pitchers," with music to accompany each mound change. I nominate "War March of the Priests" from the opera "Aida." San Diego used four hurlers on their march to an 8-6 victory over San Francisco, who employed only three pitchers — which might be why they lost.

Who knows? Had they thrown in two more they might have taken that game.

Dilbeck, Thomas, Humphreys, and Hebert took the mound for the Padres, and they were responsible for giving up sixteen hits. Epperly, Stutz, and Ballou did the pitching honors for San Francisco. They allowed twelve hits. Evidently none of them turned in a stellar performance.

The headline called it a slow, sloppy game. The fans in attendance probably wished they had gone to the movies or even the opera.

6-1-41 Padres/Angels

Wally Hebert was on the mound with a six-run lead. Everything seemed to be going his way. He was in the zone, tossing strikes and forcing infield flies, and generally making life miserable for the hapless Angels.

Baseball season in 1941 was starting on its third month. I was a lonely five-year-old only child who amused herself with two imaginary playmates named Lavory and McGuvney. But not for long. I would soon have a baby sister or brother. My mother, whom everyone called Bobbie, had a little time left before the new baby was expected to arrive, but everything was ready.

Back to the ball park, Wrigley Field in Los Angeles. Wally Hebert was on the mound systematically sending the Angels' batters back to the dugout in high dudgeon. Word came to the press box, and the Padre manager got the word that Hebert's wife had given birth to their second child. The manager, Cedric Durst, knowing how laid back his usually reliable pitcher was, sent word to the press box to share the good news over the public address system and radio.

The newspapers had a field day the following day. The Los Angeles Times had this to say.

"We've seen ball games won and lost in a lot of different ways, but we were treated to a brand new one yesterday afternoon and early evening at Wrigley Field."

Of all things it was the stork who gave the Angels victory in the second game of the twin bill.

Here's what happened. The Padres had already put the hurt on the Angels in the first game, 9-5. They were breezing along in the second game with a 6-0 lead when Los Angeles came to bat in the sixth inning.

So far Hebert had limited the home team to three skimpy singles. In fact, it looked like the game was probably over, and half of the 5,500 paying customers had gone home for supper. Then came the announcement.

"Attention everyone. We have just received word that opposing pitcher

Wally Hebert has become a father for the second time. His wife, Bobbie, gave birth in San Diego to a boy. Mother and baby are doing fine. Congratulations to Mr. and Mrs. Hebert."

Applause broke out all over the stadium in spite of the home team's woes at the hands of the enemy. His teammates were cheering, and it took a while for everyone to settle down and get back to the game. However, the normally unflappable Cajun never did settle down. No more strikeouts. No more infield flies.

Hebert subsequently gifted the Angels with four runs on four hits and four walks. Angel bats came to life and the six-run lead faded away. Manager Durst had to take Hebert out. The Angels continued the pounding against the next two Padre pitchers and ended up with a 9-8 win in extra innings.

The Times thought the whole thing rather strange because when his first baby (that would be me—Linda Fay) was born five seasons earlier, he went out and pitched a one-hit shutout.

Earl Keller, sportswriter for the San Diego Tribune, shone some light on the cause of the confusion over the gender of the newcomer. Writes Keller: "Just a line to tell you that Hebert's baby turned out to be a girl—named Hillene—so now he has two daughters. Somebody took the message for the telegram over the phone wrong, and the wire to Hebert read, 'Earl has arrived.' It should have read 'Girl has arrived.'"

Someone somewhere along the line got their facts wrong that day. I became big sister to Mary Hillene that Sunday afternoon in San Diego.

Linda Fay, Age 10, Mary Hillene, Age 5

6/8/41 Padres/Portland

Padres Defeat Portland, 6-3

It was June on the Pacific coast, and Wally Hebert was doing his best to prove the naysayers wrong about their pre-season prognostications regarding the 1941 Padres. On June 7 Hebert handed Portland a 6-3 defeat at Lane Field. This would be his seventh victory of the young season. Only one more win and he would be over halfway to his projected limit of fifteen.

Five days later, again at Lane Field, he got win number eight in the form of a six-hit shutout. The six hits were scattered over all nine innings, and none of the Oaks were ever in a scoring position.

The Oakland sports writer spent his column castigating his hapless team for serving up a goose egg diet to the Oakland faithful. It seemed they had failed to score in their last five games—twenty-two innings in a row. "Can't 'Cha Even Score?" he asked in a quote displayed over the box score.

Have faith Mr. Ward. Nothing lasts forever.

6-18-41 Padres/Stars

In mid-June the Padres took a little trip to Hollywood to face the Stars, who were known as Kings of the Mountain in their own backyard. The Hollywood bunch were looking forward to a fourteen-game home stand at Gilmore Field, where they would lord it over their unfortunate rivals in the PCL. Someone forgot to tell Wally Hebert.

He proceeded to pitch a five-hit shutout for his eighth win of the season. For the first eight innings the Stars managed to get only three balls out of the infield. In the bottom of the ninth they filled the bases—this is where my mother would have made her way to the restroom had they been playing at Lane Field. Not to worry. Hebert's playmates finished the inning off with a double play to retire the side and end the game.

The Padres were never in any real trouble since they led by the ninth inning. They had scored four in the third inning, one in the sixth, and two in the seventh. 7-0. Hebert helped his cause with a hit and an RBI.

7/6/41 Padres/Seattle

Hebert Pitches Two-Hit Eleven Inning Shutout
Padres Down Seattle

Some more bad news for the pre-season doomsayers. Southpaw Wally Hebert pitched a two-hit game on July 5, defeating Seattle 1-0 in an eleven-inning battle and tightening their hold on second place in the PCL standings.

The lone score of the marathon came in the bottom of the eleventh inning when center-fielder Hal Patchett singled to center, stole second, and was sacrificed to third. He came home on a long fly by third baseman Mickey Haslin. The Seattle pitcher had intentionally walked two men hoping Haslin would hit into a double play. It backfired.

Seattle got a hit in the second inning and another in the fourth. After that—zeroes across the board. Only thirty-four Rainiers came to the plate to face Hebert in eleven innings. It would be his twelfth victory of the season. (*Only three more to go to hit the fifteen game prediction.*)

7-11-41 San Diego/Sacramento

Pacific Coast baseball fans were abuzz about those streaking Padres after they handed the first place Sacramento Senators their collective *derrieres* three nights in a row. Wally Hebert went the distance on July 10, passing out a stingy seven hits.

In the meantime his teammates were manhandling Hollingsworth, leading pitcher in the PCL, and two other Senator hurlers to the tune of seventeen hits. The Padres scored in five different innings and showed Mr. Hollingsworth the door in the fifth.

In addition to a successful pitching excursion, Hebert helped out at the plate with a hit, a sacrifice, and a run batted in. As of July 11 San Diego was ensconced in third place—a long way from the second division spot as predicted earlier.

As of July 24 Wally had fourteen victories against six losses with fifty strikeouts and a .700 percentage. Guess when he gets that next victory he can sit back and coast till season's end—he will have fulfilled the prophecy.

7-29-41 ALL STAR GAME

Right in the middle of the 1941 baseball season the Pacific Coast League powers-that-be decided to host an all-star game with proceeds going to the Association of Professional Baseball Players of America. Players and managers were elected by a vote of baseball writers who covered the games up and down the West Coast. Purpose of the game was to parade the loop's outstanding talent. The game was set for July 30 to be played in San Francisco.

The second place Padres provided six players for the southern team in the elite game: Mickey Haslin, third base; Hal Patchet, left field; Sperry, second base; pitchers Wally Hebert and Yank Terry; and George Detore,catcher. Lefty O'Doul of the San Francisco Seals was elected manager.

O'Doul named Hebert and Detore the starting battery. Haslin and Patchett were also selected starters. Not too bad for a team that wasn't supposed to get out of the second division.

According to pre-game hype the South seemed to have an edge on the North. O'Doul had three of the four first division teams to choose from, and had a margin of .310 to .298 in team batting. However, Pepper Martin's North had great speed and seven players from league-leading Sacramento. The pundits opined pitching was most likely a toss-up. It would be the North against the South. Seattle, Portland, Sacramento, and Oakland made up the northerners. San Diego, Los Angeles, San Francisco, and Hollywood were the southerners. All in all, they agreed, it should be a great evening of baseball.

Three days before the big game all was not well in North camp. It seemed Pepper Martin, North manager, ignored Oakland's four players who had been picked for the team when he designated his starting lineup. O'Doul of the South, on the other hand, made sure all of the teams were represented in his starting lineup. The sportswriter didn't understand the snub and wrote that he hoped Oakland put the hurt on Martin's team, Sacramento, when the two teams met in regular play on September 2-7. Revenge is always best served up cold.

Bad luck struck the South two days before the game when George Detore, Padre catcher and designated starter for the game, injured a finger in an earlier game with Sacramento. He did not come north with the team and would be replaced by the catcher of either Hollywood or Los Angeles.

Under the rules every one of the thirty-six players selected—eighteen on each team—would play at least part of the game. Pepper Martin would have to get rid of the bee in his bonnet and let the Oaks take the field.

July 29, 1941.The big day arrived and a total of 11,031 excited baseball fans turned out to watch the cream of PCL take on each other in a War Between the Cities. They got their money's worth and the treat of their lives as the South won out over the North by a score of 3-1. (Eat your heart out, General Grant—the South has risen again.)

Credit for this sterling performance went to the eight pitchers who worked their magic during the evening. The South allowed three measly hits and the North gave up six, but that was sufficient to bring in enough runs for the South to prevail.

A good time was had by all except the Northern team, of course. Coast league management was already planning for another game in 1942 to be played in Los Angeles.

8-4-41 Fresno Bee

As of August 4 San Diego and Seattle were battling it out for second place behind Sacramento. To whom it may concern: San Diego's still not in the second division. In the first game of a doubleheader against Los Angeles Wally Hebert chalked up his seventeenth win of the season.

8-19-41 20 GAME WINNERS

According to the Associated Press on August 19 seven Coast League pitchers looked favorable to hit the twenty-win mark. Padre Yank Terry was already there, having recorded his twentieth victory earlier in the week. Right behind Terry was teammate Wally Hebert with nineteen wins to seven losses. With more than a month left in the season it seemed certain he would join the chosen few, thereby debunking pre-season predictions.

8-25-41 Elite Circle

August 24, 1941. Three days after he turned thirty-four, Wally Hebert joined the elite circle of twenty-game winners. In the first game of a doubleheader with Portland he scored his twentieth victory of the 1941 season. Portland got eight hits but could only translate that into two runs. Nine batters went down swinging. The Padres countered with eight runs.

Hebert did his share, and then some, on offense. Four hits on four trips to the plate, including one triple. Two runs scored. One run batted in. A good day's work by any standard. Not bad for a "mature" player.

Five days later, on August 29, Hebert delighted the home town crowd by notching his twenty-first victory when the Padres battled the unfortunate Sacramento team. He allowed six hits and one run, striking out seven along the way. Taking four trips to the plate, he got one hit, scored one run, and batted one run in. *Wonder what Curly, Larry, and Mo thought about that.*

9-4-41 Standings

As of September Wally Hebert was in second place in the pitching stats, three points behind league-leader Turpin. Hebert's teammate, Terry, was in third--six points behind Hebert. Both Padres were twenty-two game winners. On September 11 coast standings were published. Guess who sat in first place. If you said San Diego you guessed right.

9-17-41 Third Place

As usual, all good things come to an end. On September 16 San Diego played Hollywood and lost both games of a double-header, thus sinking the Padres further into third place and out of contention for a chance at winning the pennant. Wally Hebert lost the opener by a score of 8-2. The Padres dropped the second game 6-1. Bad luck, but still not in the second division as predicted, and Shaughnessy was on the horizon.

9-19-41 Wally Hebert Day at Lane Field

Sometime during the summer of 1941 a column appeared in a San Diego newspaper calling for "A Day for Wally?" The writer pointed out that in the six seasons the Padres had been in San Diego you could count on one hand the number of times when players had been publicly honored at Lane Field. He went on to say San Diego had never followed the lead of other league cities in this respect. It was time all that changed. He continued.

"Here Wally Hebert, one of the most popular Padres of them all, is on the verge of pitching his 100th victory for San Diego, and if he doesn't draw a 'Wally Hebert Day,' with appropriate ceremonies and a few gifts, then there isn't any justice after all. It behooves the club officials and a few spokesmen from the ranks of the fans to put their heads together and see what can be done about it."

The big, quiet-spoken Frenchman from the Louisiana bayous had won ninety-six games since he had come to San Diego in 1936. With any kind of pitching luck the 100-game mark was in reach before the end of 1941 season. His best season to date was 1939—won twenty, lost ten—when he finished eighth in the final PCL pitching averages. His earned run average had never been above 3.91, and until 1940 it had never been above 3.11—good pitching in any league.

"Like good whiskey," the writer continued, "Wally seems to get better the longer he sticks around. It's about time he had his day." Turns out the writer was somewhat of a prophet.

September 19 was designated Wally Hebert Day, and by then he had racked up his twenty-second win on September 1. Not bad for someone who was not supposed to win more than fifteen games.

Accolades began to arrive. He received a congratulatory Western Union from the Doerr family. Another telegram arrived from a Phil Purcell in Salt Lake City. He had some nice things to say about Hebert.

"Ever since you first reported to the Padres in spring training at Riverside you have faithfully given your all in your effort to give the Padres full benefit of your talents as a pitcher. Through it all your personal conduct has become an inspiration to hundreds of youngsters, and won for you the admiration of thousands of fans. It is very pleasing to me that the good people of San Diego have insisted upon expressing their kindly feelings towards you. Please accept my personal congratulations and appreciation of your splendid work."

He also received a page-long letter from Dr. and Mrs. Eckols, a chiropractor—two baseball fans who never missed a Padre home game and even went to Los Angeles on occasion to watch the team.

"We salute you on this 'Wally Hebert Day' at Lane Field. Your performance, either on the mound or at bat has been a credit to the good clean sport you have so ably represented. . . .While we are total strangers to you we are not unmindful of the pleasure and thrills you have given to each of us. We predict even a better year ahead for you."

Along with the letter was a card for twenty free chiropractic adjustments during the remainder of 1941 and 1942. I don't know if my parents ever took advantage of it. A card from the Coronado Hotel declared "Win or lose you will always have the admiration of the Coronado fans." There was also a list of over twenty donors—just names, no details.

His teammates donated $104—one dollar for each victory he had recorded since 1936. Fans presented him with a live chicken and a Louisiana catfish. My mother's southern cooking and hospitality were well known there.

The chicken is no mystery, but where did they get a Louisiana catfish in southern California?

9-20-41 Where's Wally?

Lane Field. September 20, 1941. The San Diego Padres took the field against the Hollywood Stars in one of the last regular season games before the start of the Shaughnessy playoffs. The fans in attendance that day cheered their favorite players as they scattered to their respective positions.

Confusion took over when they looked at the pitcher's mound expecting to see Wally Hebert. They had seen him run out of the dugout. But that wasn't him at pitcher. It was rookie Del Oliver. They looked around the diamond, puzzled. There he is, someone shouted, pointing. Puzzlement deepened. What's he doing in left field? No mistake. It was him. Oh, well. Batter up.

The Padres were rolling along with a five run lead in the fifth inning. Then it turned into a nail-biter that went two extra innings. The Stars tied it up in the ninth to force the extension. The Padres finally closed it out with two hits and one run in the bottom of the eleventh to win 10-9.

Newspaper reporting the next day said heavy hitting by pitcher Wally Hebert, playing in the outfield for the day, paced San Diego to its win which set a new season record of ninety-nine triumphs—the most they had ever won in a single season.

Hebert proved that should his left arm ever weaken he could always transfer to the outfield for a few more years. He went three for three at bat, including a triple, scored one run himself, and three runs-batted-in. The Los Angeles Times ran this headline: *Hebert Paces Padres to 10-9 Win Over Stars.* San Diegans were accustomed to these kinds of headlines concerning the popular southpaw. Folks reading the headline only would assume he had just pitched another gem.

At a meeting before the game the team voted to split the money from the Shaughnessy playoffs into twenty-two shares, in addition to two half-shares. They hoped, of course, it would be the $5,000 winner's pot.

9-22-41 Last Hurrah

Final standings of the first division for the Pacific Coast League in 1941: Seattle, Sacramento, San Diego, Hollywood.

Quite a difference from the preseason predictions of Curly, Larry, and Mo. Tied for second. Not bad for a second division team. And Wally Hebert racked up his twenty-second victory on September 1. So much for the "expert" opinions.

Time to gear up for the Shaughnessy playoffs. The winning team would receive $5,000 in prize money and the President's Cup. $2,500 would go to the runner-up. The third and fourth place teams would each take home $1,250.

Sacramento and San Diego wound up their 149-game schedule tied for second place. They were to meet on Tuesday, September 23, at San Diego to decide third place in the standings. The game would also count in the playoffs. Yank Terry was picked to pitch the first game, and Wally Hebert was tapped for the second game the next night.

Unfortunately the Padres did not fare well in the playoffs, but they went down fighting. Sacramento won four in a row to make it to the finals. Hebert pitched the second game on September 24 and lost by a score of 3-0. It was a southpaw mound battle for seven innings between the two opposing lefties. Hebert held Sacramento to four hits and an unearned run during that time. The Senators scored in the sixth, eighth, and ninth innings while holding the Padres scoreless.

Still, the season could not be called a loss. They finished in third place for the regular season, winning 101 games. Their two ace pitchers were at the top of the pitching list, YankTerry being in first and Hebert not far behind in fifth. The team qualified for some of the prize money—somewhere in the vicinity of $54 each.

Best of all they made a trio of know-it-alls eat their preseason words.

Pitching Statistics: 1941

Games: 39

Innings Pitched: 279

Won: 22

Lost: 10

Percentage: .688

Hits: 294

Strikeouts: 102

Bases on Balls: 58

Earned Run Average: 3.00

12-7-41 Conclusion

Jeanerette, Louisiana. Early December. The 1941 baseball season was a thing of the past. Time for some rest and relaxation in a sleepy little town in south Louisiana's sugar cane country. Wally Hebert had stored his mitt for the year and donned a hard hat to work in the oilfields during the off season. Our family of four was staying with my mother's parents, the Bosticks.

Between Thanksgiving and Christmas the holiday preparations were in full swing. On a quiet Sunday afternoon—December 7—my friends and I were running amok outside. No adults were out and about. Inside their houses they huddled around their radios. We didn't care. We were having too much fun. We learned why later.

The Japanese had bombed Pearl Harbor.

FIFTEEN

1942

1942 Beginning

By the end of December, 1941, the United States was at war on two fronts. The U.S., along with Canada and England, declared war on Japan December 8. Germany and Italy declared war on the United States December 11.

Everyday life changed for everyone. New plants to manufacture war goods were built. Millions of women joined the labor force because men were needed for combat operations.

The U.S. had introduced its first peacetime draft in September, 1940. All men between the ages of twenty-one and thirty-five were required to register for military service. This was later extended to eighteen through forty-four.

In order to keep up with the demand for war necessities the government had to ration a wide variety of products, including coffee, sugar, tires, and automobiles.

How would the war affect baseball? President Roosevelt sent a letter on January 15, 1942, to the commissioner of baseball. In it he said he felt it would be best for the country to keep baseball going. There would be fewer unemployed people who would be working longer hours and harder than ever before. They would need a recreational break from time to time. However, players who were of active military age would not be exempt from the draft.

For some of us life went on as usual. All I knew as I ran around Jeanerette with my friends was that it was time to pack up and head for San Diego and a new set of playmates.

1942 Preseason Prophecy

The Padres of 1941 gave the prognosticators some unpleasant memories when they had been picked almost unanimously to end up dead last. Instead, they fooled everyone—tied for second in regular season play, and made it into the post-season Shaughnessy playoffs. Wally Hebert won twenty-two games instead of the fifteen forecast by our three oracles.

The Padres got a little more respect in 1942. One sports writer dared to venture into prediction territory and gave his opinion of the final standings: (1) Sacramento; (2) Seattle; (3) Los Angeles; (4) San Diego; (5) Hollywood; (6) Oakland; (7) San Francisco; (8) Portland.

We'll find out how he did at the end of this chapter.

4-2-42 San Diego/Portland

Opening Day. April 2, 1942. Anticipation was high as the Pacific Coast League geared up for the start of the 1942 baseball season, despite the spectre of war on two fronts. Lane Field expected a crowd of 5,000 or more first nighters. The Los Angeles/San Francisco game was the only one scheduled for the afternoon. So far nighttime games were still on tap in spite of a future threat of blackouts. San Diego/Portland, Seattle/Sacramento, and Oakland/Hollywood were set for the evening.

At Lane Field a short ceremony took place for pre-game. Members of the two squads marched in parade to the outfield and a short patriotic service followed. An admiral from the 11th Naval District tossed out the first ball and the 1942 season began.

Manager Cedric Durst of San Diego picked Wally Hebert, veteran southpaw, for the honor of hurling the opening game. He was the only Padre pitcher to win an opening game since the franchise had been brought to San Diego. Lane Field was electric as the fans looked forward to another successful season like 1941.

Unfortunately, they would have to wait for another day to see their beloved Padres win. Portland, who was picked to finish dead last, used a two-run eighth-inning rally to defeat the home team by a score of 4-2.

The PCL opened its 1942 season in fine form with 24,000 fans attending despite the fear of Army bans on crowds above 5,000 persons. San Diego fans suffered a disappointment, but the season was young. One game does not a season make.

4-11-42 Padres/Seattle

Seattle was bee-bopping along with a four-game winning streak against no losses. Enter cellar dwellers San Diego with no wins against five defeats. The faithful arrived hoping to see a game listed in the "W" column, but steeled themselves to sitting through another disappointment. Hebert was on the mound, hoping to change things.

Seattle's rookie pitcher got off to a rocky start in the second inning that ended up with San Diego ahead 2-0. Seattle tied it up in the fourth, however, when Hebert gave up two base hits, and a third Rainier drove them in with a single. The Padres came back in the sixth and put the game on ice 4-2.

Hebert had given up eight hits in the first five innings, but settled down and sent Seattle batters back to the dugout empty-handed for the remainder of the game. Chalk up one "W" for the team and one "W" for Hebert. The ice had been broken. The fans breathed a sigh of relief, and the team was ready to take on the world.

4-15-42 Padres/Angels

Local '9' Snaps Out of Slump, Wins for Hebert.

The headline said it all. The Padres had been in a batting slump since opening day, and as a result were sitting alone in the cellar. The Los Angeles Angels were the recipients of a Padre awakening.

San Diego took an early lead in the first inning, and the faithful fans felt a glimmer of hope. But the Angels took over the lead 2-1 in the third inning. Gloom settled over Lane Field. *Here we go again.*

The Angel lead was short-lived, thanks to four Padres who came through at the right time: Hebert, pitcher; Detore, catcher; Jensen, left-field; and Lohrke, shortstop. Hebert evened the score in the fourth with a sharp single for a run batted in. The other two Padre runs were the result of four hard-hit doubles. Detore and Jenson hit two of them in the fifth inning, and Salkeld and Lohrke combined for two more in the sixth. When San Diego retook the lead in the fourth they never relinquished it.

Hebert, in addition to his contribution at the plate, pitched his team to a 5-2 victory, racking up his second Coast League win of the young season. The visiting Angels were limited to seven hits.

The loyalists went home feeling they had gotten their money's worth, and Hebert went home with Victory #2 on his belt.

5-13-42 Padres/Stars

As of May 13 the Padres moved to third place thanks to the pitching of Wally Hebert in a game against the Hollywood Stars. The final score was 4-2, but the game was anything but a cake walk for the victors. Two late inning outbursts by the Stars kept everyone on the edge of their seats.

Hebert gave up eleven hits—three more than the opposing pitcher—but was in control when it came to translating all those hits into runs. Hollywood managed to score first with one run in the top of the third inning. However, the Padres bounced right back with two runs in the bottom of that inning.

The game hummed along uneventfully until the sixth inning when the Padres added another run to go up 3-1. Hebert sailed along in his comfort zone until the seventh inning when two Stars got back to back singles with two away. Hebert went to work on the next batter and struck him out on an inside pitch to end the inning. A collective sigh of relief—but not for long.

Eighth inning up. Hot water again. First Star up drew a walk. Next batter hit a single to right field sending the base runner to third. Next man up singled to score the Star on third. *This is where Bobbie headed for the ladies room.* Hebert's teammates came through for him, and the scoring ended there. The Padres added another run in the bottom of the eighth, bringing the score to 4-2. Another collective sigh. Again—not for long.

Top of the ninth. First Star batter led off with a single. Next batter was called out on strikes but the base runner stole second. The next man up knocked a single into center field. Two men on base. One out. *Another trip to the ladies room.* The next two stars sent fly balls to the outfield. Game over. Five victories for the gentleman from Louisiana.

The faithful followers went home happy, but with fingernails bitten down to the quick.

5-25-42 All Star Game-Benefit

Pacific Coast League teams were more than willing to help the war effort by donating their time and talents in charity all-star games. The North/South game, consisting of All-Stars from San Diego-Hollywood, South, and Oakland-Sacramento, North, was played May 25 in Oakland, who furnished the balls and the park. Proceeds from the gate went to buy baseball equipment for army camps in the west. Beneficiary was the Army Bat and Ball Club.

San Diego placed nine on Team South: Wally Hebert and Frank Dasso, pitchers; George Detore and Bill Salkeld, catchers; George McDonald, first base; Jack Calvey, shortstop; John Hill, utility; John Jensen, left field; and Mel Mazzera, right field. Teams were chosen by baseball writers and sports editors.

The North beat the South in that outing despite the five-hit pitching of Hebert and his Southern cohorts. However, it was an opportunity for the Coast League to do their bit for the war effort. One suggestion for future endeavors was to set aside one night as Army Benefit Night, with the proceeds of all league games played that evening going to the Army Recreation Fund. A suggestion to league owners was to set aside a substantial part of its receipts for the balance of the season to be invested in war bonds.

5/42 Padres/Stars

San Diego Back in Third Place

San Diego helped themselves by taking two from Hollywood the same day. Hebert chalked up win number six in the first contest with a score of 3-2. The Padres added a second win in the nightcap 6-3.

Hebert was zinging along with a two run lead and had things his own way until the seventh inning. Up until then he had allowed five hits scattered over six innings—five hits that came to nothing. The Stars woke up in the seventh and collected four hits which they translated into two runs, tying the game at two-all. Nail-biting time again.

Padre fans again sat on the edge of their seats. The bottom of the seventh was unproductive for San Diego hitting as was the top of the eighth for Hollywood. Two more chances for the local boys to pull another one out of the fire.

Bottom of the eighth. Shortstop Calvey slashed one to right field. Hollywood right fielder miffed a shoestring catch and Calvey ended up on third base. Mazerra, Padre outfielder, zinged one into center and the runner scored, putting the locals into the lead 3-2.

Hebert cut the Stars down in convincing fashion in the ninth to end the game. Another collective sigh from the frazzled faithful as they filed off of Lane Field.

5-27-42 Padres/Stars

On May 27 the Padres paid the Hollywood Stars a visit and were not very nice guests as far as the host Stars were concerned. It was another one of those down-to-the-wire games Padre fans were accustomed to, but this time they weren't putting their own fans through the wringer. Hollywood's faithful had to sit through another defeat at the hands of southpaw Wally Hebert on his way to a seventh win.

The Stars loaded the bases in the bottom of the fourth and their fans began to hope this might be a turning point. However, Hebert clamped down in the pinch, and the scoreboard still showed zeroes.

The bottom of the sixth rolled around, and San Diego turned three hits and a walk into two runs. 2-0, San Diego. Elation for the visitors. Dejection for the home town boys, but not for long.

The top of the eighth was uneventful for the Padres. However, the bottom half of the inning brought the Hollywood fans to their feet when the hometown boys scored two runs, tying the score at two-all. Their joy was short-lived.

Top of the ninth. Last chance for San Diego to pull it out. A base on balls for center-fielder Patchett. A sacrifice by first-baseman McDonald, moving Patchett to second. A line drive into right field by third-baseman Johnny Hill scored Patchett. San Diego 3-2. The Stars fans were back in the dumps.

Bottom of the ninth. Just get three outs in succession. San Diego would go home with a win, and Wally Hebert would chalk victory up number seven. Easier said than done. The first two outs were easy—the Padres breathed easier. The next man up doubled and the next batter drew a walk. Uh-oh. Two men on base. Hollywood faithful saw a glimmer of hope. Hebert bore down again, and the next batter flied out. Game Over. San Diego 3-2, and Hebert got his seventh.

5-31-42 Padres/Stars

Gilmore Field was the scene of the crime on May 31 when the Padres of San Diego invaded the territory of the Hollywood Stars. The boys from the border city were not gracious guests, to say the least. They handed the guys from Tinsel Town not one, but two smackdowns in front of a home town crowd of 6,500.

Wally Hebert was the deliverer of the first fiasco, tossing a six-hit shutout to the Stars on his way to win number 8. This was not one of the nail-biters. Both teams hummed along with a hit here, a hit there, for eight innings. Big fat zeroes on the scoreboard in the run column. Ho-hum.

Top of the ninth. San Diego decided enough was enough. Power hitter Mel Mazzera led off with a single into center field. Catcher George Detore hit one to shortstop, and Mazzera beat the throw to second. Two men on base. Padre second baseman Mel Skelley advanced them on a sacrifice. Man on second, man on third. Up next—Wally Hebert, pitcher. Fans of the Stars breathed easier. Pitchers are not expected to do much at the plate—right? Not this time.

Hebert won his own game with an infield hit, scoring Mazerra and advancing Detore. Hal Patchett, Padre center-fielder, whacked one to right field and scored Detore. 2-0. The top of the inning ended, mercifully, with that on the scoreboard. Bottom of the ninth came up dry for the Stars. Wally Hebert notched win number eight.

The Hollywood faithful were disappointed, but held out hope for vindication in the second game of the double-header. Alas, it was not to be. Game two was worse than game one—an 11-1 shellacking. May 31, 1942, was not a good day for the Star devotee.

6-2-42 Battle of Midway

In the summer of 1942 San Diego baseball was in full swing. My father was in the middle of one of his best years ever. In June the season was still young, and the Hebert family was ensconced in San Diego. I was five years old that June—soon to be six in August. My little sister Hillene was just barely one, having had her first birthday on June 1.

I had heard the grown-ups talking about war, but I had no idea what war was and frankly didn't care. I never asked why we had ugly black shades on all the windows or why we had to turn the lights out at midnight. I asked my mother once why we had to go into the hall at kindergarten and pull our sweaters over our heads until the all-clear bell rang. She told me those were air raid drills so we'd know what to do in case the Japanese ever bombed the naval base. I didn't know why the Japanese wanted to bomb the naval base, but when school let out for the summer vacation I soon forgot all about the Japanese and their bombs. I was having too much fun with my new friend across the street.

Meanwhile, out in the middle of the Pacific Ocean at a small, little-known island, unbeknownst to the residents of San Diego, events were unfolding that would determine the fate of the California coastline.

My mother had a cousin who was a civilian worker at the large naval base in San Diego. He was a frequent visitor to our house, especially around suppertime. He had a standing invitation to drop by for a home-cooked meal any time. One night in early June—about three or four days after Hillene's birthday party—he came over for supper. When we finished eating I went into the living room with my book. The grown-ups, as usual, sat around the table talking.

Our cousin was telling my mother about the ships that were coming in from the Pacific for repairs. "They're really banged up. I don't know what's going on out there." He went on to say the ships had been coming in since the second of June badly damaged. His coworkers didn't know any more than he did about the state of affairs, but that was not normal, he said.

However, life went on as usual at the house on Oregon Street. Air raid drills were no more since kindergarten was out for the summer. We still had black shades and a curfew, but I couldn't care less about all that.

I rode my tricycle all over the neighborhood with my friends. My father still went to the ball park every day, or left for road trips every now and then. My mother still went to the home games—especially when Daddy was scheduled to pitch. Sometimes I would go with her, and sometimes I would stay home with whatever relative or friend happened to be visiting us from Louisiana. The house always seemed to be full of relatives and friends from back home.

I don't know about the adults, but my friends and I didn't worry about banged-up ships limping into the naval base.

In the Pacific Ocean a little northwest of Pearl Harbor the Battle of Midway was what was going on. The battle between U.S. and Japanese air power raged for three days—June 2 through June 4. By the time it was over the Japanese had lost four aircraft carriers, 300 aircraft, and around 3,000 sailors and aviators. U.S. losses stood at the aircraft carrier *Yorktown,* about 150 planes, and 300 troops. The battle crippled the Japanese navy and stopped Japan's advance in the Pacific. The tide had turned, and the mainland was safe.

I, of course, knew nothing about this until I was older and heard about it along with other family stories. 1942 was my father's last year to play for the Padres. When the season started in 1943 we would be up north in Pittsburgh making new friends and having more adventures.

6-5-42 Padres/Beavers

San Diego. June 5, 1942. The United States had been at war six months. The Padres played Portland in the first twilight Coast League game at Lane Field. The contest was played before dark as an experiment. A coastal dim-out was in effect—something that might force cancellation of night baseball games.

The Padres were on a roll no matter the time of day or night. San Diego used the holy trinity of baseball to rack up four straight wins over Portland and hand Hebert his ninth win of 1942. Tight pitching. Timely hitting. Great defensive plays. That's what wins ball games—and the Padres had all three going for them. Portland, in last place, did not go gently into that good night. They made a game of it.

The first inning was tit for tat. Portland center-fielder put the Beavers ahead via a homer with one out. The Padres came back in the bottom of the first and tied it. Bottom of the second: two hits and an error, put the Padres up by 2-1. Hebert got his first RBI in that inning. The home town crowd was feeling good. It didn't last long.

Portland tied it up in the top of the third and scored another run in the top of the fourth. 3-2 Portland. That would end their scoring. The bottom of that inning came up empty for the home town team, and the fans were getting antsy again.

Top of the fifth proved equally fruitless for the visitors. Hebert took a big hand in tying the score in the bottom of the fifth. He smacked a triple to right center with one out and scored to tie the game at three-all. Two and a half scoreless innings followed. Mel Mazerra, first man up in the bottom of the eighth, knocked the first pitch over the right-field wall some 350 feet away to put the home town boys ahead 4-3.

Happiness in the bleachers once again. Just hold them to three quick outs and it's over. And that's what they did.

The Padres had won twenty-three of their last thirty-three games as of

June 5, and Hebert had registered his ninth victory of the season.

About that triple. The writer said a faster man could probably have made it home for an inside the park homer, but Wally only made three bases and was huffing and puffing by the time he pulled up at the hot corner. However, let us not forget he was pushing thirty-five summers.

6-10-42 San Diego/Oakland

Hebert's Lefty Slants Stymie Oaks

It was *deja vu* at Lane Field on June 10. Wally Hebert was on the mound for the Padres. The night before, another southpaw, Lefty Olsen, was there. He fanned the first batters he faced. Hebert did the same the following night. Olsen allowed a triple to set up Oakland's lone score. Hebert did the same. When the dust settled, the final score both nights was 5-1. Oakland must have thought they had landed in the twilight zone.

On his way to victory number ten Hebert pitched a seven-hit, one-run game that was never in doubt after the second inning—zeroes across the board from then on. He also hammered three hits out of four trips to the plate, sharing batting honors with teammate Swede Jensen. This victory elevated San Diego into second place in the standings all alone, but with Sacramento one game behind.

Oakland drew first blood in the top of the second inning when another Wally—Westlake—tripled to right center, and then scored on the next batter's single. That was it for Oakland. The Padres combined tight pitching by Hebert and good fielding by his teammates to keep the Oaks in line for the remainder of the game.

The Padres didn't let up. They tied it in the bottom of the second and went ahead in the third by one run. They added two more in the fifth and another in the eighth.

The Oaks threatened once in the top of the eighth. With one out Hebert gave up two successive singles putting one on first and one on second. Luby, number three in Oakland's lineup, hit into a double play. An uneventful ninth inning ended the game.

Oakland, I'm sure, hoped there wouldn't be a three-peat.

6-14-42 San Diego/Oakland

Lane Field was the site of a double victory for the Padres over Oakland on June 14. The Dangerous Duo—southpaws Wally Hebert and Al Olsen— turned in masterful pitching performances to take both games of a double-header, delighting the fans with scores of 3-2 and 6-2.

Hebert pitched the nightcap on his way to win number eleven against five losses. The Oaks threatened in the top of the second with two hits given up by Hebert, but the Oaks were unable to translate them into runs. They went ahead in the top of the third when Hebert gave up a double and a single that delivered one run. Oakland ahead 1-0. The lead didn't last long.

The Padres bounced back in the bottom half of the same inning with two runs. They led by a score of 2-1. Hebert settled down and things hummed along until inning number six when the Oaks got busy again and scored a run on a triple and a single. Score tied at two-all. That seemed to awake the San Diego bats.

Mazerra homered with one man on base to send the Padres out front 4-2. The San Diego faithful sat back in their seats and quit holding their collective breath. Swede Jensen, who had done everything in the first game except sell peanuts in the grandstand, came to the plate and singled, made it to second on a sacrifice, then made it home on another single. Padres up 5-2. They were far from through, however. Shortstop Calvey tripled, sending the base runner in for the final score. 6-2 Padres. All Hebert had to do was hold them, and hold them he did. Victory number eleven on ice.

6-26-42 Padres/Portland

The Padres traveled up the coast to take on the Portland Beavers in a double-header. Wally Hebert was on tap for the first game that went seven innings by agreement. The second game was held to eight innings due to the league curfew ruling.

Hebert was trying for his twelfth victory of the season, and obliged the folks back in San Diego by delivering a four-hit shutout. Final score 3-0. There's nothing worse than watching your team have a big fat zero on the scoreboard. The Padres collected five hits, but four of them turned into three runs. Home runs by shortstop Whipple and left-fielder Swede Jensen helped Hebert along to number twelve.

That defeat must have angered the home town boys because they came back in the second game with an 11-1 shellacking of the visitors, who were probably suffering from a case of *grosse tete* because of their win in the first game. That's French for big head — for the non-Cajuns in the room.

6-30-42 Padres/Angels

Hebert Hurls Padres to 3-0 Win Over Angels

The Los Angeles batters of 1942, who were known to be the most powerful hitters in the league, found their batting averages somewhat lower after a game played at Lane Field on June 30 thanks to masterful pitching by Wally Hebert. Padre catcher Detore said it was Hebert's top showing of the season. He showed his fellow chuckers how it should be done as he handed the Angels a five-hit shutout on his way to a thirteenth win. The 3-0 victory pulled the Padres within one game of the second place Angels.

Until two Angel batters collected singles in the top of the ninth, Hebert had given up a paltry three hits—one of them a fluke bunt. He was in trouble in the first inning, but eased out and was the master of ceremonies the rest of the way.

While Hebert was having his way with Angel batters, Ken Raffensberger, Angel pitcher, was keeping zeroes on the Padres half of the scoreboard. It was the seventh inning before the hosts could get on the board. Raffensberger decided to walk Detore, and that proved to be a major mistake. Mel Skelley, rookie second baseman, was up next. Should be an easy out. Right? Not this time. The young man slashed a triple into right center, scoring Detore. Padres, 1-0.

Hebert had things under control and didn't need any more help from the bats, but his teammates added two more in the bottom of the eighth, bringing the score to 3-0. He disposed of the L.A. batters in the top of the ninth, ending the game.

How many men does it take for a double play? A normal one usually takes three. Infielder, second base, first base. Sometimes it only takes two. In the top of the sixth inning it took nearly the entire Padre team to complete one. Angel left-fielder walked to open the frame. The next man up bunted—a pop-up Garibaldi, Padre third baseman, couldn't get to. Two Angels on. The lead base runner tried to make it to third—unguarded when Garibaldi was chasing the bunt. All the infielders plus one out-fielder, pitcher Hebert, and catcher Detore took part in the double killing. First baseman Stinson and pitcher Hebert made the tags on the runners. A two-minute double play—something that usually took five seconds— according to the sportswriter. My math came up with seven players. Too bad they didn't have instant replay back then. Would have been fun to watch.

7-8-42 Padres/Sacramento

Hebert Pitches 14th Victory

Lane Field. July 8, 1942. The Padres took the field against the league-leading Sacramento Senators. On the mound for Sacramento would be their number one pitcher, Clarence Beers. Trepidation engulfed the hometown grandstand. They wondered which Padres would show up — the ones who sent them over the moon or the ones who sunk them to the bottom of the Pacific. They didn't have long to wait.

Wally Hebert, on the mound for San Diego, allowed one hit, no runs in the top of the first inning. The Senators took the field, and the hometown crowd held their breaths as the Sacramento ace took his warm-up tosses. At the end of the inning it looked like the good Padres had shown up. They got four hits off Beers that translated into three runs. Glimmer of hope for the faithful. Padres, 3-0.

Hebert shut Sacramento bats down once more in the top of the second — one hit, no runs. Padre bats came alive again in the bottom half of the inning for two more runs off three hits. Padres, 5-0. A good lead. The fans leaned back in their seats, expecting a ho-hum night.

Things hummed along with no action until the fourth inning when Sacramento decided enough was enough. They collected three hits off the Padre southpaw and ended up with two runs. Padres, 5-2. Not too bad, but the hometown crowd knew how fast things could change.

Hebert silenced the Sacramento bats, allowing one more hit and no runs for the remainder of the game. The Padres, however, were not finished, and they exploded in the bottom of the sixth for six hits and five runs. The visiting team went through four pitchers on their way to a 10-2 defeat by the home team. After their half of inning number seven Hebert made short work of the Sacs, and cut them down as fast as they came to bat.

Every San Diego player except the pitcher collected two hits. I guess he could be forgiven since he limited Sacramento to seven hits, with three of them being in the fourth inning rally. His one hit accounted for a run in the second inning.

7-16-42 San Diego/San Francisco

Hebert Southpaws Seals Into Defeat

This game was played in SanFrancisco, and I think it was victory number fifteen for Wally Hebert. There were no dates on the clipping, but it seemed to be between win number fourteen and sixteen.

It started off with Hebert in trouble in the bottom of the first before he even got into his normal rhythm. He allowed three hits that turned into one run. He then walked one, filling the bases. Manager Durst called for activity in the bullpen, but he needn't have worried. The next batter grounded out, and the inning was over. Hebert settled down and put zeroes on the San Francisco half of the board until the seventh inning, when he flirted with trouble again.

He walked the Seals catcher with two out. Another single, and the runner advanced. Hometown fans came alive again. Two outs and one man in scoring position. Turned out to be a false alarm when the next batter flied out to left field—and that was it for San Francisco. No more hits, no more runs. A five-hitter.

It was a different story on the San Diego side, starting with an explosion in the fourth inning—five hits and five runs. They scored again in the fifth and the eighth. 7-1 Padres.

Aside from the first inning Hebert was in charge all the way.

7-42 Padres/Seattle

Hebert Wins No. 16

Number sixteen came at the expense of Seattle playing the Padres at Lane Field in the first game of a double-header. Reliable Mel Mazzera got out of his sick bed to pinch hit for Jensen and delivered the one that gave Wally Hebert his sixteenth triumph of the year.

Hebert got into hot water in the fourth inning when Seattle bagged two runs on four hits. He got out of the hole by intentionally walking one batter to get to the next one, who obliged by striking out to end the inning. Then in the sixth inning the Seattle shortstop walked and stole second. Hebert tossed one that caused the Seattle catcher to pop out and leave the base runner stranded. That was it for Seattle. Hebert held them scoreless for the last three innings.

San Diego had taken a 2-0 lead in the bottom of the third when first baseman Stinson whacked a single to open the frame. The next two batters did nothing. Two outs. Up comes Mel Skelley, second base, and triples to right field, scoring Stinson. Centerfielder Patchett singled, sending Skelley in. 2-0, Padres.

After the fourth inning the score was tied at two-all. Mazzera worked his magic in the bottom of the sixth with two outs. Garibaldi, Padre third baseman, singled. Catcher Salkeld got an infield hit to second. Two runners on. Mazerra came in to pinch hit for Jensen and came through for the Padres. He singled off the Seattle pitcher's foot to score Garibaldi for the winning run.

Another squeaker for the home team, but a win is a win.

8-11-42 Padres/Hollywood

PADRES SHADE STARS
Hebert Scores 17th Victory

On August 11 the Padres invaded Hollywood. Wally Hebert took the mound for the visitors. On his mind—victory number seventeen. The game dragged on for four innings with neither side being able to mount any kind of offense. Goose eggs across the scoreboard.

Then came the top of the fifth; the Padres were at bat. They must have been tired of the ho-hum game they were involved in because they started smacking balls around and ended up with six hits and five runs. The Stars helped out with a couple of errors. By the time San Diego took the field in the bottom of the fifth the score was 5-0, Padres. Hebert shut the hosts down in their half of the inning.

Top of the sixth, and the Padres looked like they would start all over again. They added four hits and two more runs. 7-0. By now Hollywood followers were deep in the doldrums. Then they remembered Hebert had blown a six-run lead when they played the Angels in 1941. Hope sprang eternal.

The Stars obliged with some offense. A double and a single in the bottom of the sixth turned into a run. 7-1. Maybe. Maybe.

A scoreless inning followed for both teams. In the bottom of the eighth the Stars added two runs when Kalin, Hollywood right fielder, blasted a two-run homer over the left field wall. Hollywood fans were still hopeful, but even though they held San Diego scoreless in the ninth they couldn't get anything going in their half of the inning. Final score, 7-3.

Even though Hebert gave up ten hits, the two Stars' pitchers tallied fourteen. In fact, all hands on the San Diego side partook of the belting. Four Padres got one hit each, and five hit for two apiece—including Wally Hebert. A good night's work for the boys from the border city.

8-15-42 Padres/Oakland

HEBERT BLANKS OAKS, 5 TO 0 FOR 18TH VICTORY
Hebert Hangs Up 18th Win For San Diego

Wally Hebert and the Padres headed north one day in mid-August to Oakland to show the Oaks how it was done down south. Things couldn't have gone any better for the Padres. While Hebert chalked up win number eighteen with a nine-hit shut-out his teammates lit up the scoreboard with five runs and eleven hits.

The first inning was quiet, with neither team doing anything. George Detore, Bill Salkeld, and Jack Whipple started things rolling in the top of the second with back-to-back hits along with an infield out by Hebert that netted two runs.

Top of the third with two men out, saw a two-run homer over the left field fence by Detore. Padres up, 4-0. Oakland fans not happy. They went further down in the dumps when the Padres added another run in the top of the sixth. San Diego loaded the bases when Hebert got to the plate. He hit a slow roller to second base, permitting Detore on third to score while he was being thrown out at first.

It's not like Oakland didn't have their chances. After all, they got nine hits off Hebert. They just couldn't seem to do anything with them. They had four distinct opportunities to score--the second, fourth, fifth, and again in the ninth. The scoreboard showed goose eggs all the way across nine innings. Eleven men were left twiddling their thumbs on base waiting for that elusive smack to send them home.

8-19-42 San Diego/Sacramento

Night Baseball Is At End In Coast League

The order came down from the Army. No more night baseball. It was official. From August 20 until the end of the season PCL clubs would play only during the day-time under provisions of the dim-out order issued by the Army. Civil Defense was vigilant when it came to protecting the coast from threats of Japanese bombs.

Veteran pitcher Wally Hebert, chasing number nineteen, pitched the last night game of the season, defeating Sacramento 2-1 while allowing a stingy two hits. The one run the Senators scored off him was unearned. Along the way he struck out six and went one for three at bat.

Sacramento went ahead in the fourth inning and pleased the home town crowd by remaining in the lead until the final two innings when San Diego broke the fans' heart by scoring two runs to take the game and deflate the home team.

"Heading for an outstanding season" the headline stated, as Hebert got ready to try for number twenty.

8-25-42 Padres/Oakland

Padres Battle Oakland in Twilight Game

The questions for this game were will Wally Hebert rack up his twentieth, and will San Diego hold onto fourth place to make the Shaughnessy playoffs? First pitch was scheduled for 5:15 p.m.

Hebert, in the midst of a hot streak, had won three games in a row and needed only three more triumphs to top his 1941 record. In hurling those three straight victories he had given up only four runs in twenty-five innings.

Optimistic Oakland was still hopeful of knocking the Padres out of fourth place and taking the spot for themselves. First order of business: don't let Hebert get that twentieth win on August 25th.

Oaks Nose Out Padres in 10th, 2-1
Hebert Drops Overtime Tilt

The headlines said it all. Looked like Wally would have to wait till his next game. San Diego picked up their lone run early — in the first inning — and for six innings it looked like Hebert was on his way to number twenty. In the top of the seventh he served up his only walk of the game. It turned out to be a costly gift since it became the tying run. No harm done. They were tied at one-all. Still time to pull it out of the fire.

They coasted along, still tied when the ninth inning ended and the game went into extra innings. The Oaks grabbed two hits off Hebert that opened the door for a run in the top of the tenth. Oakland, 2-1. No problem, though. The home team still had their half of the inning. They had come through before. They could do it again.

Unfortunately, Padre bats were silent for most of the game. Even normally reliable Mazzera didn't get the ball out of the infield and struck out twice. The home team ended up with goose eggs on the scoreboard for the tenth inning and the Padres went down to defeat by a score of 2-1. They did manage to hold on to fourth place since the teams that were dogging them were defeated also.

8-29-42 San Diego/Oakland

HEBERT TAMES OAKS, 9 TO 5, FOR 20TH VICTORY

Lane Field. August 29, 1942. The San Diego faithful gathered once again, hoping to see the popular southpaw from Louisiana pick up his twentieth victory of the season. This time they weren't disappointed. However, according to newspaper accounts fans were treated to less than stellar performances by the pitching on either side. It was strictly a batters' smorgasbord.

Cotton Gives Lesson On How Not to Pitch and San Diego Liked It. This was the sub-title of one account. It seemed that two of the three Oakland pitchers combined in a demonstration of how baseball should not be pitched. According to the sportswriter they succeeded quite well.

As a result of their efforts the Padres won the game 9-5, collecting eleven hits along the way, including two home runs. The starting Oakland pitcher lasted five and two-thirds innings, giving up nine hits and six runs. The reliever worked briefly in the sixth and ran into big trouble in the seventh when he walked two batters, gave up a home run and a triple, and added a wild pitch to the debacle. He didn't last too much longer and yet another reliever took over.

Hebert completed the game and won his twentieth, but according to the sportswriter he had no reason to pat himself on the back for exceptional pitching. In fact, he wrote, in spots Hebert was almost as bad as the two Oaks pitchers. He gave out thirteen hits, two more than the Oakland mounds men. The big difference was that those thirteen hits only segued into five runs. Two of those thirteen hits were home runs. Be that as it may, a win is a win. Hebert could thank the bats of his teammates for helping him win this one. He went one for three at the plate, so he could be included.

9-16-42 San Diego/San Francisco

Wally Hangs Up 21st Win

Lane Field. September 16, 1942. The San Diego faithful filed into the ball park with some trepidation. Their beloved Padres were locked in mortal combat with San Francisco for fourth place and a chance at the Shaughnessy playoffs. A double header was on tap, and one of their favorite players, Wally Hebert, would be pitching the first game. He would be trying for his twenty-first victory of the 1942 season, which was soon coming to an end.

They hoped it wouldn't be a repeat of his win number twenty, where he gave up thirteen hits and five runs. The main reason he won, according to press accounts, was because Oakland's pitching was somewhat worse than his and gave the Padres nine runs to get him into the "W" column.

The fans needn't have worried. Hebert was back in the zone. He gave up a single in the first inning, one in the sixth, and a third one in the seventh. Zeroes across the boards in the run department.

His team came through for him at the plate, giving him a comfortable four run cushion by the end of the fourth inning.

Those who hung around for the second game were treated to another shut-out, a six-hit. A good day for players and fans alike.

9-20-42 San Diego/San Francisco

Seals Win, Gain on Padres In Fight for Playoff Berth
Rivals to Decide Fourth Place Today

Thus shouted the headlines in the San Diego papers on Sunday morning, September 20, 1942. The Padres had just suffered defeat at the hands of the San Francisco Seals the day before by a score of 6-3.

The Padres needed one game to tie up fourth place and a seat at the playoff table. Three days in a row they tried. Three days in a row they failed. One last chance that Sunday afternoon in late September when a double-header was on tap at Lane Field, the first game scheduled for 1:30. The Seals had to win both games for them to advance. Manager Cedric Durst held southpaw Wally Hebert and Norman Brown, the Padres' most consistent right hander, in reserve for the final test.

Padres Capture Twin Bill, Qualify for Playoffs
Hebert Racks Up 22nd Victory in Hurling Clincher, 12-4

The 1942 Padres were never a team to do things by halves, either riding prolonged winning streaks or slogging through equally lengthy slumps at various stages in the pennant race. The 6,000 wild-eyed, rabid fans at Lane Field that Sunday afternoon were treated to an old-fashioned 12-4 Seal barbeque.

Wally Hebert put the clincher on fourth place and the playoffs by running his personal string for the season to twenty-two triumphs. He gave up nine hits that translated into four runs. His teammates pounded five Seal pitchers for fifteen hits and twelve runs. Hebert himself contributed to the score with two singles and a run batted in. The second game of the double-header was *lagniappe* for the fans. Padre hurler Dasso pitched a two-hit shutout and the home town team was headed for a share of Shaughnessy prize money.

9/23/42-9/28/42 Playoffs Padres/LA

Padres Open Playoff Drive Against Angels Here Today

Following a close shave which saw the Padres clinch a playoff spot on the last day of the regular season thanks to a fine pitching performance by southpaw Wally Hebert, the Padres rested for three days before opening their bid for a share of the $5,000 President's Cup booty. They were set to meet the Los Angeles Angels at 4:30 on September 23 at Lane Field. The two teams were scheduled to play the first three games in San Diego and finish up in Los Angeles. Winner of the series would then play the Sacramento-Seattle victor for the big share of the $10,000 prize money. The loser would split $1,250 and be eliminated from the competition.

The Angels won the first game 6-5 on the 23rd. Wally Hebert took the mound for the second game the next day. LA got a lone run in the first inning. Hebert gave up five hits, and after the first inning the Angels didn't get a runner beyond second base. Even that was not good enough for a win. Some help at the plate would have helped. Another one-run defeat.

Fast forward to September 28. Los Angeles led the series 3-2. A double-header was scheduled. All they needed was one more win to make it to the finals. The only thing that stood in their way was Hebert.

He allowed six hits in the game, but the Angels scored a run in the bottom of the fifth. The top of the sixth, however, saw Padre bats come alive. They scored all their runs then. 3-1. The Angels scored once more in the bottom half, but Hebert shut them down the next three innings, and squeaked out a 3-2 victory. Series tied at three-all, forcing game number seven.

Unfortunately, the big money was not on the horizon for the boys from down south. Los Angeles took the second game by a score of 5-1 and the Padres got the $1,250. They headed south, their season over. That 3-2 victory that kept them in the hunt turned out to be Hebert's last game in a Padre uniform.

Pitching Statistics for 1942

Games: 40

Innings Pitched: 319

Won: 22

Lost: 15

Percentage: 5.94

Hits: 324

Strikeouts: 125

Bases on Balls: 78

Earned Run Average: 2.37

11-2-42 Pittsburgh gets Wally for 1943

Owners Buy "Old Men" For Teams

Eleven major league baseball teams decided to spend $139,000 to obtain twenty players off the draft lists. The Pittsburgh Pirates got two. Wally Hebert was one of them. The emphasis in many cases was on age and selective service status rather than 1942 performances.

Hebert's 1942 performance would stand up against anyone's. His won-lost record was twenty-two to fifteen. He was thirty-four years of age and was married with two children. His draft status was Three-A. According the press accounts, he was worth $7,500.

The draft that year was the heaviest in many seasons. The large number of players selected was attributed to the efforts of major league clubs to replace younger players who had been drafted into the military. The Pacific Coast League was well represented — six Coast leaguers got the call.

If Connie Mack hadn't needed help in his infield Hebert might have been wearing a Philadelphia Athletics uniform instead of a Pirate one. Mr. Mack sent his scout to San Diego to look over the list of prospects for the upcoming draft who would be playing in the Shaughnessy playoffs. The day he arrived he was sidelined with a bout of the flu.

He missed the playoffs, but he was a San Diego boy and familiar with Hebert. He wrote his boss urging him to make Hebert his number one choice in the player draft. Mr. Mack analyzed his team needs and decided to bolster his wavering infield first and take Hebert in the second round. The Pirates wanted him above all others and nailed him when their turn to choose came up.

Earl Keller, writing in the San Diego Tribune, said the Pirates had gained a manager's ball player. Hebert was strictly a team player, always pulling his hardest whether he was on the mound or not. For the seven years he played for the Padres he averaged eighteen wins a year. He pitched 163 complete games, including twenty-five in 1941 and thirty-three in 1942 — a record for him. Not once in 1942 did he need relief. Not once.

During those seven years he won 126 and lost 95. In only two seasons did he lose more than he won—twelve wins and sixteen losses in 1938, and fifteen victories against eighteen defeats in 1940. He pitched 1,899 innings, gave up 1,980 hits, walked 451, and struck out 713. His unofficial earned-run average for 1942 was 2.29, a record performance "for the likeable lefthander, whose actions are more like a righthander's." (Hm. Does Keller mean lefties are usually somewhat flaky?)

Hebert became known as a willing, hard worker. "You could count on Wally anytime," according to manager Cedric Durst. While with the Padres he earned recognition as one of the best southpaw pitchers in league history.

In late November he got a letter from Bill Brandt officially welcoming him as a member of the Pirate organization. A new set of adventures awaited the Hebert clan.

SIXTEEN

1943

2-7-1943 Muncie, Indiana Training Camp

Wally Hebert quit the sunshine of California at the end of his 1942 Padre season in September and headed for the swamps and bayous of his Louisiana home. Before he left California he told the boys of the press that he had no intention of returning to the coast in the spring of 1943 if the war was still going on.

What he didn't know was that he might be drafted by the Pirates, which he was in November. What else he didn't know at the time was the Pirates had already announced they would be training at El Centro if it did not interfere with the war effort. It's not clear what happened between November and March, but the press reported the Pirates were headed for Muncie, Indiana, for spring training. The Lake Charles paper reported Hebert was to leave on March 16 for training camp.

When they gathered in Muncie to bask under sun lamps instead of the California sun, manager Frankie Frisch would have thirty-four players to start spring training, provided everyone's military status remained unchanged. Fifteen of those were pitchers.

Hebert's contract with the Pirates arrived in Pittsburgh on March 8. Although he was thirty-four years old he was considered by the experts to be a better pitcher than ever. He improved so much during his seven-year stint with San Diego that he had become one of the most talked-about players in baseball.

One Pittsburgh sportswriter wrote of his "whistling fast ball, a sharp curve, and an effective change of pace." His value was not only to mechanical ability; he had a ballplayer's ideal temperament and was always in shape.

Manager Frisch took an advance party of twenty-two Pirates on the train for Muncie at 9 o'clock one night in mid-March with the main guard due to arrive the next morning around 8:30. Wally Hebert was among the latter group.

Frisch intended to lose no time getting spring practice started. As soon as everyone had been assigned their living quarters he intended to call the first session. Mid-March in Indiana was not the same as March in California. If the weather was good the workout would be outside. Bad weather would bring no rest—Frisch intended to move it into the Muncie High School Field House.

A bright development coming out of the early workouts had to do with the oldest recruit on the squad—Wally Hebert, 35-year-old former Padre. Frisch didn't expect to see him report in such good shape as to be able to fire his fast ball in drills during the first week.

Temperatures were down around the freezing point when the manager assembled the squad for their workout. The thermometer climbed about ten points when batting practice got under way. Hebert took over the mound for about fifteen minutes, and he had the batters swinging and missing most of the time—especially the lefties among them. Indeed, they were more than happy when Frisch replaced the "veteran rookie."

The manager never had much of an opportunity to study Hebert's style and manner, but he had confidence in coach Hollis Thurston's judgment. Thurston said Hebert seldom had the stuff and class he was showing in training camp. He went on to assure Frisch that Hebert was a major leaguer in every sense.

3-5-43 Muncie Bound

Wally Hebert Leaves for Buc Camp March 16
Lake Charles American Press

The headline announced the third stage of Wally Hebert's baseball life. Having been sold to the Pittsburgh Pirates of the National League by San Diego earlier, he was due to leave Lake Charles to report for spring training in Muncie, Indiana. This would be his second excursion into the top tier of professional baseball. We had been living in the house on Foster Street and were expected to join him in Pittsburgh when the 1943 season began.

Meanwhile, back in Muncie batting practice was under way. Manager Frankie Frisch didn't expect to see his oldest recruit, Wally Hebert, report in such fine shape as to be able to fire his fast ball in the drills of the first week.

And so it came to pass that my mother, my sister Hillene, and I headed north that summer in 1943 to a most interesting city and new adventures. I got lost on the second day we were there, but that's another story.

Adventures In Pittsburgh

Pittsburgh was different from San Diego—no black shades on the windows, no blackouts after ten o'clock, no air raid drills, and no dog tags. But it was baseball season again, in a different city and with a different team—the Pittsburgh Pirates.

My dad got us settled into a house in a quiet neighborhood and left the next day on a two-week road trip. Our family at that time consisted of Mama and Daddy, my sister, Hillene, age two, and me, Linda, age six.

It was a Sunday morning, and my mother needed her morning newspaper. Hillene was asleep, so Mama couldn't leave, but she saw a drugstore on the corner about eight houses down. She decided to send me. After all, I was six going on seven.

She stood on the porch and watched as I walked down the sidewalk, a quarter in my hand. The clerk gave me change, and I left with a newspaper under one arm and a nickel and two pennies in the other hand.

I got back outside and started down the street, but I didn't see my mother anywhere. All the houses looked alike, with tall sets of steps leading to porches. I didn't know which one was mine, and she wasn't where she said she'd be.

I kept walking and looking, getting farther away, but she wasn't anywhere. The money was making my hand sweat, and the paper was getting hard to hold on to. I looked down the sidewalk and saw a woman walking toward me. She wore a hat and gloves and carried a Bible. I had been told repeatedly not to talk to strangers, but being from the Bible Belt I knew people on their way to church were probably okay to approach.

She took my hand, and we started back the way I had come. We reached the drug store and went inside. Then I saw the other door. I had gone in one door and out the other, and was headed in the opposite direction of our house.

The lady and I left through the other door and saw a crowd of people down the street in front of our house, and my mother and a policeman running toward us. I got a big hug from Mama and a lecture from the policeman about talking to strangers. However, I knew someone was looking out for me.

About a week later my mother was sweeping the front porch and noticed a small crowd of people across the street talking and pointing to our roof. She went upstairs to see what was going on. The window was open to let in the breeze, and my curious younger sibling, two-year-old Hillene, sat on the porch surveying the world below.

Thus the Hebert girls invaded Pittsburgh, but we survived and enjoyed our summer. Mama met all the neighbors through my little adventure. I had several playmates, and we spent our days sliding down cellar doors, climbing trees, and riding our tricycles down the high porch steps. We only did that once; one of my friends had to get some stitches in her forehead.

Hillene got a few more licks in, like the time she poured a whole container of *rationed* coffee all over the kitchen floor. Two people from south Louisiana who can't have their morning coffee? Not a good thing.

4-3-43 Pittsburgh/Cleveland-Preseason

In early April the Pirates, still in Muncie, hosted the Cleveland Indians in a pre-season game For the first seven innings it was an Indian show. They scored a run in the second inning and two more in the fourth. Cleveland, 3-0. The Pirate section of the scoreboard showed zeroes across until inning number eight.

Left fielder Barrett led off with a single. The next two batters made outs. Third baseman Elliott walked. Two men on. Right fielder Colman tripled and both base runners scored. Cleveland, 3-2.

Lanning had pitched the first five innings for Pittsburgh and allowed four of the five Indian hits and all three runs. Hebert relieved him in the sixth and allowed Cleveland one hit, holding them scoreless for the next three innings. In the bottom of the ninth Frisch pulled Hebert for a pinch hitter and the Pirates tied it up, sending the game into extra innings. Rescigno came in for Hebert and put the Indians away one-two-three. Score still tied at 3-3. In the bottom of the tenth an error resulted in a man on base for the Pirates. Clean-up batter Elliott whacked a triple and the game was over when the base runner scored. Resigno pitched one inning and got the win.

4-11-43 Pirates/Detroit Exhibition Game

Pirates Slam Tigers Hard, 13 to 2
"Vet" Rookie Tames Tigers
Bucs Pound Outer, Double and Single: Hebert Stars

On April 11 the Pirates met the Detroit Tigers at their training camp in Evansville, Indiana. The Pirates had been in a batting slump, but lurched out of it in a big way at the expense of the Tigers. Wally Hebert was on the mound for Pittsburgh and pitched five scoreless innings, allowing five hits and both Detroit runs.

By then the Pirates had a comfortable lead of 6-2 which they never relinquished. Nevertheless, Frisch replaced Hebert with a pinch hitter in the top of the seventh. Rescigno took over mound duties in the bottom half and pitched scoreless ball.

In the meantime, Pirate batters added five runs in the seventh and two more in the eighth. Vince DiMaggio, Hebert's former Padre teammate, blasted a two-run homer, a double, and a single. Final score: Pittsburge 13, Detroit 2. Hebert got the credit for the win. The game was on ice in the third inning.

5-2-43 Pittsburgh/Chicago Cubs

Hebert, Klinger Hurl Shutouts In Double Win
Bucco Moundsmen In Rare Form

Wally Hebert and Bob Klinger served up a double dose of whitewash at Forbes Field in Pittsburgh as 16,491 cheering fans braved the threat of menacing weather. They watched as the Pirates swept the first home series with the Cubs by taking two games, 3-0 and 1-0.

It was strictly a pitcher's afternoon for both games. Wally Hebert and Cub hurler Bithorn battled all the way through in the opener. The Cubs started off by tapping Hebert for three safeties in the first inning. However, they failed to turn those three hits into a single run.

Hebert settled down and for the next eight innings he was scarcely threatened. He allowed three other hits scattered throughout the following innings, but once again nothing came of them. Visitor scoreboard showed zeroes across.

Pirate batters did their part and won the game, technically, in the bottom of the third when they scored two runs. Pirate catcher Baker lined a single to right. Hebert sacrificed him to second. Russell, left fielder, tripled to right center and Baker scored. Russell crossed the plate after right fielder Barrett flied out to center. They added run number three in the bottom of the sixth, but the game was already on ice. Hebert got out of his jam in the first inning and never looked back.

5-26-43 Padres/Brooklyn

Pirates Overwhelm Dodgers, 17 to 4

The league-leading Brooklyn Dodgers took on the Pittsburgh Pirates at Forbes Field on May 26, but the hosts were not at all nice to their guests. The Pirates pasted a 17-4 shellacking on the visitors, a rude awakening indeed for the first place team, who might have come into town carrying an aura of invincibility with them. There was nothing remotely resembling a big league contest in the affair. In fact, it looked more like a tee ball game.

The Dodger debacle started out in the first inning when Pittsburgh scored their first run. The second inning saw five Pirates cross the plate. Things looked somewhat better for the visitors in the top of the third when the Dodgers managed to put two on the board. 6-2 Pirates. Then came the bottom of the third. Nine Pirates scored. 15-2 Pittsburgh. One would wonder if there were any Dodger fans still sitting next to their radios in New York by then.

Wally Hebert was on the mound for Pittsburgh. He went the full route and gave up twelve hits to the guests—but who cared? The Dodgers scored only four runs. Three Dodger pitchers gave up sixteen hits between them, and Pittsburgh turned them into seventeen runs.

Pirate bats were on fire. Every batter except one hit safely at least once. Vince DiMaggio, Hebert's teammate from San Diego, homered twice and sent five runners ahead of him. Hebert got two hits, two runs, and an RBI. A good time was had by all. Almost all.

5-30-43 Pittsburgh/Philadelphia

Bucks Whip Phillies Twice, 4-3, 2-1.
Hebert Captures Ten-Inning Game; Take Fourth Place

The 7,297 paying fans at Forbes Field enjoyed a double dose of victory when their hometown heroes took two from the visiting Phillies on May 30. Wally Hebert engaged in a southpaw duel that went ten innings—a low scoring affair in which the Pirates squeaked out a 2-1 victory.

The Pirates drew first blood. Both teams had buzzed along for three innings, putting batters away with regularity. Bottom of the fourth saw Pittsburgh convert two hits into a run, thanks to a sacrifice by Lopez, the catcher.

The lead didn't last long. Philidelphia came right back in the top of the fifth inning with one run, thanks again to a sacrifice hit that sent a base runner to third base.

Things settled down for four ho-hum innings in which neither team could muster any offense. The ninth inning rolled around with the game still knotted at one-all. Extra innings needed. Hebert kept Philly bats quiet in the top half. Three singles gave the Pirates their victory.

With one out, Pirate right-fielder O'Brien singled to left, and first baseman Fletcher lined one to right field. Two men on. Pinch hitter Colman smacked one to the second baseman who tossed it to first base to retire the batter. Both runners advanced. Up came DiMaggio, who ended it all with a single that got past the shorstop. The man on third crossed the plate with the winning run. DeMaggio never hit a homer that looked better to Frankie Frisch than that game-winning single.

The fans there that day got to sit through two nail-biting, one-run games. A good day for the team and a good day for the fans.

6-7-43 Pittsburgh/Brooklyn

Late Dodger Rally Jars Pirates, 4-1
Hebert Victim of Uprising After Hurling Shutout Ball For Seven Frames

The Pittsburgh faithful—19,000 plus—turned out to see what they hoped would be a walloping of their old rivals, the Brooklyn Dodgers. What they got was eight innings of great pitching and fielding by Hebert and his teammates, and a disastrous four-run inning for the visitors.

The Pirates got on the board in the bottom of the first inning thanks to second baseman Frank Gustine, who got four of Pittsburgh's seven hits and crossed the plate for the home team's lone tally. Things settled down as the two teams hummed along in a dozer contest for the next six innings, even though there were some great feats of fielding on both sides.

They eased into the top of the eighth inning and soon found things could change in an instant. With one out, the second Dodger batter started the trouble with a single. He advanced to third on another single. The next batter was tagged out at first, but the runner on third scored. 1-1. The Dodgers added three more runs, raising the score to 4-1.

The home town boys could do nothing in their half of the eighth. They held the visitors scoreless in the top of the ninth. The game would not be over till it was over, and until the last batter made the last out, there was always hope. Unfortunately, it would not happen that night. An inning like that can shut down the home crowd in a heartbeat.

The winning Dodger pitcher got the win in spite of a hit batter, a wild pitch, and a balk while allowing seven hits.

6-13-43 Pittsburgh/St. Louis Cards

Bucs Bid Cards Goodbye With Base Hits
Pirates Win And Tie As Attack Clicks

The Pirates had been hanging out in St. Louis for a five-game series that left manager Frisch none too thrilled with his squad. They had lost the first three games and were set for a double-header on Sunday afternoon. They redeemed themselves somewhat by winning the first game by a blowout and fighting the host Cardinals in the second game to a 4-4 tie that had to be called because of darkness. The game had started at 3 o'clock and lasted three hours and ten minutes. No night baseball because of the war.

Both games were slugfests, with twenty-seven hits in the first game and twenty-five in the second. However, the majority of the 18,000 plus fans who witnessed it did not leave happy; a blowout and a why-even-bother game.

Wally Hebert took the mound for the Pirates in the first game and racked up win number four for him in a game that lasted two hours and thirty-five minutes. He gave up eleven hits, but coasted all the way because when it looked like the Cards might get something started he always managed to shut them down.

The game was actually on ice in the top of the first inning when Pirate batsmen scored seven times. Then in the bottom half of the first inning the Cards crossed the plate twice and that was it for them until the eighth inning when they scored once more. The Pirates added one in the fifth inning and twice in the sixth. Final score, 10-3.

The second game was more exciting to watch, but turned out to be a big letdown for both teams. A tie decides nothing; makes you wonder why you even spent the time and money.

7-17-43 Pittsburgh/St. Louis Cards

Run String to 4 Straight Over Leaders
Butcher Wins First, Hebert Triumphs in Nightcap

Back in pre-season the experts got together and declared the St. Louis Cardinals a shoo-in for the National League pennant. The Cards seemed to have fallen on evil days in mid-July, dropping a double-header to the Pirates on July 17 by scores of 7-3 and 3-2. This made four straight games they had lost to the Pirates.

According to the sports writer, in both games of the double-header they did not look like pennant contenders, and played more like a second division club. Pittsburgh, on the other hand, played heads-up ball all the way. Butcher scored his fifth victory against two losses, and Hebert won his fifth versus six defeats.

That was the first time in the '43 season the Cards had dropped both ends of a twin bill. The double loss set a new mark for losses at four straight. They came to Pittsburgh with a comfortable five-game lead over Brooklyn and ten and a half over third-place Pittsburgh. After the double-header they found themselves only three and a half games over Brooklyn, and six and a half games ahead of the Pirates.

In the second game, with Hebert on the mound, Pittsburgh took an early lead in the bottom of the second inning by a score of 1-0. They added another score in the third. 2-0. The Cards picked up their first run in the top of the sixth and added another in the eighth. Score knotted up at 2-2. Another nail-biter. In the bottom of the eighth with darkening skies threatening to shut the game down, the home town boys came through. Barrett, right-fielder, doubled with two out, and the usually alert Cardinal shortstop, Marion, let a blooper fall behind him, allowing the base runner to score the winning run. 3-2. A nice way for Pirate fans to end the day.

7-25-43 Pirates/Dodgers

PIRATES RAID DODGERS TWICE WITH SAME SCORE
30,309 See Klinger, Hebert Hurl Pirates to Dual Win
Bucks Crowd Dodgers Win Two by 7-1 Edge

Superb pitching by Bob Klinger and Wally Hebert, and timely batting by the Pirates gave Frisch's crew a double sweep by the identical score of 7-1, delighting 30, 309 screaming fans on a Sunday afternoon in Pittsburgh. Klinger turned in a two-hit effort, and Hebert held Durocher's boys to four singles. The outcome was to pull the Pirates to within a half a game behind Brooklyn.

Hebert's victory was his sixth of the season against the same number of defeats. The Dodgers sent five pitchers to the mound while Hebert was the lone Pirate to do the hurling honors for his team. He also led the Pittsburgh offense with a triple, double, and single, while driving in one run and scoring three himself.

Hebert got in trouble in the seventh inning when the Dodgers got three of their four hits and their lone tally. After their score an error and a single loaded the bases with one out. Time for Bobbie Hebert to head to the ladies' room. Hebert, however, came through by forcing a double play to end the inning.

The teams played scoreless ball for two innings. The bottom of the third proved to be the biggie for Pittsburgh. Vince DiMaggio started things off with a double to right. The next batter flied out, and brought Hebert to the plate. He smacked a two-bagger over third base, scoring DiMaggio. 1-0.

Second baseman Coscarart was safe on second on an error, followed by a wild pitch, and Hebert hustled to third. Left fielder Russell doubled to left, scoring Hebert. 2-0. Coscarart pulled up at third. A walk following a strikeout filled the bases. Fletcher, Pirate first baseman, came through with a single to center, scoring two base runners. 4-0, Pirates.

DiMaggio, who started the rally, ended it by fouling out to the Dodger first baseman. That was basically the ball game. The last three runs scored by the

Pirates were *lagniappe*, and the lone run tallied by Brooklyn in the seventh inning was too little, too late.

It wasn't because Leo Durocher didn't try. He was so aggravated by his team's dismal performance in the first game, won by southpaw Klinger, that he stripped his outfit of all the lefties in his lineup and replaced them with a complete array of right-handers. To no avail. The replacements did little better with the shakeup than the left-handed batters had done in the first game—a two hitter by southpaw Klinger. On top of that they cut loose with five fielding bobbles that didn't help their cause at all.

Some days it pays to just stay in bed.

8-7-43 Pirates/Cardinals

Wally Hebert Checks Cardinals, Pirates Win, 4-1
Southpaw Nicked For 13 Bingles
Big Lefty Given Superb Support

The Pirates of Pittsburgh were in St. Louis trying to catch up with the league-leading Cardinals. Wally Hebert took the mound on August 7 and served up thirteen hits, which was usually enough for the team on the receiving end to take home a mark in the win box.

Not so this time. The Cards managed one run in spite of the embarrassment of riches handed to them by the gentleman from Louisiana. The Pirates, on the other hand, got ten hits off three Cardinal pitchers, and managed to turn them into four runs—enough to take home the goodies.

The victory was the seventh for Hebert and moved the Pirates one game closer to the top, being only eleven games out. He got a lot of defensive help from his teammates, including three great double plays. The prize fielding play of the day was made by shortstop Gustine when he jumped high into the air for a line drive in the sixth inning, batted the ball up with his glove, and caught it as he fell flat on his back.

The second inning was the big one for the Pirates. All the runs they scored came when they put together three hits and two bases on balls for the four tallies. After that none of the visitors reached second base.

Hebert was in hot water most of the time, but managed to keep the Cards at bay every inning except the third. That's when the home team put their lone tally on the board. They threatened again in the bottom of the ninth with a man on first and third and one out. A double play ended the threat and the game.

8-16-43 Lefty Grove Winning Streak

An interesting story appeared in the Pittsburgh Press in August of 1943. A correspondent of the newspaper, Mr. Campbell, remembered a long winning streak of sixteen consecutive games piled up in 1931 by Robert "Lefty" Grove, the fireball master of Connie Mack's Athletics. He went up against the St. Louis Browns for a stab at number seventeen. Since the Browns of 1931 were the league doormat, it was a foregone conclusion he would keep the streak alive.

Grove was beaten that day by a score of 1-0, and Mr. Campbell said he thought a little-known left-hander, Wally Hebert, was the one who ended the streak. Then he asked the paper if it was the same Hebert who was pitching in 1943 for the Pirates. The Wally Hebert who was with the Browns was indeed the Hebert in a Pirate uniform in 1943. However, he wasn't the one on the mound that day; it was Dick Coffman who stopped Grove.

Hebert remembered that game along with an interesting back story. The Browns had been to Canada for an exhibition game. After the game they boarded the train bound for Philadelphia and the game with Lefty Grove. While in Canada the drinkers among them bought liquor to bring back into the states. Hebert, being a non-drinker, had two bottles belonging to his roommate, Walter Stewart.

The team was already in their sleepers when a policeman came in and said, "I don't guess any of you guys got any liquor in your bag." Dick Coffman sat up in his bunk and blasted the officer with a nice loud Bronx cheer. The policeman made everyone empty their bags onto the floor and he confiscated all the spirits.

Manager Killefer was not amused and told Coffman, who was feeling no pain, that he had just drawn the pitching assignment the next day against one of the best pitchers in baseball.

Grove was chasing a record, which seventeen straight would have been, but that afternoon the fans would not see that. The Browns scored their lone run on an error, and Coffman got the last laugh by keeping the Athletics off the scoreboard. Maybe more should try pitching with a hangover.

8-19-43 Pittsburgh/NY Giants

Pirate Homers Help Hebert Win

Seven of the eight runs in the Pirate victory over the Giants were brought about by home runs, giving Wally Hebert his eighth win of the season. Vince DiMaggio whacked one against the balcony of the left field stands for his number 14 in the fourth inning with two men on. The Pirates had already scored once in the first inning, and DiMaggio's clout gave Pittsburgh a 4-0 advantage.

In the fifth inning Jim Russell hit one into the upper deck of the right field stands with one on base. 6-0, Pirates. The Giants got their solo run in the bottom of the fifth when Mel Ott and Sid Gordon singled. Ott took third base on an infield out and scored on an infield fly. That was all the offense they could generate in spite of the eight hits handed them by Hebert. 6-1, Pirates.

Jim Russell came through again with an inside-the-park homer with one on. Pirates final, 8-1. Hebert shut down New York bats in the bottom of the ninth to finish the job.

8-26-43 Backstage

Wally Hebert and catcher Al Lopez cut up two large, yummy-looking cakes in the clubhouse before the game on August 26. The ladies, who never forgot team members' birthdays, gave them each a box of candy along with the cakes. Lopez's birthday was the previous Friday, August 20, and Hebert's was the next day on the 21st.

Some three weeks later a bit of bad news came down the pike. Hebert had received notification from his draft board in Lake Charles that he had been reclassified from 3-A to 1-A and subject to induction soon. He was thirty-five years old, married with two children.

This was something neither I or any of my siblings ever knew. I found out about it when I ran across the newspaper clippings online. As far as I know none of them had ever heard about it either. Neither of our parents ever said anything. I, for one can't imagine my father in the army. He never heard anything else about induction, however.

9-29-43 Pittsburgh/Brooklyn

Hebert and Brandt Record DoubleVictory
Bucs Fight To Hold Newly Won Position

The Pirates elbowed the Dodgers out of third place in September 1943; all they had to do was keep "Dem Bums" from returning the favor. They took over third by beating the Dodgers twice on September 28 by scores of 5-2 and 4-2.

Wally Hebert went the distance for the Pirates in the first game, giving up ten hits but managing, along with his teammates, to limit Brooklyn to two tallies on the scoreboard. The Dodgers got on the board early — second inning — without hitting the ball out of the infield.

One man drew a walk, and the next two men rapped singles, loading the bases. (Ladies Room time for Bobbie.) Next batter up hit into a double play, but the man on third scored. 1-0, Dodgers.

The Pirates tied things up in the bottom of the third. The Dodger pitcher couldn't seem to control the ball and gave away three freebies. Hebert , on third, scooted home when DiMaggio flied to left.

The next two and a half innings were uneventful, but Pirate bats woke up during the bottom of the sixth. They turned five of their six hits into three more runs to break the tie. 4-1, Pirates. After holding Brooklyn scoreless the next inning, the Pirates added another run when right-fielder Jack Barrett smacked an inside-the-park homer. 5-1.

Brooklyn made some noise in the eighth inning with three singles bunched together and one out. One run scored, but Hebert tightened up and snuffed out the rally. This would be Hebert's last full game in baseball.

Pitching Statistics: 1943

Games: 34

Innings Pitched: 184

Won: 10

Lost: 11

Percentage: .476

Hits: 197

Strikeouts: 41

Bases on Balls: 45

Earned Run Average: 2.98

2-6-44 Pittsburgh Press Dick Fortune

As early as February the baseball community was beginning to make plans for the upcoming 1944 season. On February 6 Dick Fortune, writing for the Pittsburgh Press, informed the Pittsburgh fans about the prospects of their beloved Pirates. "Barring strikes, insurrections, rebellions, Acts of God and the Selective Service and general wear and tear, the Pittsburgh Pirates will have thirty players when the training season opens at Muncie, Indiana, on March 15." There were thirteen pitchers, three catchers, eight infielders, and six outfielders.

Seven of the pitchers were listed as holdovers from the 1943 season, including Wally Hebert, who was working in the off season at Firestone Rubber Company in the Lake Charles area. Pirate management had received word in late February that he had signed his new contract.

Pirates Head for Muncie Training Camp on Tuesday

This was the headline in the Pittsburgh Press on Sunday, March 12. Twenty-one Pirates were headed to Indiana to start the third wartime grind. Two Pirates were absent from the advance guard—Wally Hebert and Vince DiMaggio. DiMaggio hadn't signed his contract as of then and Hebert's employer had asked him to remain on the job until April 1. Pirate management gave him permission to remain in the south for that period. He said he would do his own conditioning while he was away from camp.

Hebert Quits Pirates for War Plant Job

This headline appeared in the Pittsburgh Press on March 27, 1944. The writer reported that the Pirates lost another badly-needed pitcher and one of their two remaining left-handers when Wally Hebert notified manager Frisch he had decided to remain on his war plant job. He asked to be placed on the voluntary retired list.

This decision was a solid blow to Pittsburgh's plans. At the age of thirty-four the southpaw was an iron man on the Pacific Coast League in 1942 and was figured to be a real help to the Pirates in 1944. Frisch had figured on Hebert to bring his staff to nine.

Pittsburgh lost one Hebert when Wally decided to stay in Louisiana, but they picked up another one — Billy Hebert, who hoped to make Pirate fans forget Wally. He was only twenty-one to Wally's thirty-five. He had been discharged from the Marines. His home was Bay City, Michigan, so it's probably certain he pronounced his name Hee-bert instead of A-bear.

Wally's baseball life had come to an end; he moved on to the next phase of his journey. He spent fourteen years with an elite group, with men he would remember forever. Men who lived the dream, like him.

SEVENTEEN

MEMORIES

BABE RUTH

During an interview when he was ninety-one Preacher shared these memories. One thing Ruth apparently couldn't master was a slow curve. Pitching in relief Hebert allowed a lead-off single to Jimmy Reese; the next man up was Ruth.

"I guess I was pretty nervous," he recalled. "I was only twenty-four. And Ruth was swinging with everything he had. I threw him a slow curve, and he hit a little squibber to second base. Grounded into a double play. As he was running back to the dugout, he looked at me and yelled 'You can stick that slow curve right up your ass.' After that I never gave him a fast ball to hit. I'd never throw him a strike on a fast ball. He didn't like the slow stuff at all. I pitched him every kind of way except a fast ball over the plate. I don't know if he ever hit a home run off me."

Ruth hit three home runs off the rookie. Once in each of the years he pitched for the Browns.

LOU GEHRIG

"To me, Lou Gehrig was one of the best hitters I ever pitched to. He hit flat-footed and had few weaknesses. He was quiet, but could he play."

TED WILLIAMS

Ted Williams broke into baseball in 1936 with the newly named Padres. Hebert was pitching for San Diego. The Hollywood team had moved down south from Los Angeles, and sported a new team name as well as a new ball park, Lane Field. Ted was a skinny seventeen-year-old, still in high school.

Williams was born and raised in San Diego. When he connected with the ball it would take off low like a bullet, and when it hit the boards at the rear of the stadium it sounded like a dynamite detonation. If he hit it over the fence, cars were on the endangered species list; dents and broken windows were a common occurrence . They weren't the kind of home run balls that went high and landed soft.

Pitchers didn't like pitching to him. They would walk him on purpose about every four times he came to the plate. He hated that.

When he first signed on to the team he was too young to drive. Hebert, living in the same neighborhood, picked him up for rides to the ball park for practice and games.

One day I was volunteering at the library selling used books for Friends of the Library. I got up to stretch my legs and ran across a book in the sports section—a biography of Ted Williams by Leigh Montville. The title is simply *Ted Williams.*

Knowing my father played with Williams in San Diego, I turned to the index just for the heck of it, and what do you know—there was Wally Hebert's name directing me to page 28. And there on page 28 were two lines.

"Fun was Ted going hunting with a kid named Wally Hebert. They had two bullets between them—bullets were expensive—but they came home with two rabbits."
None of my siblings ever remember that story, but someone must have told Mr. Montville. One thing I need to correct—my dad was not a kid in 1936. He was in his late twenties.

Dad was an avid hunter and fisherman, and he enjoyed those pastimes with Ted Williams, but he wouldn't go to the movies with him because Ted made so much noise there. He said you could always spot Ted in a theater; there was usually a circle of empty seats around him. The Padres' young bat boy did enjoy the movies with Williams.

I discovered an interesting coincidence while reading through the Montville book. Williams grew up in a modest house on Utah Street in San Diego. He had a friend in elementary school named Joe, who walked to school with him every morning. Joe lived at 4335 Oregon Street. Ted would walk from 4121 Utah to Oregon, and they would go on to school from there. Oregon Street rang a bell with me, and I dug out my old dog tag from my time in San Diego during the war. Our address was 4527 Oregon Street. I guess I must have walked the same streets as one of the greatest hitters of all time, albeit a few years apart.

THE DIMAGGIOS: VINCE AND JOE

Wally Hebert played several seasons in San Diego with Vince DiMaggio, older brother of Joe, the Yankee star, and Dominic, who played for Boston in later years. Back in the mid-thirties Vince was playing for San Francisco of the Pacific Coast League, and Hebert was playing in Hollywood before the franchise was transferred to San Diego in 1936.

He had an interesting story of how Vince came to leave San Francisco and ended up in San Diego. It seems that one day Vince took younger brother Joe to spring training at the San Francisco camp. The powers that be were so impressed with Joe that they decided to keep him and Vince got sent to Hollywood in 1933.

According to Hebert, Vince could hit the ball as hard as Joe, but every time he hit a home run he tried too hard to hit another and ended up with a string of strikeouts. When he settled down and quit trying so hard, he would hit another homer. Vince was a good outfielder, and one of the best sun fielders around, rarely losing the ball in the sun the way some outfielders did.

An ongoing Monopoly game sat on a table at the Hebert house awaiting whichever visitors ventured over to take up where someone else had left off. Vince loved to play and was a frequent participant as was teammate Ed Wells. Sometimes the game would go on well into the night.

"Don't ask Vince to sing," Ed would tell the wives. Vince had an operatic voice and sang loud, long, and high. Ed was afraid the neighbors would start complaining when the soaring tenor notes started wafting through their windows.

Someone wrote a song about Joe when he played for the Yankees. Vince would sing it for the team, but he used his own name instead.

Hebert was also acquainted with the elder DiMaggios, who lived in the San Francisco area back then. Whenever Vince, Wally, and the Padres played in San Francisco, the team ate dinner at the DiMaggio home. They played double-headers on Sunday, and had chicken spaghetti with the DiMaggio family.

An old-timers baseball game was being played in Houston many years after they had all left baseball. One of the players was Joe DiMaggio, the Yankee Clipper. Hebert was able to attend the game and made his way to the dugout area. Joe recognized him at once.

"Well hello, Wally. It's been a while."

PART III
Back to the Bayou

THE LATER YEARS
1943 To 1999

EIGHTEEN

LAKE CHARLES & WESTLAKE

Summer 1944

The Hebert family returned to the house on Foster Street in Lake Charles in the fall of 1943. My father went to work at Firestone Rubber Company. I started second grade at Fourth Ward School, three houses down from ours. As usual, I had missed the first week of classes and had to have help to catch up with the other students. By the end of the school year I learned we wouldn't be returning to Pittsburgh for another baseball season. Dad decided to hang it up for good and stay on at Firestone. Travel was hard because of the war, and my parents didn't want me missing any more school. Also, he was coming up on thirty-seven. It was just time.

That summer my parents broke the news that I would start third grade in a place called Westlake, a little town across the lake from Lake Charles. There was a horse, a cow with a calf, a pig, and some chickens. The house was a gabled structure a story and a half high, sitting on three and a half acres of mostly overgrown land.

Our first trip there seemed to take forever to my eight-year-self. I had never been so far out in the country before. We were at the very end of Westwood Road, which ran all the way through the town and beyond, starting at the lake and ending at the West Fork of the Calcasieu River.

We went into the house, looked it over, and tramped around what part of the grounds we could get to. Even at my young age I wondered what had possessed my parents to buy that place.

The house, to me , was huge. Downstairs was a living room, dining room, large kitchen with breakfast nook, a den with knotty pine walls, and a huge bathroom. Upstairs—three large bedrooms, a half-bath, and two attic rooms next to two of the bedrooms.

It seemed too large for just the four of us. That's when I learned three more people would be arriving the next week; my grandparents and my great-grandmother would be living with us, but I was still apprehensive about everything else. My dad took me to the upstairs bedroom that would be my parents' for several decades. We stood at the window and looked out.

"What do you see on the other side of the trees?"

The trees weren't very tall. On the other side a river drifted along in the summer heat. Every now and then a silver fish would break the water and disappear back into the depths.

"Let's go have a look," he said.

The four of us left the house and took a short walk through the woods. That's the first time I saw the West Fork of the Calcasieu River, and that's when I knew I was home.

San Diego was fun and Pittsburg was fun, but this was where I wanted to be.

The Wallace branch of Clan Hebert increased by three more after the move to Westlake. Wally Jr. came along in November 1945, followed by John David in March 1951, and Stephen Lee in May 1952. After Stephen came along the house at the end of Westwood Road had a total of ten permanent residents within its walls.   That number quite often increased as relatives, friends, schoolmates, etc. showed up from time to time to spend anything from overnight sleepovers to several days to a couple of weeks.   Seems like there was always an extra cousin or two around.   Many nights the youngsters slept on the floor with a quilt and a pillow.   When you're twelve who needs a bed?

David, Linda, Wally Jr., Hillene, and Stephen

The Westlake Homeplace

He's Still Got It

Just because he was no longer fanning National League batters didn't mean Wally Hebert had lost his stuff. The only thing he seemed to have lost was his baseball moniker—Wally. Back home in southwest Louisiana he was "Preacher" once again.

He worked for Firestone Rubber Company making tires for the war effort. The plant worked around the clock, dividing the twenty-four hour period into three shifts: first—day; second—evening; and third—midnight or graveyard. He shared rides to the plant with two neighborhood co-workers—Red McGuire and James George.

One day Preacher and Red were waiting for their ride in the McGuire's front yard. The kids were in the yard playing baseball, and Preacher was pitching to them. A tractor sat in the corn field next to the yard, some forty or fifty feet away. Red decided to offer a challenge.

"Hey, Preacher. Bet you can't hit that smokestack. Go ahead. I dare you."

"Nah. Better not. I don't want to break it."

"Break it? Heck. You won't even hit it. Go ahead."

Preacher let it fly just as he had a million times before. The ball hit the narrow smokestack, which tumbled to the ground in a cloud of dust. Their ride arrived, and the last thing the McGuire kids heard was their dad grousing as he got into the car.

Preacher's fellow Firestone workers knew he hadn't lost his stuff, having seen it first hand. Insects swarming around light poles in the parking lot attracted a lot of nuisance critters to the *smorgasbord* around the base of the pole.

"See if Preacher's here," someone would say.

If he was on shift he would arrive with valve stem covers in hand, and proceed to pick off the nuisances until the survivors ran to safety. I wonder what his coworkers did when he retired in the seventies.

He still hunted well into his nineties, and there was always a duck or two in the crock pot during the season. However, one day he returned empty-handed.

"I guess I better get my eyes checked," he told my mother. "I shot the decoy."

A Chapter From Wally Jr.

For all five Hebert siblings, growing up was framed by the West Fork
River, barely a hundred yards from our house. It was a slow moving hundred-
foot-deep branch of the Calcasieu River about a quarter-mile across with deeply
forested banks of oak, cypress, and sweet gum. Clear and teeming with fish, it
became brackish in the summer and sharks, salt-water fish and, blue crabs came
upriver.

Heberts were all early swimmers for safety reasons, and the swimming
hole behind our house was always full of kids swinging off ropes and diving off
40-foot platforms into deep water. Our dad had trot-lines on the river and caught
crabs at night in the summer, but we were more interested in the adventure the
river provided.

Two rival social groups had emerged by 1960: the swimmers and the
skiers. It was not unusual for us to bait the river with a lone swimmer 30 feet off
the bank and swing off a rope to ambush any skier malicious enough to take the
lure.

One summer day the three Hebert boys were playing baseball when
Preacher said, "You boys come with me." He told us to cut some bamboo the size
of fishing poles. He stripped off the leaves, trimmed them with his pocket knife
and down we went to the swimming hole. "Get some of that orange and gray
clay," he said, pointing to a particular stratum on the 15-foot bank. We had no
idea what was happening, but he pinched a golf-ball-sized lump, rolled it in his
hand, and fastened it to the bamboo knuckle on the thin end of the cane. Very
casually he used his pitching motion to whip the cane forward. The clay ball
went across the quarter-mile river, over the fifty-foot longleaf pines, and, still
climbing, vanished from our sight!

This weaponry, as can be imagined, revolutionized the river rivalries.
Clay balls enabled us to break up profane picnics in Sam Houston Jones State
Park on the other side of the river with no possibility of retaliation. It would have

taken a half hour for anyone to drive roundabout to our location. We left them alone as long as they did not hurl insults across the river. If they transgressed, we walked up the hill to their taunts and cut some bamboo.

Occasionally a Westlake girl would be there with a Chennault Air Force Base airman, and call us out by name. One large boat sporting a platter-sized flattened-out clay ball came close to the bank, and the driver said, "I'm not upset; I just want to know how you did it!"

In the 1950's our Dad labored for months on a special project in the garage. He was building a fishing boat from scratch, using a hand-held plane, shaping each piece of wood. When it was complete, he used resin and sheets of fiberglass to render it totally waterproof. A masterpiece of wood-and-water craft, it was his pride and joy and he kept it tied at the river in a little inlet.

One day it went missing, and Dad visited the entire neighborhood asking if anyone had seen his boat. One neighbor said, "No, Preacher, I haven't seen your boat." Three years later, Dad was picking huckleberries across the river in the park, and came to a small natural pond in the swampy area. In the middle was this neighbor, sitting in that boat, with all his gear and an outboard motor attached. Daddy didn't say a word; he just waded out into the water and turned the boat over, dumping the nefarious neighbor, his motor and gear, all overboard. We still have that handmade Preacher Hebert boat in the family today, and the youngest son, Stephen, makes his home on the West Fork River. (Note from me: the last time I saw the boat it was in Stephen's yard at an outdoor wedding filled with ice and all manner of beverages.)

After the passing of our Dad and brother David, Wally Jr. wrote this song about the river and what it meant to all of us.

The River Our Life Flowed By

June 21, 2010 Words and Music by Wally Hebert

Dedicated to
Preacher Hebert, 1907-1999
John David Hebert, 1951-2010

We learned to swim in the West Fork River when we were two years old.
Our Daddy tossed us away from him into waters deep and cold.
We did our best dog paddle and swam with all our might.
We knew if we got back to those strong hands everything would be all right.

Blue crabs boiling in a big black kettle, Mama's huckleberry pie
Cannonballs off a rope swing, clay balls launched at the other side.
Black lab playing with a cottonmouth, tree house way up high.
Flying squirrel in Stephen's shirt pocket, snapping turtle on Daddy's trotline.

Life took me away from the West Fork River when I was seventeen.
Whenever I came back home again I told it where I'd been.
I showed it to the girl I loved and saw it in her eyes.
What seemed so wide when I was young, now small against the sky.

The River was deep and wide and clear, an eternity across
It saw all our joyful times, every pain and loss.
To our Dad it was a good old friend, a highway to his life.
It fed our bodies and our souls with summer days and nights...
And that was life on the West Fork River, the river our life flowed by.

Life brought me back to the West Fork River in 1999.
My Dad and I went down to see in December's cold sunshine.
We sat without a word and watched the water flow on by.
"We can go now," Daddy said, but he knew that was good-bye.

Now I'm back here ten years later but still it's way too soon.
My brother David fights for life in the same place he was born.
There's no way we can let him go; there's no way he can stay.
We know he rests in God's strong hands and wakes to that bright day.

This morning I took my coffee cup and looked at the other side.
I know I could be there in just one step and not even really try.
I held my grandsons in my arms and told them the river's name.

Like me, they'll learn from the West Fork River, some things will never change.

The River was deep and wide and clear, an eternity across
It saw all our joyful times, every pain and loss.
To our Dad it was a good old friend, a highway to his life.
It fed our bodies and our souls with summer days and nights...
And that was life on the West Fork River, the river our life flowed by.

His Toughest Foe—A Family Story

Hebert was well-liked at Firestone, and his coworkers enjoyed talking sports with him. One afternoon several of them were sitting around on a break. One of the men asked him a question about his high school football career. Who was the toughest footballer he had ever played against? Preacher's answer was a quick one—a one-armed Chinaman from Opelousas. Everybody laughed and shook their heads. He had the reputation of being a big kidder, and of course they thought he was having them on again.

He told us he really did play against a boy of Chinese descent with one arm. He was on the football team in the small town of Opelousas, Louisiana. He said that kid was like a tree stump when the offensive line tried to move him out of the way for the running backs. I must say, when I first heard the story I was somewhat skeptical. A one-armed Chinaman from Opelousas?

The Great Watermelon Heist

When I was still in high school, back in the fifties, we had two pit bulldogs—Missy, black and white, and her son, Cougar, a tan. Preacher Hebert had a first-class crop of watermelons ready to pick in a field adjoining Phillips Road. There were watermelons everywhere, and we couldn't wait.

One day my mother's cousin and husband came from Texas to spend a weekend with us. They brought along their dog, Cougar's litter mate, Buddy, also a tan. Cougar and Buddy could pass for each other—same size, same markings—and they became fast friends after reconnecting. Chasing squirrels and birds was their favorite pastime. Missy slept under the house all day.

Night fell and everyone, worn out after an afternoon in the river, ate supper and went to bed. Buddy was in the house with his people. Cougar, being a night wanderer, was chained to the clothesline so he had plenty of room to maneuver without being able to leave the yard.

Along about midnight the dogs went crazy. We could hear Missy barking. We heard the chain zipping back and forth on the metal clothesline as Cougar tried to get loose. The next morning Shirley, Mama's cousin, said Buddy had growled and paced around the room. We just figured someone was walking down the road. We were in the country, after all, and dogs barked at everything.

Preacher went out to water the garden like he did every morning before the sun got too high. He came back in sooner than usual. Took off his hat, and sat down on the breakfast nook bench. He looked around at those of us who were there eating. Shook his head and ran his fingers through his dark, curly hair.

"What's wrong, Preacher?" Shirley asked.

"Forget watermelon after swimming this afternoon," he said. "There's not one melon left. Looks like a truck parked next to the field and took 'em all. Pretty deep ruts in the road."

"The dogs tried to tell us," my mother said. "

"Yep. Doing their job," Daddy said. "Guess I better get busy. I've got a whole field to plow under today."

I don't know what would have happened, but I have a feeling that had we turned those two big males loose we would have been chowing down on watermelon the next afternoon after our time in the river. Also, there might have been some folks missing a portion of their *derrieres*

That was a long time ago and the dogs are long buried, but I'm sure they'll be waiting for us at the rainbow bridge.

A Hunting Tale

As usual, during duck season in Louisiana, it was one of those sunless days when dampness penetrated through layers of padded camouflage all the way to the bone. The exhausted hunters filed onto the camp's porch and began to shed their hunting gear. One man seemed to be having difficulty getting his boots off.

My father, already free of his paraphernalia, watched his fellow hunter try for the third time to remove his boot. Ever the good Samaritan, my dad could stand it no longer. He strode to where the man was sitting and reached out.

"Here, let me help." He grasped the boot and gave it a yank.

The good Samaritan found himself holding a boot and an artificial leg. Everyone else was equally surprised. This man had been their hunting companion ten years and nobody had a clue. They stood around trying to think of something to say. Finally my dad stepped into the breach.

"Well, at least your toes don't get cold."

Remembering Christmases Past

I've been a scribbler as soon as I learned how to write. Little two-page endeavors in elementary school and up to fifty or so pages of purple prose when in high school. As far as I know Hillene never did any of that until we were grown. However, she made it into print before I did with an essay in a Christmas anthology — *Christmas is a Season! 2009,* edited by Linda Busby Parker.

" 'His Hands' is an essay about a remarkable man, my father, Preacher Hebert, who stood six feet two inches tall and was a renaissance man in every sense of the word. This story is a child's view of a man, bigger than life, whose children were always fascinated watching his hands as he went about such things as making a wreath, stringing his lures, mending his nets, or making functional Indian moccasins for their playtimes."

His Hands

Hillene Hebert Deaton

As the holidays approach, I think back with fondness of my father and childhood Christmases so long ago. It was rumored that my father once held nine baseballs in his hand at one time, yet he could beat his sisters at playing jacks.

His hands could skin alligators, yet they could pick out the smallest splinter from a tiny finger.

His hands could tie the thinnest strings through his fishing lures and hand-sew leather moccasins to fit tiny feet.

We lived in a big, white two-story house in the country. There were four generations of us living together: my great-grandmother, my grandparents, Mom and Dad, and five of us — three boys and two girls. Everyone grew excited as Christmas approached.

The day my grandmother went to the attic and began moving the boxes that held the Christmas ornaments signaled to us that Christmas was not far away. It was time for our annual trip across the river.

We made our plans and gathered our tools—baskets, cutting shears, handsaw, shotgun, and a long piece of rope. We were going Christmas tree hunting, and this was the time of year that we five children looked forward to with great excitement. The delicious smells coming from the kitchen assured us that it was going to be a full-belly Christmas.

Back in those days we had colder winters, so Mom dressed us like the little brother in the movie, *A Christmas Story*, when his mother encases him in his bulky snowsuit, boots, mittens, and hat. I think we too would have bounced had we fallen over. On top of all that, we had to wear life jackets because we would be in a boat on the river behind our house.

My three brothers were younger, so it was up to my sister and me to organize the younger ones. But we didn't mind. We were thrilled because we were going in Daddy's fishing boat. I had ventured out with him one other time to fish, and once had been enough. I talked the whole time and wound my line around a tree several times. When I had the line in the water, I made pretty designs by moving my fishing pole up and down in circles. Who knew that fish could hear, and that they didn't like a lure to be jumping around in the water? But this was different. This was Christmas!

In the boat that Christmas season, we crossed the river and started looking for the perfect tree. We searched the tree tops for mistletoe. When it was spotted, Daddy blasted away with his shotgun, raining mistletoe down upon us. My three brothers' job was to pick up the mistletoe and place it in one of the baskets we had brought with us.

When we spotted our favorite holly tree, Daddy cut off some of the smaller branches. We were very careful as we put them in a basket so as not to dislodge the beautiful red berries.

Trying to find the right Christmas tree elicited many opinions. My

337

brothers wanted a tree tall and skinny. My sister and I wanted a tree fat and full. We compromised. Daddy spotted the top of a tree that was just right.

With much laughter and good-natured arguing, Daddy commandeered the handsaw and began cutting. He tied the branches of the tree together, loaded our treasure into the boat and crossed the river back to our side.

Grandmother had hot chocolate and cookies ready for the intrepid crew. The house smelled of baking, pine, and chocolate. We took our cookies and hot chocolate outside. We wanted to watch Daddy's strong hands as he carefully wove the holly branches around a clothes hanger that he had shaped into a circle. When he finished, we had a beautiful, real holly wreath to hang on our door for everyone to see.

We left the tree up until New Year's Day. By that time, although it still smelled of pine, the needles were beginning to fall off. By then our perfect Christmas tree looked pretty pathetic. The season was officially over when we put the ornaments back into their boxes and into the attic.

Fast forward to the next Christmas season. We prepared to go across the river to cut our favorite holly branches, gather our mistletoe, and find our Christmas tree. We piled into Daddy's boat and took off. As we stepped onto the other bank, what do our wondering eyes see? Not a reindeer or a sleigh, but a NO TRESSPASSING sign: SAM HOUSTON STATE PARK! DO NOT CUT ANY TREES! PROPERTY STATE OF LOUISIANA!

No more beautiful wreaths. No more mistletoe raining down on us. No more friendly haggling over the best tree. We crossed the river back to our side in silence.

We were a dejected bunch that walked back into the kitchen. We gathered around Daddy to discuss plan two. After a lively discussion, and Daddy's absolute refusal to buy a tree, we took the handsaw, the length of rope, and a wagon, and walked out of our yard to the woods across the road from us. We found a tree, and it was all right, but somehow it wasn't filled with the magic of years past. We had lost the fun and excitement of our family's river search.

We had an evergreen tree in the yard, and Daddy cut some of the branches and made a wreath. We watched his large hands as they wove those beautiful pieces together. He hung it on our front door, and my sister trimmed it with a bright red ribbon. But that didn't feel as festive either.

Many Christmases have come and gone, but the ones I remember now are the Decembers when my brothers and sister and I got into Daddy's fishing boat with him and went on adventures across the river in search of our perfect Christmas tree. The excitement and fun of those trips were bigger than life.

I still have some of Grandmother's handmade ornaments that I put on my artificial tree each year. I have the ugly Santa with his reindeer and sleigh that used to scare us as children because when she would plug it in, the light made him look really weird. Some of the legs and antlers have broken off. Santa's light doesn't work anymore, but I put him out each year because it brings back the memories of Christmases long ago. And of hands we thought could do anything.

Thanks to Hillene Hebert Deaton for permission to use her remembrances of Christmases past. And thanks to Preacher and Nannie Hebert, Hill and Bessie Bostick, and Lizzie Stratton for giving the Hebert kids such wonderful childhoods.

Alligator Skinning. Preacher Hebert Comes Full Circle.
By Wally Jr.

The increase of alligator populations allowed Louisiana to reinstate hunting in the late 1970's. Strictly regulated, alligator "tags" were allocated according to the nests counted in winter flyovers by wildlife department personnel. A tract of private land containing habitat would be issued a number of tags for hunting, and the hides could be taken and sold.

In order to prevent out-of-season poached hides from being taken for sale, wildlife officials devised an ingenious solution: Each hunting season a diagram was issued of a special pattern of intricate cuts which had to be performed at the time the alligator was taken. Older hides with those cuts would be easily weeded out in the process, as they were noticeably different from a "fresh" hide. This meant the alligator skinner was perhaps the most important person in the hunting party, and in everyone's opinion Preacher Hebert was the best ever.

Usually a fish, blackbird, or chicken quarter was suspended just over the bayou on a stout hook attached to a cable draped over a tree limb. The cable was tied to the trunk of a large tree, and the line was checked regularly. The submerged alligator was pulled to the surface (sometimes a very difficult and dangerous proposition) and dispatched with a firearm, put in a boat and brought to a shed where Preacher and his skinning knives awaited.

This process was described in the National Geographic Magazine of August, 1979, when Preacher was featured in an article by Peter Jenkins, "Walk Across America, part II."

6-25-05 San Diego/Seattle

On June 24, 2005, my sister Hillene, brother David, and I boarded a plane out of Houston bound for San Diego. We were to meet our brother Stephen and his wife Jane, as well as brother Wally and his wife Brenda in San Diego. Also, traveling with Stephen and Jane were family friends Robert and Sue Moss, staying at the legendary Coronado Hotel.

The occasion? Our dad, Wally Sr., was to be inducted into the PCL San Diego Padre Hall of Fame along with some of the other Pacific Coast League players. Those from the original 1936 club besides Hebert: Jim (Tiny) Chaplin, Dom Dallassandro, Bobby Doerr, Cedric Durst, George McDonald, Steve Mesner, Frank Shellenback, Yank Terry, and Ted Williams. The only original 1936 Padres still living in 2005 were George McDonald, first baseman , and shortstop Bobby Doerr.

Bill Swank, San Diego baseball historian, met us at the airport to take us to our hotel (*not* the Coronado). We had been in touch with him before we left, and he told us we'd recognize him—just look for Santa Claus. As it turned out he found us first. As soon as he saw David, he said, he knew it was some of the Hebert kids.

The next morning—Saturday, June 25—as guests of the Padre organization, we gathered at the PCL Bar and Grill along with sixteen former PCL Padres, their families, and the families of deceased players. We attended the unveiling of thirty-four plaques on a wall of honor. Sandy Alderson, Padres team president, welcomed everyone to Petco Park. Former Padre broadcaster, Bob Chandler, introduced the players and deceased players' families with brief biographies of each.

After the ceremony at the PCL Bar and Grill we were taken on a tour of Petco Park where modern day Padres plied their trade.

We found our seats in the stadium and settled in to watch a regular scheduled game between San Diego and Seattle. The Seattle Mariners became the

Seattle Rainiers of earlier times. They wore throwback road gray uniforms. San Diego wore throwback pin-striped uniforms from 1936. Everyone there liked the throwbacks, but observed the pants weren't baggy enough. Also, there were no logos on the dark blue caps. It was said that Bill Lane was too cheap to pay extra for logos.

George McDonald was chosen to throw out the first pitch. He was eighty-eight in 2005 and said he was afraid his arm was going to go with the ball. An amusing side note: McDonald hit the longest home run in history—120 miles. The ball cleared the fence, landed in a railroad car, and was later retrieved in Los Angeles.

The Padres won the game 8-5. To be sure the lead was preserved, starting pitcher Jake Peavy was relieved in the ninth by Padre closer Trevor Hoffman. The scoreboard began flashing "Trevor Time" accompanied by a deafening rendition of "Hell's Bells" that probably could be heard by folks in Los Angeles some 120 miles to the north. McDonald said he had never seen or heard anything like that before. We in the Hebert contingent couldn't have agreed more.

Hillene and Stephen got to go down to the diamond while introductions were being made of attending players and families of deceased players. Stephen called our mother, who was at home in Louisiana, to tell her he was standing on the first base line. Then some guy dressed like a 15th Century Spanish monk goosed Hillene.

After the game Wally, Brenda, David, Hillene, and I went to downtown San Diego, which resembled Bourbon Street in New Orleans. All the shops were open, as were the eating places, and people were out and about everywhere. Most restaurants had outdoor seating and were doing overflow business. We passed by Jim Croce's place and decided to eat there as soon as we could get a table. It was operated by Croce's widow, Ingrid. She stopped by our table and chatted awhile. I can't speak for the others, but I've never forgotten the meal I had there—meat loaf made with ground *filet mignon* and the best mashed potatoes I have ever eaten, before or since.

We went home to Louisiana and resumed our somewhat quiet, unobtrusive lives, but I've never forgotten our season in the sun in the border city where our dad spent most of his professional life doing what he loved.

Hillene and the Retro Uniform

David, Linda, Hillene, Brenda & Wally at the Hall of Fame Game

History of Hebert Siblings

There were eight children born to John Aurelian and Matilde Smith Hebert. The four oldest were born in what is now Creole, Louisiana. It was called Cameron back then. Austin Willey was born in 1906. My father, Wallace Andrew, was born in 1907. The oldest girl was Bessie Mae, who made her entrance in 1909. The youngest boy was Charles Francis, born in 1910. Grandpa Aurelian was sharecropping the property there in Creole.

They moved to Grand Lake, still in Cameron Parish, and sharecropped land there, starting to save money to buy their own land.

Three more girls were added to the family after the move to Grand Lake. Winnie Olive Ann was born in 1913. Hilda Mary and Violet Grace were only fourteen months apart—1915 and 1916 respectively. That made seven children between the years 1906 and 1916. I would say my grandmother had her hands full.

They were able to buy a farm in Sweet Lake and lived there until the hurricane of 1918 destroyed everything. They lived with Hebert relatives for a year, but when the schools there could not reopen they decided to move to Lake Charles in Calcasieu Parish so they could get the oldest four into school. However, Grandpa Aurelian continued to farm the land in Sweet Lake for awhile even though they resided in Lake Charles.

The last daughter, Genevieve Betty, was born in Lake Charles in 1925. Somewhere along the way five of them acquired nicknames that stuck with them the rest of their lives. Uncle Austin was known to all as Foots. My father was Preacher. Charles was always Uncle Charlie. Hilda was Aunt Peanut and Violet was Aunt Pug. Genevieve was Gin or Bebe, but I always called her Genevieve since she was only eleven when I was born.

They were a hardy bunch, all but two having lived into their nineties. Aunt Winnie was eighty-nine, just a few months shy of her ninetieth birthday, and Aunt Peanut was eighty-six. Uncle Austin was ninety-six, Aunt Bessie was ninety-five, and Uncle Charlie lived to be 102. Aunt Pug was ninety-five. Genevieve, in her nineties, is still with us.

At the age of ninety-two, my father was the first of the siblings to depart this life on December 8, 1999—twenty-three days before the world ushered in a new century. He went out the same way he lived his extended stay on earth—at peace with humankind. Reading one of his favorite Louis Lamour books, he laid it on his chest, turned his head to one side, and took his last breath.

Austin, Wallace, Genevieve, Hilda, Winnie, Violet, Charlie, Bessie Hebert

Postscript: Genevieve—last of the Hebert clan—left this world on August 12, 2019, at the age of ninety-four.

Wally "Preacher" Hebert Award at Westlake High

In May of 2018 the baseball program at Westlake High School established an annual award to be presented to the Westlake player who exemplified everything Westlake baseball stood for — a selfless teammate and a humble person. The award is the Wally "Preacher" Hebert Memorial Scholarship of Westlake High School Baseball. According to Blake Reed, current baseball coach, the recipient is selected by a vote of team members and coaches.

A "humble person" is one who is not proud or haughty, not arrogant or assertive. That describes Preacher Hebert to a "T." A "selfless teammate" would be someone who had no concern for one's self, instead putting the welfare of the team and teammates ahead of their own. That's my dad — true during the baseball years and true when those days were over.

The 2018 recipient of the award was Hunter Witherwax, who played first base for the Rams. He was also the designated hitter, a position unheard of back in the early days of the game. The 2019 winner was Mark Ashworth, who covered the infield at shortstop. It so happens these two young men are first cousins, the grandsons of Jimmy Ashworth, who is a good friend and fellow WHS alumnus.

The legacy of Wally "Preacher" Hebert lives on.

Mark Ashworth and Hunter Witherwax

Epilogue

Wallace Hebert was a "oner", and he picked up his nickname—Preacher—in grammar school. It followed him through his long, diverse life. Will Rogers once said he never met a man he didn't like. Preacher went him one better. He never met anyone who didn't like him. As the years passed more and more of his friends and coworkers said goodbye to this world.

"There won't be anyone left to see me off," he often joked. He left this world December 8, 1999, and would have been surprised at the steady stream of condolers on visitation night and the standing-room-only crowd in the chapel the day of the funeral. There were plenty there to see him off: wife, children, grandchildren, great-grandchildren, former coworkers, hunting and fishing buddies, seven siblings, and assorted extended family members. The eulogies went on for some time. Nearly everyone had a "Preacher" story to tell.

He was in my life from the day I was born until the day he died. I observed nearly every phase of his life. I remember those dark Cajun looks. The curly hair, the laughing eyes, the pug nose that's a strong familial trait. Tall and solidly built, he had an athlete's fluidity of movement. I remember his hands, so big they could hide a baseball, strong enough to skin an alligator, yet with a touch so delicate he often beat his sisters playing jacks. The dark, curly hair grayed and thinned over the years, but the laughing eyes were there until they closed for the last time.

He excelled in all sports, but his passion was baseball. He was amazed he could actually get paid for doing something he loved. However, when it was time, he hung up his cleats and went on to the next chapter— employment with the Firestone Rubber Company. He never tried to relive the past through his children. Of the five of us, only three showed any real interest in sports when growing up, but that was okay with him. .

His retirement years afforded him the opportunity to pursue his other passions. He hunted ducks in the fall and winter. Spring and summer were the time for fishing and gardening. He skinned alligators during 'gator season and read "shoot-em-up" paperbacks when the weather was too bad for anything else.

His talents extended to the kitchen as well, where he could whip up a mean gumbo or fried fish, filleted by him, of course, so we wouldn't swallow bones.

A snapshot shows him sitting in his pirogue in a quiet backwater of the Calcasieu River, an old man fishing, his face shaded by a battered baseball cap. A stranger might be surprised to know he'd been equally at home on the pitcher's mound in St. Louis, Hollywood, San Diego, or Pittsburgh. That snapshot is only part of his story. He was in my life a long time, and I regret he's no longer part of it.

A dictionary definition: Oner — *A unique or extraordinary person or thing. One of a kind.* That's my dad.

A Reunion of Clan Hebert

Wally "Preacher" Hebert

1972 at Age 65

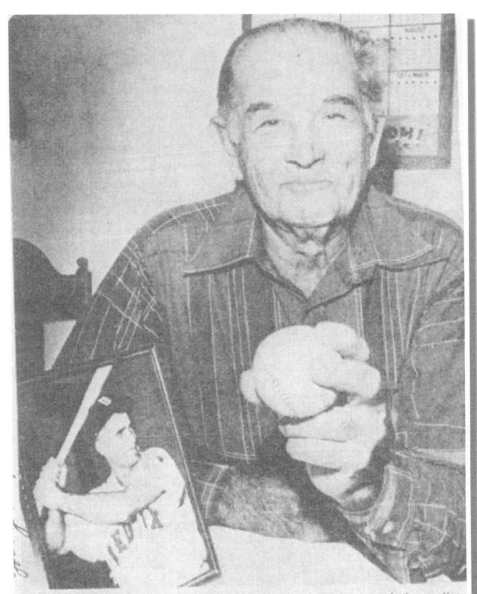

Preacher Hebert relaxes in his West Lake home and shows the bubbling good humor that made professional baseball 'fun.' Now 70, Hebert still keeps in touch with former Boston Red Sox great Bobby Doerr, shown in the autographed photo.

Hillene stuck her head into the den where Preacher was in his recliner, a paperback copy of The Haunted Mesa by Louis L'Amour in his hand.

"Hi, Daddy. We're going to the movies to see "The Babe," she said. "John Goodman's playing Babe Ruth. Wanna go?"

He laid his open book on his chest and looked up at her. "Deal around me on that. I knew the real thing."

ACKNOWLEDGMENTS

Many thanks to those who helped make this book a reality.

My siblings: Hillene, Wally, David, and Stephen.

Our mother, Bobbie Hebert, who saved the clippings.

Bill Swank, who organized the scrapbook.

The Bayou Writers Group, who encouraged me to take my writing to the next level.

Pam Thibodeaux and Randy Dupre, founders of the Bayou Writers Group.

The gang at Stellar Beans, the best critique group around—Cliff, Beverly, Marcia, Marsha, Bob and Georgia, Ellen and Joey.

Jess Ferguson, my mentor, who gives me excellent advice about all things writing and research leads in writing this book.

Heather Duff, webmaster and cover designer *extraordinaire.*

My daughter—Micki—who got the manuscript to the printer.

My other children—Katy, Mollie, Donna, and Dan—for their encouragement.

Michael Hall, my instructor at the 2017 Writers League of Texas retreat who helped me get this project started.

My class at the 2018 WLT retreat who told me what needed fixing.

Carol Dawson, who showed me how to revise.

My beta readers, Norma, Wally, and Hillene.

Jimmy Ashworth who supplied the pictures for the Wally Hebert Award.

ABOUT THE AUTHOR

Linda Hebert Todd is a retired librarian who spends her time writing poetry and prose from the bayous of Louisiana. She is the author of a novel—*Wild Justice*—a crime novel with a revenge theme. It received an Honorable Mention in the Writer's Digest Self-Published Book Awards in 2016. She is also the author of a collection of short stories—*Sidonie and the Loup-Garou: Stories From The Bayou*, as well as a book of poetry—*Stardust In My Hand*. Several of her short stories and poems have won various awards. *From The Bayou To The Big League* is her first attempt at non-fiction. She resides in Westlake, Louisiana, which is the setting for most of her writing.

BIBLIOGRAPHY

BOOKS

Jenkins, Peter and Barbara Jenkins. *The Walk West: A Walk Across America 2,* William Morrow & Company, Inc. 1981

Larwin, Tom, Carlos Bauer, Dan Boyle, Frank Myers, and Larry Zuckerman. *San Diego's First Padres and "The Kid:" The Story Of The Remarkable 1936 San Diego Padres And   Ted Williams' Professional Baseball Debut*, Montezuma Publishing, 2019

Salin, Tony, *Baseball's Forgotten Heroes: One Fan's Search For The Game's Most Interesting Overlooked Players*, Masters Press, 1999

Swank, Bill, *Baseball In San Diego: From The Padres To Petco*, Arcadia Publishing, 2004

Swank, Bill, *Echoes From Lane Field: A History Of The San Diego Padres 1936-1957*, Turner Publishing Company, 1997

Wells, Donald R., *The Race For The Governor's Cup: The Pacific Coast Playoffs, 1936-1954*, McFarland & Company, 2000

NEWSPAPERS

American Press, Lake Charles, Various issues 1928-2000

Ithaca Journal, various issues, 1931

The Morning News, various issues, 1931

Reading Times, various issues, 1931

St. Louis Post-Dispatch, various issues, 1932-33

St. Louis Star and Times, various issues, 1931-33

Star Gazette, various issues, 1931

Bakersfield Californian, various issues, 1941

Los Angeles Times, various issues, 1934-41

Oakland Tribune, various issues, 1937-42

Ogden Standard-Examiner, various issues, 1940

Petaluma Argus-Courier, various issues, 1937-1942

Press-Democrat, various issues, 1937-42

San Bernardino County Sun, various issues, 1934-1942

San Diego Tribune-Sun, various issues 1936-1942

San Diego Union-Sports, various issues, 1939

San Francisco Examiner, various issues, 1936

San Mateo Times, various issues, 1937-41

Santa Ana Register, various issues, 1938-41

Santa Cruz Evening News, various issues, 1937-41

Santa Cruz Sentinel, various issues, 1941-42

Statesman Journal, various issues, 1942

Baltimore Sun, May 3, 1943

Daily Press, Newport News, VA, March 28, 1943

Daily News, Opelousas, LA, September 19, 1943

Democrat & Chronicle, Rochester, NY, July 26, 1943

Ogden Standard Examiner, September 19, 1943

Pittsburgh Post-Gazette, various issues, 1943

Pittsburgh Press, various issues, 1944

Standard-Sentinel, Hazelton, PA, May 27, 1943

Wilkes-Barre Record, July 26, 1943

Made in the USA
Columbia, SC
04 February 2021

31570069R00200